LAYOUT
ESSENTIALS

100 Design Principles for
using grids

BETH TONDREAU

ROCKPORT

Quarto.com

© 2009, 2019 Quarto Publishing Group USA Inc.

First published in 2009; this edition published in 2019 by
Rockport Publishers, an imprint of The Quarto Group,
100 Cummings Center, Suite 265-D, Beverly, MA 01915, USA.
T (978) 282-9590 F (978) 283-2742

Rockport Publishers titles are also available at discount for retail, whole-
sale, promotional, and bulk purchase. For details, contact the Special
Sales Manager by email at specialsales@quarto.com or by mail at The
Quarto Group, Attn: Special Sales Manager, 100 Cummings Center, Suite
265-D, Beverly, MA 01915, USA.

ISBN: 978-1-63159-631-5
Digital edition published in 2019
eISBN: 978-1-63159-630-8

Originally found under the following Library of Congress Cataloging-in-
Publication Data
Tondreau, Beth.
 Layout essentials : 100 design principles for using grids / Beth Ton-
dreau.
    p. cm.
 Includes bibliographical references.
 ISBN-13: 978-1-59253-472-2
 ISBN-10: 1-59253-472-4
1. Grids (Typographic design) 2. Layout (Printing) 3. Graphic design
(Typography) I. Title.
 Z246.T65 2008
 686.2'252--dc22
                                        2008035091

Design: BTDNYC
Design Associate: Patricia Chang
Diagrams: Punyapol "Noom" Kittayarak and Patricia Chang

[FSC logo]

CONTENTS

"Just as in nature, systems of order govern the growth and structure of animate and inanimate matter, so human activity itself has, since the earliest times, been distinguished by the quest for order."

—JOSEF MULLER-BROCKMANN

GRIDS AT WORK

"A grid is truly successful only if, after all of the literal problems have been solved, the designer rises above the uniformity implied by its structure and uses it to create a dynamic visual narrative of parts that will sustain interest page after page."

—**TIMOTHY SAMARA**
Making and Breaking the Grid

INTRODUCTION

*"Grids are the most
misunderstood and misused
element in page layout.
A grid is only useful if it is
derived from the material
it is intended to handle."*

—DEREK BIRDSALL
Notes on Book Design

A grid system organizes space and supports a range of material for many kinds of communication; it ordains and maintains order, oftentimes without being obvious. A grid is a plan and not a prison.

Although grids have been used for centuries, many graphic designers associate grids with the Swiss, whose rage for order in the 1940s led to a systematic way of visualizing pretty much everything. Towards the end of the last century, grids were considered monotonous and boring, but currently, with so much data and imagery moving swiftly along multiple platforms, grids are again viewed as essential tools, relied upon by both newbies and seasoned practitioners alike.

This book is a primer, a short take on how grids can be used. Each of the 100 principles offers a nugget that is helpful in building a layout or communciation system—and each contains images of projects in a range of media by designers or design firms throughout the world.

No single principle works on its own. Often, projects or systems incorporate multiple precepts. So, this update lists how some principles cross refer to different portions of the same project or to a completely different project. One case shows components of communication system in more than one principle. This edition contains more examples of design's applications to print, desktop, tablet, device, or all of the above.

The strength of this book stems from the work of talented and generous designers whose work is inspiring, solid, delightful, controlled, and augment the topic. I hope the examples in *Layout Essentials* will instruct, intrigue, and excite, while guiding you to recall the most essential precept of communication: Ensure that your work reflects and enhances what you or the author want to communicate.

GETTING STARTED

1. Know the Components

The main components of a grid are margins, columns, markers, flowlines, spatial zones, and modules. Starting a new project can be hard. Begin with your content, then set up your margins and columns. You'll need to make adjustments. Just start.

COLUMNS

are vertical containers that hold type or images. The width and number of columns on a page or screen can vary, depending on the content.

MODULES

are individual divisions separated by consistent space, providing a repeating, ordered grid. Combining modules can create columns and rows of varying sizes.

MARGINS

are buffer zones. They represent the amount of space between the trim size, including gutter, and the page content. Margins can also house secondary information, such as notes and captions.

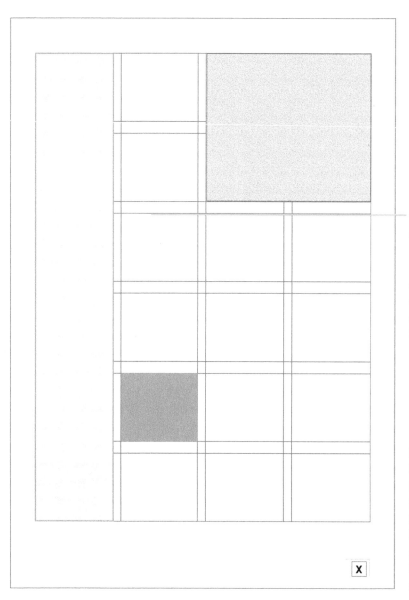

SPATIAL ZONES

are groups of modules or columns that can form specific areas for type, ads, images, or other information.

FLOWLINES

are alignments that break space into horizontal bands. Not actual lines, flowlines are a method for using space and elements to guide a reader across a page.

MARKERS X

help a reader navigate a document. Indicating placement for material that appears in the same location, markers include page numbers, running heads and feet (headers and footers), and icons.

2. Learn the Basic Structures

Although the diagrams below show common structures, there are additional variations on the basic configurations. The multicolumn grids of newspapers and their sites extend beyond three columns to five or more.

A **SINGLE-COLUMN GRID** is generally used for continuous running text, such as essays, reports, or books. The block of text is the main feature on the page, spread, or device screen.

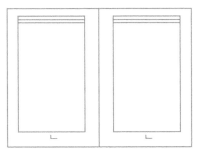

A **TWO-COLUMN GRID** can be used to control a lot of text or to present different kinds of information in separate columns. A double-column grid can be arranged with columns of equal or unequal width. In ideal proportions, when one column is wider than the other, the wider column is double the width of the narrow column.

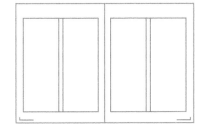

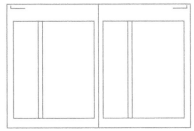

MULTICOLUMN GRIDS afford greater flexibility than single- or two-column grids, combine multiple columns of varying widths and are useful for magazines and websites.

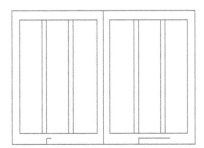

MODULAR GRIDS are best for controlling the kind of complex information seen in newspapers, calendars, charts, and tables. They combine vertical and horizontal columns, which arrange the structure into smaller chunks of space.

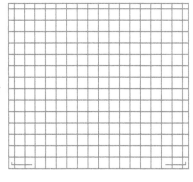

HIERARCHICAL GRIDS break the page into zones. Many hierarchical grids are composed of horizontal columns. Some magazines organize contents pages horizontally. For ease and efficiency, many devices break material into horizontal bands.

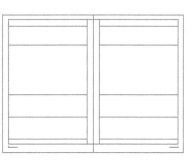

START BY ASKING
- What is the material? Is it complicated?
- How much of it is there?
- What is the goal?
- Who is the reader/browser/user?

3. Assess the Material

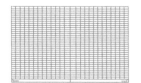

Content, margins, amount of imagery, desired number of pages, screens, and panels all factor into deciding how to set up a grid. Above all, the content determines the structure of the grid. The grid you use depends on each specific design problem, but below are some general guidelines:

- Use a **SINGLE-COLUMN GRID** when working with continuous text, such as an essay or a book. A single column of text can seem less intimidating and more luxurious than multiple columns, making it suitable for art books or catalogs.

- For more complicated material, **TWO-COLUMN** or **MULTICOLUMN** grids afford flexibility. Columns that can be further broken into two provide the greatest number of variations. Multicolumn grids are used for websites to manage a huge range of information that includes stories, videos, and ads.

- For a lot of information, such as that in a calendar or schedule, a **MODULAR** grid helps to arrange units of information into manageable chunks. A modular grid can also be applied to newspapers, which have many zones of information.

- **HIERARCHICAL** grids divide pages or screens **HORIZONTALLY** and are often useful for simple websites, in which chunks of information are ordered, to provide easier reading while scrolling down a page.

All grids create order, and all involve planning and math. Whether a designer is working in pixels, picas, or millimeters, the key to the rational order of a grid is making sure the numbers add up.

PROJECT
Good magazine

CLIENT
Good Magazine, LLC

DESIGN
Open

DESIGNER
Scott Stowell

Sketches by a master designer show how a grid evolves.

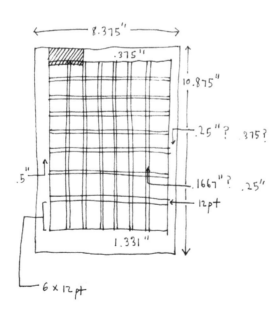

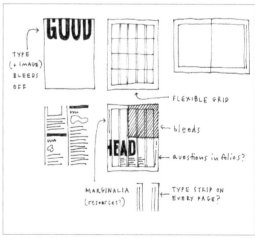

Developmental sketches show possible grids for the format of a magazine.

4. Do the Math

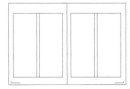

Consider the main text first and analyze the project's complexity—most projects have restrictions, such as size, number of pages, and colors. When paying attention to the content, also factor in any project criteria.

Once you know the sizes of the page or screen and your basic text, figure out how the elements fit on the page. If you're working with text only, you can fit your text into the allotted number of pages. If you also need to include images, headings, boxes, or charts, first determine the amount of space needed for the text. The remainder is the amount of space left for imagery, charts, and other information. Often, you will need to simultaneously calculate numbers for all elements.

When you have determined the basic approach to the material and its fit, you can dive into the details of headings and hierarchies. (See next principle.)

TYPOGRAPHY TIPS

Type's texture springs from size, space, width, and line breaks. Consistent color of running copy is easy for the reader to follow. If the text is lengthy, it must be large enough, with enough leading (space between the lines), to support an easy reading experience. If the columns are narrow, avoid gappy word spaces, by either setting type small or, alternatively, flush left, unjustified right.

Because different typefaces set differently, there is no perfect criterion for type sizes For instance, 10 pt. Helvetica looks a lot bigger than 10pt. Garamond. With the exception of the words Helvetic and Garamonhe, the bulk of this paragraph is set in 8 point Interstate with 4.5 points of space between lines. It's worth studying typefaces.

PROJECTS
Astronomy and
Symbols of Power

CLIENT
Harry N. Abrams, Inc.

DESIGN DIRECTOR
Mark LaRivière

DESIGN
BTDNYC

DESIGNER
Beth Tondreau, Suzanne Dell'Orto, Scott Ambrosino (for *Astronomy* only)

Single or double-column grids depend on the content and extent of the text.

A single column of text for this book of astronomical images echoes the idea of deep space.

A catalog with reams of text employs two columns to contain text and frame images.

5. Go Easy on the Reader

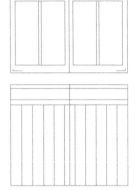

Does the material have headings? Subheadings? Lists? Bullets? If not, does it need any or all of the above? Make the most important information larger or bolder, or set it in another face to distinguish it from less-important text. Varying fonts as well as text size and weight can also help set apart different types of material, but keep it simple. If each style doesn't have a clear purpose, many different styles can be confusing.

Although size matters, space matters just as much. The location of a head and the amount of space surrounding it can also convey importance.

To make a lot of disparate or varied material easy to parse, break it into segments for easy reading. Pull quotes are the visual equivalents of sound bites. Use sidebars and boxes to break information into chunks that can be easily skimmed. Typography can help a user immediately understand the content.

PROJECT (ON LEFT)
Symbols of Power

CLIENT
Harry N. Abrams, Inc.

DESIGN DIRECTOR
Mark LaRivière

DESIGN
BTDNYC

Classical typography using the face Bodoni reflects the Napoleonic time period of the artifacts shown.

PROJECT (ON RIGHT)
Blueprint

CLIENT
Martha Stewart Omnimedia

DESIGN DIRECTOR
Deb Bishop

DESIGNER
Deb Bishop

Contemporary typography is clean, informative, and assertive.

For those starting out and using only one typeface, a rule of thumb is to set up a hierarchy by incorporating roman upper- and lowercase and italic upper- and lowercase fonts. For more complex information, use various typefaces and sizes to set off chunks of text.

Varying typefaces and sizes and setting material within boxes are ways to handsomely contain a large range of information.

6. Determine an Order

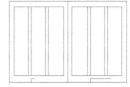

Rarely are all images in a piece used at the same size. Just as text conveys information, image size indicates the importance of an event or subject. Some companies rank images in size order prior to proceeding to layout. Others rely upon the designer to define an order or bring drama to a piece by varying size. Of course, some complex images need to be larger simply for readability's sake. In addition to function and dynamics through size, projects also need variation to keep the reader engaged.

Images can be half a column, one column, or two columns wide. Occasionally breaking the grid can add drama and call attention to an image. It's possible to signal the importance of an image by the amount of space it fills.

PROJECT
étapes: magazine

CLIENT
Pyramyd /*étapes:* magazine

DESIGN
Anna Tunick

Images of varying sizes establish a pecking order for visuals.

7. Consider All Elements

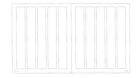

Depending on the medium or project, grids can isolate elements, by presenting type in one column or zone and images in another. Most grids integrate type and image, giving each enough emphasis to clarify information for the reader.

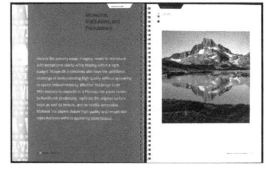

Emphasis on text. Here, the text is by itself on one page, with the image on another.

LEFT AND BELOW: A grid can let an image march across columns in a horizontal fashion, with captions below, or it can stack images vertically, with captions to either side of the image.

PROJECT
MOHAWK VIA
THE BIG HANDBOOK

CLIENT
Mohawk Fine Papers Inc.

DESIGN
AdamsMorioka, Inc.

DESIGNERS
Sean Adams, Chris Taillon

Grids control varied imagery in a paper promotion.

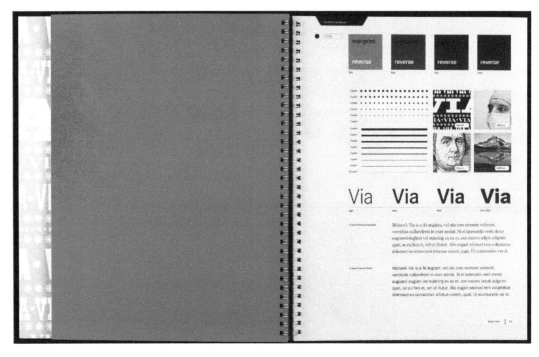

8. Define Space with Color

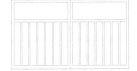

Color is a way to make modules or sections stand out. Color defines space as well as helps to organize elements within a space. Color also enlivens a page and provides a psychological signal for the kind of message that's being conveyed. When setting up colors, consider the audience. Saturated colors attract attention, while desaturated colors support the material in a more understated way. Too many colors can cause a piece to be busy and hard to navigate.

COLOR ON SCREEN VS. ON PAPER

We live in an RGB world, in which both clients and designers view almost everything on screen. Colors on screen are luminous, saturated, beautiful, and RGB. However, there is a big difference between color on screen and on paper. Traditional four-color printing requires the careful choice of paper and rounds of color correcting to approximate onscreen luminosity.

Colors can act as containers for separate bits of information.

Color sets off information, whether it is used in modules, boxes, or blocks. Modules can be quasi-ornamental—setting off colored boxes against boxes containing text—or functional, helping to differentiate between various kinds of boxed text.

PROJECT
Color Design Workbook

CLIENT
Rockport Publishers

DESIGN
Sean Adams

Spreads from this book demonstrate how color can serve a strong function as well as add a strong and bright presence to a piece.

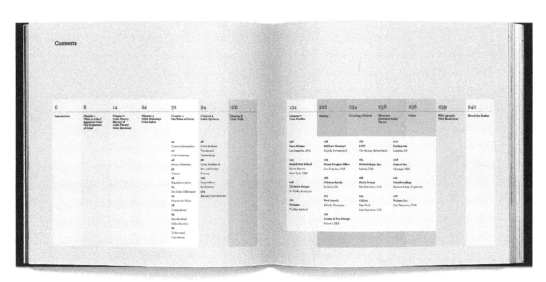

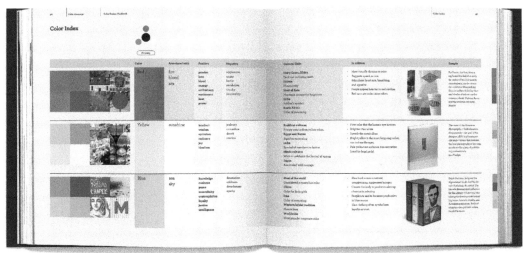

9. Use Space as a Graphic Element

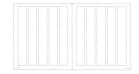

Space communicates volumes. Although a grid must be strong and clear enough to hold rafts of information, it's not necessary to fill every part of it. Space sets off the message, giving appropriate room for reading and understanding text. By design, a large amount of space creates drama and focus. Space can signal luxury or importance, and the absence of anything else on the page transmits a definite aesthetic.

Also see pages
176–177

Self Portrait (5 Part), 2001.
Five daguerreotypes, each 8 1/2 x 6 1/2 in (21.6 x 16 cm)

The use of space is a conscious design decision to give the reader pause.

PROJECT
Chuck Close | Work

CLIENT
Prestel Publishing

DESIGN
Mark Melnick

Like design, art is about space.

10. Maintain Interest With Pacing

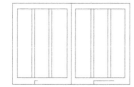

Some grids include mechanical, clear, repeated, or marching columns of images or information to catalog as much material as possible. However, most grids also allow for lyrical movement from one block of information to the next, from spread to spread, or from screen to screen. The pacing of material on the page makes a difference in attracting or sustaining interest. Pacing can stem from variation in sizes and positions of images and typography as well as the amount of margin around each image.

While designing a landmark publication replete with thoughtful essays and historical images, Bobby Martin and his team at OCD put the spreads on a wall to review and rejig position, drama, and flow.

PROJECT
King, a special-edition issue commemorating the fiftieth anniversary of the assassination of Martin Luther King Jr.

CLIENT
The Atlantic

CREATIVE DIRECTOR
Paul Spella

ART DIRECTOR
David Somerville

DESIGN FIRM
OCD | Original Champions of Design

DESIGNERS
Bobby C. Martin Jr.,
Jennifer Kinon

The flow of layouts tells a 100% clear story.

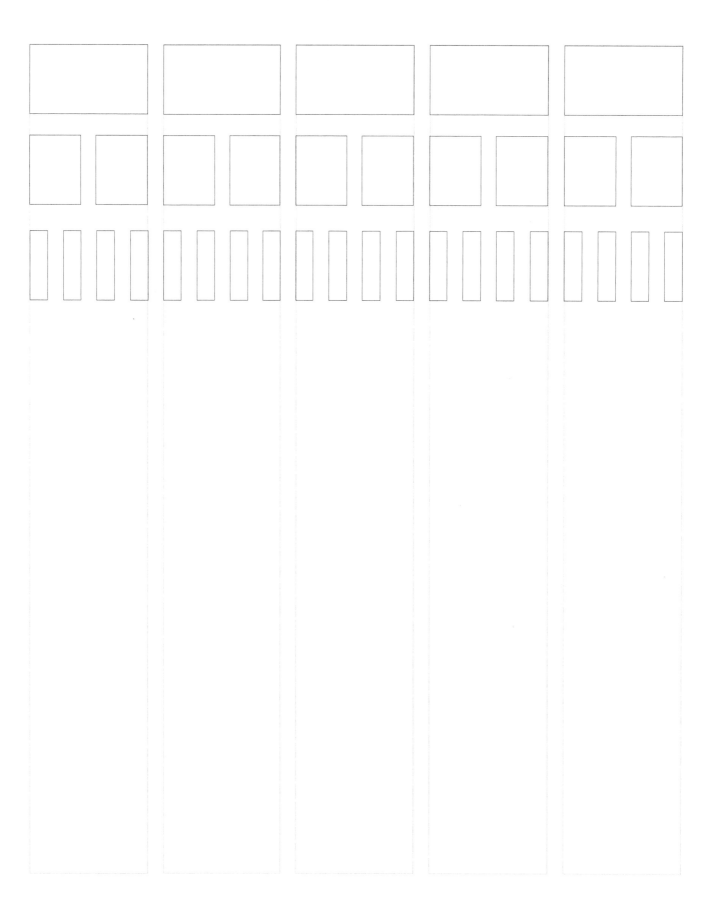

GRIDS AT WORK

11. Give the Subject a Face

When choosing an appropriate typeface for a page or spread of a single-column grid, consider the subject matter. Some faces are classic and neutral and work with most material, while other faces give a point of view and nearly mimic the topic. A typeface can help set an attitude or it can recede discreetly. Do historical research to give a sense of a time period. Conversely, work against type—ie. overturn typographical clichés. Type width, type size, and leading (interlinear space) all affect the overall fit and feel.

Also see page
25

For this project, the sans serif typeface Geometric avoids the cliché of a pretty script face for the color pink and instead establishes
punk power.

PINK

THE HISTORY OF A
PUNK, PRETTY, POWERFUL
COLOR

EDITED BY
VALERIE STEELE

Thames & Hudson

there were at least "two pinks" in the 1950s: a feminine pink and "young, daring—and omnisexual" pink.[69]

THE NAVY BLUE OF INDIA

Pink has long been a very popular color in India for both men's clothing and adornment. In Rajasthan, for example, it is still commo men wearing hot pink turbans. India's polychromatic sensibility h many Westerners. Already in 1956, Norman Parkinson did an infl

Carefully consider the leading, or interlinear space. Allow enough space to avoid typesetting that looks like a dense, gray mass. Conversely, setting too much space can result in type that looks more like texture than readable text.

The sample to the left shows the faces in their reproduction sizes, which are 10/15.75 pt Geometric caps and 10/15.75 pt Meridian. Note how the sans serif sets larger than the serif.

PROJECT
Pink

CLIENT
Thames and Hudson

DESIGN
BTDNYC

A spare page in a clean serif typeface for text is set off by a no-nonsense, unfrilly sans serif.

FEMININE DESIRE AND FRAGILITY: PINK IN EIGHTEENTH-CENTURY PORTRAITURE

A. Cassandra Albinson

A SURVEY OF OBJECTS MADE IN FRANCE AND BRITAIN IN THE EIGHTEENTH CENTURY REVEALS A REMARKABLE NUMBER OF PINK ITEMS: coverings for furniture; colored prints; porcelain; paint for interiors; paint for works of art; suits for men; and especially dresses and ribbons for women. Aside from its plentitude, what did the color pink represent in women's clothing? Portraiture provides us with a fruitful entryway because we often have indications about the sitter's life and circumstances that can provide further understanding of the choices they made in terms of costume and adornment.[1]

In comparable portraits of Jeanne-Antoinette Poisson, Marquise de Pompadour, (1721–1764) and Frances Abington (1737–1815), each woman is depicted close to the picture plane and from the waist up. Both Pompadour and Abington were exceedingly famous at the time they were painted, and their fame and fortune rested in large measure on their physical beauty and prowess. And each woman had the means to be painted by the most famous artist of her day: François Boucher for Pompadour, Joshua Reynolds for Abington.[2] Each woman gestures toward herself and suggests a touch, either in the immediate future—in the case of Pompadour, who holds a rouge brush as if poised to apply color to her cheeks—or concurrently with being painted in the case of Abington in the role of Miss Prue. Hands in each portrait are as important as faces and are stressed by the inclusion of bracelets at the wrist. Both portraits also feature a second figure around the sitter's midriff. In the case of Pompadour we see a miniature portrait of her lover, the French king, Louis XV, while a fluffy white dog sits on

83. François Boucher, *Jeanne-Antoinette Poisson, Marquise de Pompadour*, 1750, with later additions. Harvard Art Museum.

82. Joshua Reynolds, *Mrs. Abington as Miss Prue in "Love for Love" by William Congreve*, 1771. Oil on canvas. Yale Center for British Art, Paul Mellon Collection.

---

without one." A few years later, it was back, "beautifully refreshed" in a variety of styles—"pink evening shirts, pink-shirt dresses, even a pink swimming shirt," not to mention "one of 1953's prettiest little-evening blouses."[47]

"Across the US, a pink peak in male clothing has been reached as manufacturers have saturated more and more of their output with the pretty pastel," reported *Life* magazine in 1955. "Sole responsibility lies with New York's Brooks Brothers," whose pink shirt "was publicized for college girls and caught on for men too." Gradually, pink neckties, dinner jackets, golf jackets, trousers, and other garments also became increasingly visible. "Like most male fashions, including the Ivy League Look, this pink hue and cry has taken some time to develop." But by 1955, the "traditionally feminine color" had become "a staple for [the] male."[48]

Elvis Presley not only wore pink suits, jackets, and trousers, he also drove a pink car and slept in a pink bedroom. Was he influenced by African-American style? His fans wore lipstick in Heartbreak Hotel Pink, and rock and roll extolled the color with songs like "Pink Pedal Pushers" (1958), "Pink Shoe Laces" (1959), and "A White Sport Coat (and a Pink Carnation)" (1957). Meanwhile, the warm carotenoid pink of flamingos was increasingly associated with newly affordable, warm-weather vacations in places like Florida and the Caribbean. So perhaps there were at least "two pinks" in the 1950s: a feminine pink and an emerging "young, daring—and omnisexual" pink.[49]

THE NAVY BLUE OF INDIA

Pink has long been a very popular color in India for both men's and women's clothing and adornment. In Rajasthan, for example, it is still common to see many men wearing hot pink turbans. India's polychromatic sensibility has influenced many Westerners. Already in 1956, Norman Parkinson did an influential photo shoot in India for British *Vogue*. One of his striking images juxtaposed a Western model in the latest fashion with an Indian girl in a hot pink sari. Another, shot in Jaipur, the "Pink City," posed the model in pale pink with a group of Indian men in bright pink coats and turbans. Diana Vreeland, then editor of *Harper's Bazaar*, saw the images and allegedly said, "How clever of you, Mr. Parkinson, also to know that pink is the navy blue of India."[50]

Traditionally, there were many rules about color in clothing related to age, region, caste, occasion, complexion, and time of day. More recently, the individual's personal taste has played an increasingly important role. In their book

43. Unknown artist, *Portrait of an Indian Prince Wearing a Wedding Sehra (headgear)*, ca. 1920–40, Rajputana Photo Art Studio. Gelatin silver print and watercolor, 14⅜ × 11 in. (36.5 × 28 cm). The Alkazi Collection of Photography.

12. Determine Margins

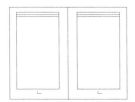

Also see pages
22–23

I f a printed project has a long page count, there's a danger that material could get lost in the gutter. Therefore , a good practice is to leave a gutter margin large enough to keep the text from disappearing into binding. When the project is a book, a spread that looks proportionate on screen or in laser printouts can change radically once the book is printed and bound. The amount of spatial loss in the gutter depends on the length of the book or brochure as well as the binding method. Whether the piece is perfect bound, sewn, or saddle stitched, it's a good idea to make certain that nothing goes missing.

BINDING METHODS AND MARGINS

Depending on the number of pages in a project, some binding methods cause type to get lost in the gutters more than others. A project with a sewn or notch binding can be opened flatter than a perfect-bound (glued) project. Type may get lost in the gutter of a perfect-bound project and readers may be reluctant to crack the binding when pulling the book open. If the project is spiral bound, leave enough space in the gutter for the spiral holes.

PROJECT
Sauces

CLIENT
John Wiley and Sons

DESIGN
BTDNYC

Eight hundred-plus pages of hard-core cooking information begs for—and receives—healthy portions of gutter space.

Images are from *Sauces*, published by John Wiley & Sons, © 2008 by James Peterson. Reprinted with permission of John Wiley & Sons, Inc.

Generous margins ensure that important recipe instructions remain easy to read, without text slipping into the gutter. In addition, wide margins take into account elements such as subheads and charts, which may appear outside of the text block. Generous margins for markers such as running feet and folios also give a sense of calm and leisure.

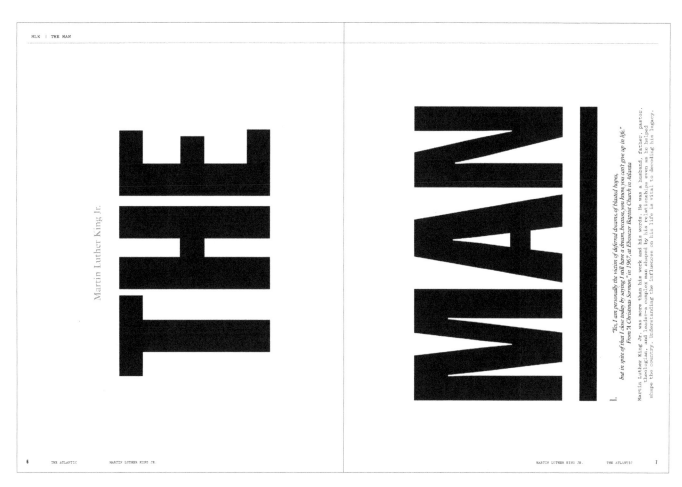

Martin Luther King Jr.

"Yes, I am personally the victim of deferred dreams, of blasted hopes, but in spite of that I close today by saying I still have a dream, because, you know, you can't grow up in life." From "A Christmas Sermon," in 1967, at Ebenezer Baptist Church in Atlanta

Martin Luther King Jr. was more than his work and his words. He was a husband, father, pastor, theologian, and leader—a complex man shaped by his relationships even as he helped shape the country. Understanding the influences on his life is vital to decoding his legacy.

1.

PROJECT
King, a special edition issue commemorating the fiftieth anniversary of the assassination of Martin Luther King, Jr.

CLIENT
The Atlantic

CREATIVE DIRECTOR
Paul Spella

ART DIRECTOR
David Somerville

DESIGN FIRM
OCD | Original Champions of Design

DESIGNERS
Bobby C. Martin Jr.,
Jennifer Kinon

Dynamics of size and space, with tight margins for markers add energy and tension.

O n the other hand—and this works for situations that are not solely single column—certain margins may be intentionally tight in order to add a sense of tension and of history on the edge. Page numbers and section information designed dangerously near the head or foot trim contrast with white space in the case of this spread or, in the case of the spreads on page 85, heighten awareness of the material's importance.

RULE OF THUMB

A common question is what the rule of thumb for print margins is. There is no magic solution, but I suggest starting with .5"(1.25cm) and adding or subtracting from there. Less than a .25"(6mm) outside marging can mean flirting with something called bounce on press. The final decisions depends on the proportion of your page and your material and, if a print project, your output provider. A common error in print is too large a text for too small a margin. On the web, tablet, or device, margins are important as well, but less margin can lose less information.

Although this is technically a single-column layout, the principle of smaller margins applies throughout the issue of this magazine. For a trim size of 7³/₄" x 10⁷/₁₆" (19.5 x 26.4 cm), the outside margins of ⁷/₃₂"(5 mm) from top trim down to running head and bottom trim up to the base of the folios and running feet push the limits of printing and trimming. It works.

13. Work in Proportion

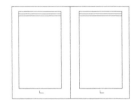

K eep proportions in mind, including for the foot margin. Even a seemingly simple page involves a deliberate use of space that will set off material on a printed page and, ideally, a screen.

PROJECT
The Plague of Doves

CLIENT
HarperCollins

DESIGN
Fritz Metsch

An example of crystal goblet design, this simple text page allows the work of a major literary talent to shine. In her book, *The Crystal Goblet: Sixteen Essays on Typography*, typographer and scholar Beatrice Warde wrote that "printing should be invisible," and noted that quiet design is like a crystal goblet: "Everything about it is calculated to reveal rather than the hide the beautiful thing which it was meant to contain."

THE PLAGUE OF

DOVES

LOUISE ERDRICH

HarperCollins*Publishers*

The foot margin (the margin at the bottom of the page) is slightly larger than the head margin. The screened, patterned art delicately presents the title type, set in bold for a strong texture but in a small size for an understated look.

The Plague of Doves

IN THE YEAR 1896, my great uncle, one of the first Catholic priests of aboriginal blood, put the call out to his parishioners that they should gather at Saint Joseph's wearing scapulars and holding missals From that place they would proceed to walk the fields in a long sweeping row, and with each step loudly pray away the doves His human flock had taken up the plow and farmed among German and Norwegian settlers Those people, unlike the French who mingled with my ancestors, took little interest in the women native to the land and did not intermarry In fact, the Norwegians disregarded everybody but themselves and were quite clannish But the doves ate their crops the same When the birds descended, both Indians and whites set up great bonfires and tried driving them into nets The doves ate the wheat seedlings and the rye and started on the corn They ate the sprouts of new flowers and the buds of apples and the tough leaves of oak trees and even last year's chaff The doves were plump, and delicious smoked, but one could wring the necks of hundreds or thousands and effect no visible diminishment of their number The pole and mud houses of the mixed bloods and the bark huts of the blanket Indians were crushed by the weight of the birds They were roasted, burnt, baked up in pies, stewed, salted down in barrels or clubbed dead with sticks and left to rot But the dead only fed the living and each morning when the people woke it was to the scraping and beating of wings, the murmurous sussuration, the awful cooing babble, and the sight, to those who still possessed intact windows, of the curious and gentle faces of those creatures

5

A centered page number, or folio, is a signal of a classical design.

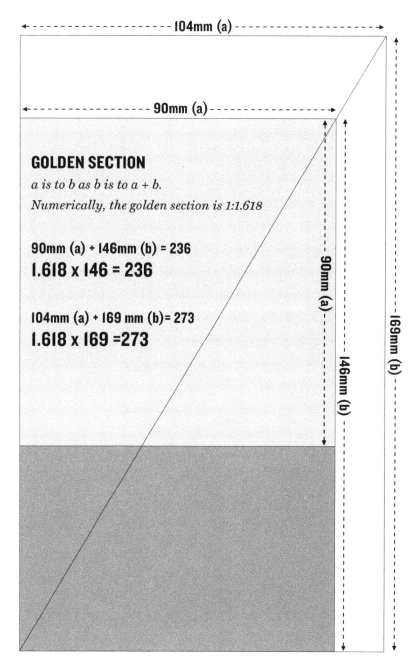

cousin John kidnapped his own wife and used the ransom to keep his mistress in Fargo Despondent over a woman, my father's uncle, Octave Harp, managed to drown himself in two feet of water And so on As with my father, these tales of extravagant encounter contrasted with the modesty of the subsequent marriages and occupations of my relatives We are a tribe of office workers, bank tellers, book readers, and bureaucrats The wildest of us (Whitey) is a short order cook, and the most heroic of us (my father) teaches Yet this current of drama holds together the generations, I think, and my brother and I listened to Mooshum not only from suspense but for instructions on how to behave when our moment of recognition, or perhaps our romantic trial, should arrive.

The Million Names

IN TRUTH, I thought mine probably had occurred early, for even as I sat there listening to Mooshum my fingers obsessively wrote the name of my beloved up and down my arm or in my hand or on my knee If I wrote his name a million times on my body, I believed he would kiss me I knew he loved me, and he was safe in the knowledge that I loved him, but we attended a Roman Catholic grade school in the early 1960's and boys and girls known to be in love hardly talked to one another and never touched We played softball and kickball together, and acted and spoke through other children eager to deliver messages I had copied a series of these second hand love statements into my tiny leopard print diary with the golden lock The key was hidden in the hollow knob of my bedstead Also I had written the name of my beloved, in blood from a scratched mosquito bite, along the inner wall of my closet His name held for me the sacred resonance of those Old Testament words written in fire by an invisible hand Mene, mene, teckel, upharsin I could not say his name aloud I could only write it on my skin with my fingers without cease until my mother feared I'd gotten lice and coated my hair with mayonnaise, covered my head with a shower cap, and told me to sit in the bathtub adding water as hot as I could stand.

The bathroom, the tub, the apparatus of plumbing was all new Because my father and mother worked for the school and in the tribal offices, we were hooked up to the agency water system I locked the bathroom door,

9

Bold, letterspaced running heads (headers) and folios (page numbers) give texture to a full page of type. Reading is easier with generous margins and ample leading.

THE GOLDEN RATIO

The golden ratio has been used in art and architecture for thousands of years. Also called the golden section, the golden ratio describes a ratio of elements, such as height to width. The ratio is approximately 0.618 or 1: 1.618. In other words, the smaller segment, for example, the width or (*a*), is to the larger segment, the height or (*b*), as the larger segment is to the sum of both segments. So, a designer could have a measure that is 22 picas wide with a height of 35 picas 6 points. The diagram to the right shows two different rectangles that mathematically work out to the golden ration. Designers often work by eye and instinct instead of using exact numbers, but they achieve pleasing proportions.

14. Consider Equality

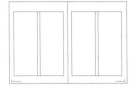

Agrid with two even columns can control a large amount of material on a page. Symmetrical columns give a sense of great order and can support variations in image sizes and amouns of space. Perfect for publications with international audiences, two even columns can present the same information in two different languages, coexisting equally.

Traditional justified columns provide a sense of order and comfort for conservative editors and readers.

EVGENY CHUBAROV
ЕВГЕНИЙ ЧУБАРОВ

PROJECT
Return to the Abstract

CLIENT
Palace Editions, for the
Russian State Museums

DESIGN
Anton Ginzburg, Studio RADIA

Two columns present
information in two languages,
Russian and English.

If the column width is wide enough and the text small enough, each of the two columns will present a uniform and readable texture. A tidy text setup can support all sorts of other information, such as boxes, charts, or images.

15. Design for Function

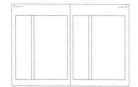

Although a typical approach to a two-column grid employs columns of equal widths, a two-column grid can consist of two unequal columns. When the purpose of an information-rich piece is to be open, readable, and accessible, an option is to construct a grid containing a narrow column and a wider column. The wider column works well for running text and enables the author(s) to deliver a coherent running narrative, while the narrow column can hold material such as captions, images, or tables.

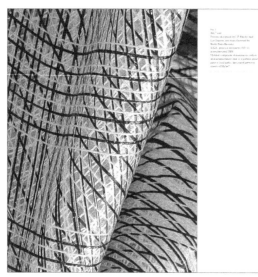

Used for captions, a narrow column can work readably, whether the caption appears on a chapter opener or a text page. Note that chapter openers often have more space before the text starts (also known as a sink, or drop) than a normal text page.

PROJECT
Extreme Textiles

CLIENT
Smithsonian, Cooper-Hewitt, National Design Museum: Extreme Textiles Exhibition Catalog

DESIGN
Tsang Seymour Design

DESIGN DIRECTOR
Patrick Seymour

DESIGNER
Susan Brzozowski

An exhibition catalog weaves different formats together, depending on the needs of the material.

Successful and balanced grid construction employs a wide column that is double the width of the narrow column. The type in the narrower column is set in the same typeface as the running text but in a lighter-weight font. Using varying font weights adds rich texture.

When there are few or no images, the structure of two uneven columns can support a page with nothing in the smaller text column.

Rules can function as devices to either divide the space or connect columns within the space. Here, the blue rules become part of the weave of the page without overwhelming the material; they also denote new paragraphs.

fig. 3
Impressions left by the airbags of the Mars Exploration Rover (MER) Opportunity on Martian soil. January 24, 2004

This classic plain weave has the greatest strength and stability of the traditional fabric structures. While no textiles survive from the earliest dates, impressions in clay of basic woven cloth demonstrate its use from at least 7000 BC.[3] Older than metal-working or pottery-making, perhaps even older than agriculture, cloth-weaving has a very primary relationship to the pursuits of humankind.[4]

It is fitting, then, that among the first marks made by man in the soil of Mars was that of a plain woven fabric: an impression made by the impact of the airbags (fig. 3).[5] Each bag has a double bladder and several abrasion-resistant layers made of tightly woven Vectran. Like most synthetic fibers, Vectran liquid crystal polymer is extruded from a liquid state through a spinneret, similar to a shower head, and drawn into filament fibers. The stretching of the fiber during the drawing process orients the polymer chains more fully along the fiber length, creating additional chemical bonds and greater strength. Vectran provides equal strength at one-fifth the weight of steel. Weight is of premium importance for all materials used for space travel, and Warwick Mills, the weaver of the fabric for the bags, achieved a densely woven fabric at a mere 2.4 ounces per square yard, but with a strength of 350 pounds per inch.[6]

The materials are also required to perform at severe temperatures. Because impact occurs two to three seconds after the inflation of the airbags, the fabrics endure their greatest stresses at both extremes of temperature: the explosive gasses that inflate the bags may elevate the temperature inside the bladder layers to over 212°F, but the temperature on the Martian surface is −117°F. Retraction of the airbags to allow the egress of the rovers required that the fabrics remain flexible at these very low temperatures for an extended period of time—about ninety minutes for the deflation and retraction process. Two other fiber types, aramid fibers (Kevlar 29 and Technora T-240) and ultra-high molecular weight polyethylene (UHMWPE) Spectra 1000, were also considered during the development of the Pathfinder airbags. Spectra, a super-drawn fiber, is among the strongest fibers known—fifteen times stronger than steel. However, it performs poorly at extreme temperatures, and so was eliminated early in the development process. Vectran was ultimately selected for the best performance at low temperatures, but Kevlar 129 was used for the tethers inside the bags because of its superior performance at higher temperatures.

The rovers themselves are also textile-based: they are made from super-strong, ultra-lightweight carbon-fiber composites, which are being widely used for aerospace components as well as high-performance sports equipment.[7] As composite reinforcements, textiles offer a high level of customization, with regard to type and weight of fiber, use of combinations of fibers, and use of different weaves to maximize the density of fibers in a given direction. Fiber strength is greatest along the length. The strength of composite materials derives from the intentional use of this directional nature. While glass fibers are the most commonly used for composites, for high-performance products the fiber used is often carbon or aramid, or a combination of the two, because of their superior strength and light weight.

One advantage of composite construction is the ability to make a complex form in one piece, called monocoque construction. A woven textile is hand-laid in a mold; the piece is wetted out with resin and cured in an autoclave. The textile can also be impregnated with resin and cured without a wet stage. The same drape or hand that makes twill the preferred weave for most apparel is also desirable for creating the complex forms of boats, paddles, bicycle frames, and other sports equipment. The weft in a twill, rather than crossing under and over each consecutive warp, floats over more than one warp, and with each subsequent weft the grouping is shifted over one warp, creating the marked diagonal effect typical of twills (fig. 8).

Boat builders were among the first to experiment with carbon-reinforced composites. One early innovator, Edward S. ("Ted") Van Dusen, began making carbon-fiber composite racing shells in the 1970s (fig. 7). The critical factor in shell design is the stiffness-to-weight ratio, with greater stiffness meaning that more of the rower's power is translated into forward motion. Van Dusen found that all of the standard construction materials had about the same specific stiffness, or stiffness per unit weight, and began experimenting with glass, boron, and carbon fiber–reinforced composites.[8]

For his Advantage racing shells, Van Dusen uses glass fiber in a complex twill commonly known as satin weave. In a satin, each weft may float over

---

CARBON

Thomas Edison first used carbon fiber when he employed charred cotton thread to conduct electricity in a lightbulb (he patented it in 1879). Only in the past fifty years, however, has carbon developed as a high-strength, high-modulus fiber.[9] Oxidized then carbonized from polyacrylonitrile (PAN) or pitch precursor fibers, carbon's tenacity and modulus vary depending on its starting materials and process of manufacture.[9]

Less dense than ceramic or glass, lightweight carbon-fiber composites save fuel when used in aerospace and automotive vehicles. They also make for strong, efficient sports equipment. Noncorroding, carbon reinforcements strengthen deep seawater concrete structures such as petroleum production risers.[10] Fine diameter carbon fibers are woven into sails to minimize stretch.[11] In outer apparel, carbon fibers protect workers against open flames (up to 1000°C/1,800°F) and even burning napalm: they will not ignite, and shrink very little in high temperatures.[12]

ARAMIDS

Aramids, such as Kevlar (DuPont) and Twaron® (Teijin), are famous for their use in bulletproof vests and other forms of ballistic protection, as well as for cut resistance and flame retardance. Initially developed in the 1960s, aramids are strong because their long molecular chains are fully extended and packed closely together, resulting in high-tenacity, high-modulus fibers.[13]

Corrosion- and chemical-resistant, aramids are used in aerial and mooring ropes and construction cables, and provide mechanical protection in optical fiber cables.[14] Like carbon, aramid-composite materials make light aircraft components and sporting goods, but aramids have the added advantages of impact resistance and energy absorption.

LIQUID CRYSTAL POLYMER (LCP)

Although spun from different polymers and processes, LCPs resemble aramids in their strength, impact resistance, and energy absorption, as well as their sensitivity to UV light. Compared to aramids, Vectran (Celanese), the only commercially available LCP, is more resistant to abrasion, has better flexibility, and retains its strength longer when exposed to high temperatures. Vectran also surpasses aramids and HMPE in dimensional stability and cut resistance: it is used in wind sails for America's Cup races, inflatable structures, ropes, cables and restraint-lines, and cut-resistant clothing.[15] Because it can be sterilized by gamma rays, Vectran is used for medical devices such as implants and surgical-device control cables.[16]

HIGH-MODULUS POLYETHYLENE (HMPE)

HMPE, known by the trade names Dyneema (Toyobo/DSM) or Spectra (Honeywell), is made from ultra-high molecular-weight polyethylene by a special gel-spinning process. It is the least dense of all the high-performance fibers, and the most abrasion-resistant. It is also more resistant than aramids, PBO, and LCP to UV radiation and chemicals.[17] It makes for moorings and fish lines that float and withstand the sun, as well as lightweight, cut-resistant gloves and protective apparel such as fencing suits and soft ballistic armor. In composites, it lends impact resistance and energy absorption to glass- or carbon-reinforced products. HMPE conducts almost no electricity, making it transparent to radar.[18] HMPE does not withstand gamma-ray sterilization and has a relatively low melting temperature of 150°C (300°F)—two qualities that preclude its use where high temperature resistance is a must.

POLYPHENYLENE BENZOBISOXAZOLE (PBO)

PBO fibers surpass aramids in flame resistance, dimensional stability, and chemical and abrasion resistance, but are sensitive to photodegradation and hydrolysis in warm, moist conditions.[19] Their stiff molecules form highly rigid structures, which grant an extremely high tenacity and modulus. Apparel containing Zylon® (Toyobo), the only PBO fiber in commercial production, provides ballistic protection because of its high energy absorption and dissipation of impact. Zylon is also used in the knee pads of motorcycle apparel, for heat-resistant work wear, and in felt used for glass formation.[20]

PIPD

PIPD, M5 fiber (Magellan Systems International), expected to come into commercial production in 2005, matches or exceeds aramids and PBO in many of its properties. However, because the molecules have strong lateral bonding, as well as great strength along the oriented chains, M5 has much better shear and compression resistance. In composites it shows good adhesion to resins. Its dimensional stability under heat, resistance to UV radiation and fire, and transparency to radar expands its possible uses. Potential applications include soft and hard ballistic protection, fire protection, ropes and tethers, and structural composites.[21]

HYBRIDS

A blend of polymers in a fabric, yarn, or fiber structure can achieve a material better suited for its end use. Comfortable fire-retardant, anti-static clothing may be woven primarily from aramid fibers but feature the regular insertion of a carbon filament to dissipate static charge. Yarns for cut-resistant applications maintain good tactile properties with a wrapping of cotton around HMPE and fiberglass cores. On a finer level, a single fiber can be extruded from two or more different polymers in various configurations to exhibit the properties of both.

COMPARISON OF YARN STRENGTH

COMPARISON OF MODULI

DECOMPOSITION TEMPERATURE

DENSITY

16. Regulate Rules

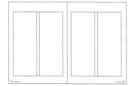

Sometimes, instructional material includes so many discrete chunks of information that a page needs more than mere space between the columns for readability. In such cases, a vertical rule can function as a dividing line between columns.

Horizontal rules can separate information within columns by dividing running text from boxed material, or by separating the overall text area from the running feet and folios by means of another horizontal rule. Caution: Too many rules can dull a page.

This vertical rule keeps chunks of different information, sometimes with different type attributes—such as bolds, all capitals, italics, fractions—in their respective columns.

PROJECT
America's Test Kitchen Family Cookbook

CLIENT
America's Test Kitchen

ART DIRECTION
Amy Klee

DESIGN
BTDNYC

Horizontal rules at the head and foot can set off information or frame an entire box.

NONFAT ROASTED GARLIC DRESSING

MAKES about 1 ½ cups
PREP TIME: 10 minutes
TOTAL TIME: 2 hours (includes 1 ½ hours roasting and cooling time)

To keep this recipe nonfat, we altered our usual technique for roasting garlic, replacing the oil we typically use with water.

2	large garlic heads
2	tablespoons water
	Salt
2	tablespoons Dijon mustard
2	tablespoons honey
6	tablespoons cider vinegar
½	teaspoon pepper
2	teaspoons minced fresh thyme, or ½ teaspoon dried
½	cup low-sodium chicken broth

1. Adjust an oven rack to the upper-middle position and heat the oven to 400 degrees. Following the photos on page 000, cut ½ inch off the top of the garlic head to expose the tops of the cloves. Set the garlic head cut side down on a small sheet of aluminum foil, and sprinkle with the water and a pinch of salt. Gather the foil up around the garlic tightly to form a packet, place it directly on the oven rack, and roast for 45 minutes.

2. Carefully open just the top of the foil to expose the garlic and continue to roast until the garlic is soft and golden brown, about 20 minutes longer. Allow the roasted garlic to cool for 20 minutes, reserving any juices in the foil packet.

3. Following the photo on page 000, squeeze the garlic from the skins. Puree the garlic, reserved garlic juices, ¾ teaspoon salt, and the remaining ingredients together in a blender (or food processor) until thick and smooth, about 1 minute. The dressing, covered, can be refrigerated for up to 4 days; bring to room temperature and whisk vigorously to recombine before using.

LOWFAT ORANGE-LIME DRESSING

MAKES about 1 cup
PREP TIME: 10 minutes
TOTAL TIME: 1 hour (includes 45 minutes simmering and cooling time)

Although fresh-squeezed orange juice will taste best, any store-bought orange juice will work here. Unless you want a vinaigrette with off flavors make sure to reduce the orange juice in a nonreactive stainless steel pan.

2	cups orange juice (see note above)
3	tablespoons fresh lime juice
1	tablespoon honey
1	tablespoon minced shallot
½	teaspoon salt
½	teaspoon pepper
2	tablespoons extra-virgin olive oil

1. Simmer the orange juice in a small saucepan over medium heat until slightly thickened and reduced to ⅔ cup, about 30 minutes. Transfer to a small bowl and refrigerate until cool, about 15 minutes.

2. Shake the chilled, thickened juice with the remaining ingredients in a jar with a tight-fitting lid until combined. The dressing can be refrigerated for up to 4 days; bring to room temperature, then shake vigorously to recombine before using.

Test Kitchen Tip: **REDUCE YOUR JUICE**
Wanting to sacrifice calories, but not flavor or texture, we adopted a technique often used by spa chefs in which the viscous quality of oil is duplicated by using reduced fruit juice syrup or roasted garlic puree. The resulting dressings are full bodied and lively enough to mimic full-fat dressings but without the chemicals or emulsifiers often used in commercial lowfat versions. Don't be put off by the long preparation times of these recipes—most of it is unattended roasting, simmering, or cooling time.

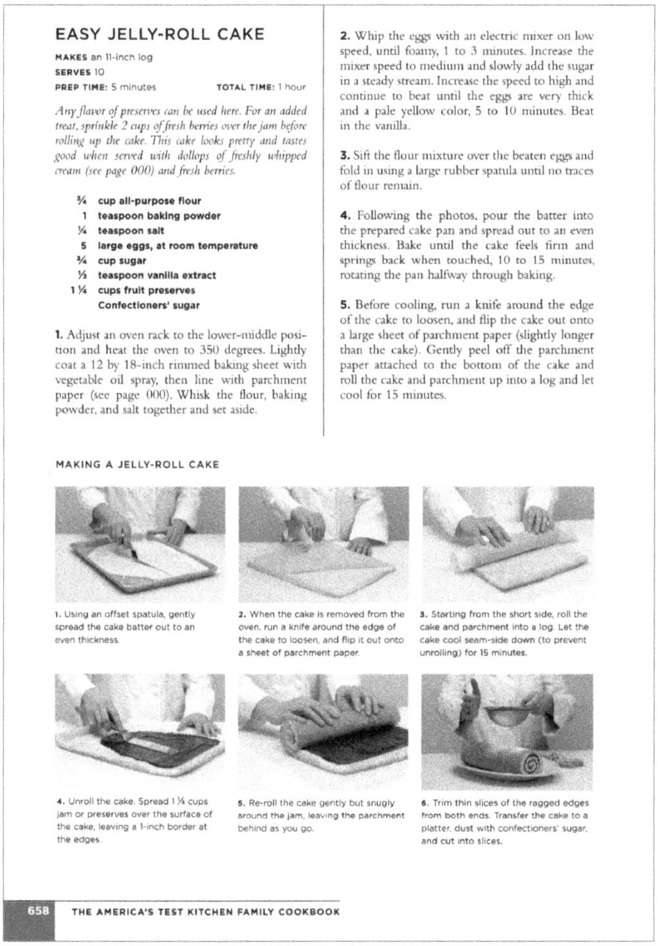

EASY JELLY-ROLL CAKE

MAKES an 11-inch log
SERVES 10
PREP TIME: 5 minutes   **TOTAL TIME:** 1 hour

Any flavor of preserves can be used here. For an added treat, sprinkle 2 cups of fresh berries over the jam before rolling up the cake. This cake looks pretty and tastes good when served with dollops of freshly whipped cream (see page 000) and fresh berries.

¾	cup all-purpose flour
1	teaspoon baking powder
¼	teaspoon salt
5	large eggs, at room temperature
¾	cup sugar
½	teaspoon vanilla extract
1 ¼	cups fruit preserves
	Confectioners' sugar

1. Adjust an oven rack to the lower-middle position and heat the oven to 350 degrees. Lightly coat a 12 by 18-inch rimmed baking sheet with vegetable oil spray, then line with parchment paper (see page 000). Whisk the flour, baking powder, and salt together and set aside.

2. Whip the eggs with an electric mixer on low speed, until foamy, 1 to 3 minutes. Increase the mixer speed to medium and slowly add the sugar in a steady stream. Increase the speed to high and continue to beat until the eggs are very thick and a pale yellow color, 5 to 10 minutes. Beat in the vanilla.

3. Sift the flour mixture over the beaten eggs and fold in using a large rubber spatula until no traces of flour remain.

4. Following the photos, pour the batter into the prepared cake pan and spread out to an even thickness. Bake until the cake feels firm and springs back when touched, 10 to 15 minutes, rotating the pan halfway through baking.

5. Before cooling, run a knife around the edge of the cake to loosen, and flip the cake out onto a large sheet of parchment paper (slightly longer than the cake). Gently peel off the parchment paper attached to the bottom of the cake and roll the cake and parchment up into a log and let cool for 15 minutes.

MAKING A JELLY-ROLL CAKE

1. Using an offset spatula, gently spread the cake batter out to an even thickness.

2. When the cake is removed from the oven, run a knife around the edge of the cake to loosen, and flip it out onto a sheet of parchment paper.

3. Starting from the short side, roll the cake and parchment into a log. Let the cake cool seam-side down (to prevent unrolling) for 15 minutes.

4. Unroll the cake. Spread 1 ¼ cups jam or preserves over the surface of the cake, leaving a 1-inch border at the edges.

5. Re-roll the cake gently but snugly around the jam, leaving the parchment behind as you go.

6. Trim thin slices of the ragged edges from both ends. Transfer the cake to a platter, dust with confectioners' sugar, and cut into slices.

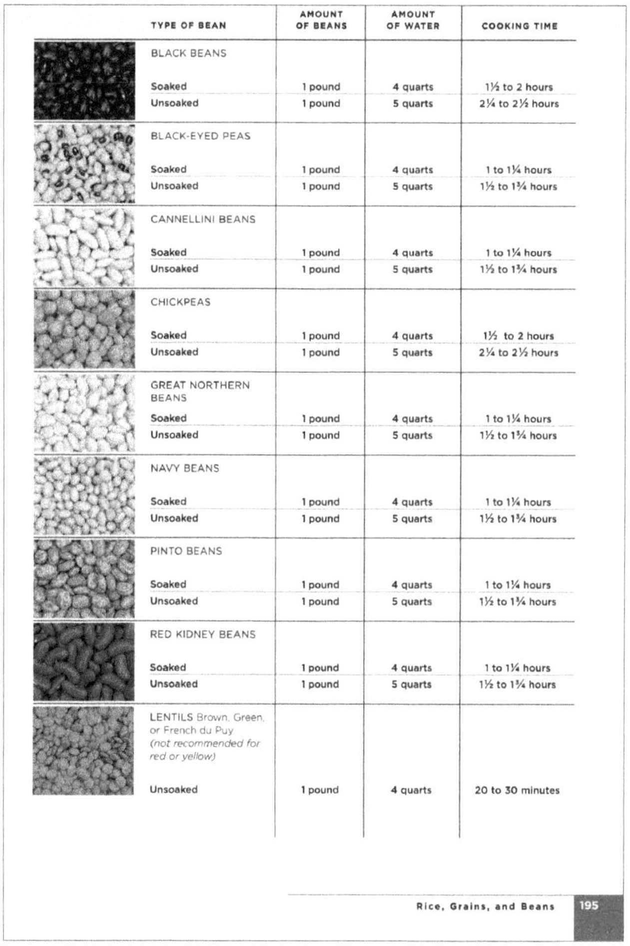

TYPE OF BEAN	AMOUNT OF BEANS	AMOUNT OF WATER	COOKING TIME
BLACK BEANS			
Soaked	1 pound	4 quarts	1½ to 2 hours
Unsoaked	1 pound	5 quarts	2¼ to 2½ hours
BLACK-EYED PEAS			
Soaked	1 pound	4 quarts	1 to 1¼ hours
Unsoaked	1 pound	5 quarts	1½ to 1¾ hours
CANNELLINI BEANS			
Soaked	1 pound	4 quarts	1 to 1¼ hours
Unsoaked	1 pound	5 quarts	1½ to 1¾ hours
CHICKPEAS			
Soaked	1 pound	4 quarts	1½ to 2 hours
Unsoaked	1 pound	5 quarts	2¼ to 2½ hours
GREAT NORTHERN BEANS			
Soaked	1 pound	4 quarts	1 to 1¼ hours
Unsoaked	1 pound	5 quarts	1½ to 1¾ hours
NAVY BEANS			
Soaked	1 pound	4 quarts	1 to 1¼ hours
Unsoaked	1 pound	5 quarts	1½ to 1¾ hours
PINTO BEANS			
Soaked	1 pound	4 quarts	1 to 1¼ hours
Unsoaked	1 pound	5 quarts	1½ to 1¾ hours
RED KIDNEY BEANS			
Soaked	1 pound	4 quarts	1 to 1¼ hours
Unsoaked	1 pound	5 quarts	1½ to 1¾ hours
LENTILS Brown, Green, or French du Puy (not recommended for red or yellow)			
Unsoaked	1 pound	4 quarts	20 to 30 minutes

The space between units of information separates horizontal elements and gives a page clarity.

Horizontal rules can also help control components. When there's a lot of informational action going on, a horizontal rule can separate a page number or a running foot from the rest of the hard-core information.

17. Add Fluidity to Order

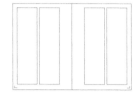

Variations include making the images wider and using various type widths.

A two-column grid is a pronounced framework that makes a piece easy to follow. Images can fit comfortably within a column, with captions above or below. But why stop there? Once the basic framework is determined, there is room to vary the spreads. Wider images, sized to two columns, or captions set out into the margin, can enliven the overall project, adding rhythm as well as order.

PROJECT
Design for the Other 90%,
exhibition catalog

CLIENT
Smithsonian, Cooper-Hewitt,
National Design Museum

DESIGN
Tsang Seymour Design

DESIGN DIRECTOR
Patrick Seymour

ART DIRECTOR/DESIGNER
Laura Howell

The flow of layouts tells a 100% clear story.

Fig. Felix Munari with his MoneyMaker Hip Pump on his farm in Maragua District, Kenya

lawn mowers, and cell phones. They are made in large quantities in big factories. The economy of scale created by centralized manufacturing lowers the price, making the product affordable and ensuring higher quality and reliability. KickStart does the same thing. By centralizing our manufacturing in the most advanced factories available, we can produce high-quality, durable products at a lower cost. Wholesalers and middlemen move these goods from factory to marketplace, making a profit in the process. A network of more than 900 local retail shops in three countries stock and sell our pumps. This supply chain needs no artificial support, and will exist as long as there is consumer demand. KickStart also uses donor funds to market the new technologies and generate demand. As with any new product, it takes both time and money. When you are selling an expensive item to the poorest people in the world, it takes even longer and is more expensive. But eventually, we will reach a point where we can end our marketing efforts and sell each pump at a profit, which we will then reinvest in developing new technology and expanding into new countries. This is a sustainable supply chain.

Third, there is a question of fairness. I have heard people say that it is not "fair" to ask poor people to invest in their own future, but is it fair to give one person or one village a gift when there are others just as needy? By making our products available through the marketplace, they are available to everyone, without patronage or favoritism. This is perhaps the hardest lesson for someone who wants to do good in the world. We see people in desperate need and want to alleviate their suffering. This spirit of generosity is human nature at its best. But as noble as this motivation is in the giving, it is demoralizing in the receiving. When people invest in themselves and their own futures, they have full ownership of their success, and that creates dignity.

INDIVIDUAL OWNERSHIP WORKS BEST

A good question to ask about any program is: Who will own the new technology? If the answer is unclear, or vague, then the program is unlikely to succeed in the long term. We have learned that individual ownership works better than group ownership. Africa is covered with failed community-owned technologies—tractors, water pumps, ambulances, water purification and irrigation systems, etcetera. The list goes on.

There is a common idea that poor people will come together for the collective benefit, or that "investing" in a community is more cost effective or efficient than working with individuals. There are some situations where this works, like building roads or farmers cooperatives. But it is much less likely to be effective with the joint ownership of a physical asset. The problem is that if everybody owns an asset, in reality, nobody owns it, and if nobody owns it, nobody will maintain it. Unless there is a way to extract a payment from everyone who uses the asset to cover the

costs of maintenance, repair, and replacement, you have the classic free-rider problem.

It comes down to this. The poorest people in the world are just like you and me. No matter how community minded we are, we will take care of the needs of our family first. And we value the most the items we had to work for.

DESIGN FOR AFFORDABILITY

Our best-selling Super MoneyMaker Pump can be used to irrigate more than two acres of land, and on average the users make $1,000 profit from selling fruits and vegetables in the first year of use. We continue to work to reduce the cost, but at $95, it is still too expensive for many families.

In response, we designed the Hip Pump, which can irrigate almost an acre and retails for less than $35. It looks like a bicycle-tire pump pivoted on a hinge at the end of a small platform. However, unlike a bicycle pump, it uses the operator's whole body. It is lightweight, portable, and extremely easy to use.

The Hip Pump has been a tremendous success. Its initial production run of 90 units sold out almost immediately. One of them was bought by Felix Murani, a young man from rural Kenya. He had a wife and three children to support, but they owned no land. Felix left his family to seek work in the city, where he managed to earn $40 a month working in a restaurant in the city's slums, sending what he could home to his wife and children. When he saw the Hip Pump, he realized he could make more money farming back in his village. He saved his money, bought a pump, went home, and rented a small plot of land. He grew tomatoes, kale, baby corn, and French beans, which he sold to middlemen who took them to the city. Felix planted different crops on each of his small plots so he would have harvests at different times of the year. When we visited Felix three months after he started using his pump, he had already made $350 profit, and he and his wife were talking eagerly about buying land and building their own house. This small pump had enabled Felix to turn his own sweat and drive into cash, look after his family, and plan for his future.

MEASURE THE IMPACT OF WHAT YOU DO

Measuring real impact or outcomes is where many would-be social entrepreneurs fail. The number of products you have sold or distributed tells the world nothing. You have to measure the change you are hoping to create in the world or invention. It is hard and expensive to do, but it is vital. We have learned a great deal from our impact-monitoring efforts. Not only does it enable us to measure ourselves against the goals we have set, it has also been hugely valuable in the design and improvement of our products and marketing efforts.

These are KickStart's core values, and they come together to create a very cost effective and sustainable way to help people help themselves out of poverty. None of these principles are unique to KickStart or our technologies.

Fig. A farmer waters her French bean crop with water from a MoneyMaker pump outside of Nairobi, Kenya

Fig. Kenya Vehicle Manufacturers (KVM), located in Thika, north of Nairobi, is one of the companies KickStart partners with to manufacture MoneyMaker Pumps.

They can be applied to many other technologies to make a real difference in the world. Each of these is important individually, but in our experience it is their combination that makes them truly effective.

Finally, for those people who are driven to innovate for the developing world (and also for those who are eager to fund such efforts), I offer this test. A truly successful program to develop and promote new technologies and/or business models needs to meet the following four criteria:

DOES THE PROGRAM CREATE MEASURABLE AND PROVEN IMPACT? This means that you need to carefully define the problem you are trying to solve, then carefully monitor and measure the actual impact you are having on that problem. In the case of KickStart, we are trying to bring people out of poverty by making them able to earn more money. So we carefully measure how much more money the buyers of our technologies make as a result of owning them. If a program cannot create and prove real impact, then it is not worth implementing.

IS THE PROGRAM COST-EFFECTIVE? There are limited funds for developing and promoting new technologies, and we need to ensure that whatever is done uses these funds efficiently. "Cost effective" is a subjective measure, so we offer this comparison. KickStart spends about $250 of donor funds to take an average family out of poverty, whereas a more traditional aid program claims on the Web site to do the same for $7,950.

IS THERE A SUSTAINABLE EXIT STRATEGY? One has to ensure that the benefits will continue to accrue for both the existing and new beneficiaries, even after the donor funds are depleted. Creating a program that continues to depend on donor funds forever is not a viable

solution. There are four different ways that an effort can become sustainable: 1) build and leave in place a profitable supply chain to continue providing the goods/services; 2) hand over the program to a government which will fund it using tax money; 3) create a local situation that can continue to prosper without the injection of any new outside funds, for instance, establishing a local group savings and loan (merry-go-round) system; 4) completely eliminate the problem, such as eradicating a disease.

IS THE MODEL REPLICABLE AND SCALABLE? The problems we are trying to solve—poverty and climate change, among others—are very large in scale, and it is expensive to develop new technologies and new business models. So we want to ensure that the technologies themselves as well as the dissemination models are not too dependent on specific local conditions, and can be easily adapted to many different settings and locations.

Incorporating all of these guidelines into your work will be a challenge, but great invention and designers enjoy a challenge. I can tell you that this experience has been an exciting, sometimes frustrating, often exhausting, and immensely satisfying journey. I wish you a fantastic journey of your own.

18. Define Understandable Zones

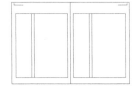

Good design reflects and relates to the material and, therefore, to the reader. Successful typography defines clear and understandable zones, no matter the publication's purpose. Zones can work both horizontally and vertically within a spread or story and still maintain orderly integrity. The key is to make certain that material corresponds. Specifically, make sure the reader understands the basic material at a glance. Make certain the headline or headlines stand apart. Ensure that captions are positioned so they correspond with their images and help the reader—especially when the piece is instructional.

PROJECT
Croissant magazine

CLIENT
Croissant magazine

ART DIRECTION AND DESIGN
Seiko Baba

Croissant, a Japanese magazine geared to women over thirty, makes instructions handsome and clear. This particular magazine is a MOOK, a special edition published by *Croissant* editors. The title is *Mukashi nagara no kurashi no chie*, which roughly means "time-honored wisdom of living."

Headlines are set in an area separate from the text—in some cases on the right edges of the page. In other cases, headlines are set in the center of the page. Sections of text are set off by space or rules, with a distinct area for captions.

左・大根の二杯酢柚子香り漬け。こうしておくと、いつまででももち、いつ何どきお弁当でも、煮てでも合せるし、お菜とでもお酒とでもおいしい。
中・大根の皮はキンピラにする。「ちょっとだけ砂糖を入れる。で、唐辛子入れて――一種もらないとダメよ。煮上がっちゃうからで、お醤油をタラッときわらせて、味は自分の好みでね」
右・大根の葉は油揚げとかめ。味付けはショウガ醤油で。この葉っぱと皮のるのは、37ページで見た大根。

大根は、葉っぱから尻尾まで全部食べられるのよ、皮はキンピラにして、ね。

薬用酒各種。「山椒の実、カリン、アロエ、ビワの葉、ニンニク、ナナカマド、タコ、クロモジ、毒草各種は、みんな庭用品になります。焼きます。左からな2つ目のアロエのお酒の作り方は、アロエの葉の皮を立てことらすり、1cmの厚さに切った、水分を同じくらいの厚さのお砂糖にする。ビン口にアロエとレモンを入れ、果実酒焼酎等を入れて、冷暗所で保存、漬けて2〜3か月したら飲める。」

上左・押し寿司の押し箱、上右・塩漬のお弁当箱と、色々なったお弁当時は「梅の、いきを使わないと薄く塗れないって」「杉、手前・おつまみ入れ。「全部、お盆に伏せると早らになって、上にものがのっかるの」

右・お客さん用の靴袋。玄関に靴が並びらず、思いついた。また入はこの袋に自分の靴を入れ、帰下に、「愛されわいように、誰も続く、いろいろな色で作ったんですよ。よ・下駄箱の戸は空気が通るよう細密がある。

薬用酒なんて、台所の納戸にい〜っぱい！　昔のものは、一つのものに効くんでなく、「効くんだもさ」、なんです

「この酒は、いくさの産地の九州は八代で作ってもらったの」。葉、マットの上に巻いて寝れば冷暖房し。「ヨガにも使うし。巻いとけば場所とらないしね」

[Japanese vertical text body — running text and step-by-step directions]

Type in different zones can distinguish various kinds of information. Here, running text and step-by-step directions are in separate areas.

19. Mix Quirks with Consistency

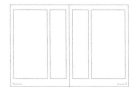

The most successful grids have consistency, order, clarity, and a strong structure—then they shake things up. A two-column grid can be set with columns of different widths, which add visual tension and movement to a project. Even when quirky variations are used to enliven a design, a stable basic structure provides a clear framework while allowing drama.

Consistent elements in many projects are

- a heading area at the top of the page
- a consistent text box in the same location on both left and right pages that acts as an effective signpost for the reader
- running feet and folios at the foot of the page to help the reader navigate through the piece

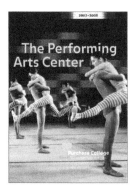

This project has a master format to support key information used throughout the brochure. Key descriptive text with auxiliary information is easy to find. The clear structure holds its own against an energetic ornamental device.

PROJECT
Brochure for the Performing Arts Center, Purchase College

CLIENT
SUNY Purchase

DESIGN
Heavy Meta

ART DIRECTOR
Barbara Glauber

DESIGNER
Hilary Greenbaum

A sound organizational structure allows quirky variation to enliven a design.

Mark Morris Dance Group

FRIDAY, SEPTEMBER 28, 2007, 8 PM
CONCERT HALL

The **MARK MORRIS DANCE GROUP** was formed in 1980 and gave its first concert that year in New York City. In 1988, MMDG was invited to become the national dance company of Belgium and spent three years in residence at the Théâtre Royal de la Monnaie in Brussels. The company returned to the United States in 1991 as one of the world's leading dance companies, performing across the U.S. and at major international festivals. MMDG is noted for its commitment to live music, a feature of every performance on its full international touring schedule since 1996. The company's 25th Anniversary celebration included over 100 performances throughout 26 U.S. cities and ten U.K. cities.

PROGRAM:
The Argument
Sang-Froid
Italian Concerto
Love Song Waltzes

DANCE SERIES SUBSCRIPTION
$225, 165, 125

SINGLE TICKETS $85, 65, 45
CYO $59, 50, 41

Beijing LDTX Modern Dance Company

"These were some of the greatest dancers Tampa Bay audiences have seen in years."
—TAMPA TRIBUNE

FRIDAY & SATURDAY, OCT 19 & 20, 2007, 8 PM
PEPSICO THEATRE

Integrating China's traditional culture with influences from abroad and contemporary dance technique, **BEIJING LDTX** offers a unique and seamless blending of these three elements in a repertoire that shows off unsurpassed technical skill and choreographic excellence.

FRIDAY'S PROGRAM: *The Cold Dagger* is the company's new full-evening work, choreographed by Li Han-zhong and Ma Bo. Based on the traditional Chinese game of Weigi, this intricately choreographed look at human confrontation juxtaposes incredible acrobatics with paired movement that would be otherwise impossible on a normal stage.

SATURDAY'S PROGRAM: A rep program that includes *All River Red*, a striking piece performed to Stravinsky's classic, *The Rite of Spring*; coupled with the company's newest commissioned work *Pilgrimage*, featuring music by the "father of Chinese rock," Cui Jian.

DANCE SERIES SUBSCRIPTION
$225, 165, 125

SINGLE TICKETS $45, 35, 25
CYO $41, 32, 23

OPPOSITE PAGE: Most images are used as full-page horizontals, but text boxes and color bars cutting into some images add movement and drama. Names of performers, positioned in clear but different areas of the image add texture and a sense of play.

Colors harmonize with the information.

RIGHT: Silhouettes and white space vary the pace.

ABOVE: Along with a strong structure, this project has a clear typographic hierarchy. The first use of the heading is larger; subsequent headings are repeated in a box of the same size but with smaller type. Dates and locations are found in a color bar with the same color code but a more straightforward treatment. Consider all relationships and keep the hierarchy clear.

20. Alternate Formats

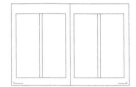

Within one piece, it's legitimate to combine a number of grid and typographic systems. When there are different kinds of information, even a clear two-column grid needs to be altered a little so that there's clarity and balance.

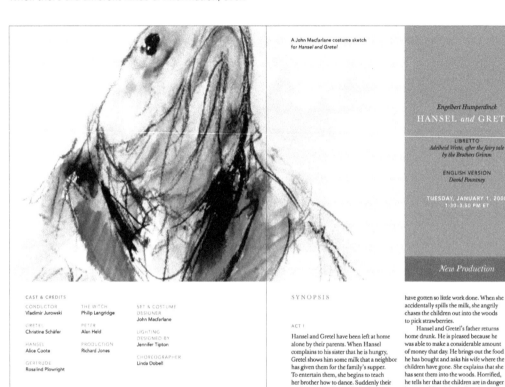

A John Macfarlane costume sketch for *Hansel and Gretel*

PROJECT
2007–2008 HD Program Guide

CLIENT
The Metropolitan Opera

DESIGN
AdamsMorioka, Inc.

CREATIVE DIRECTORS
Sean Adams, Noreen Morioka

ART DIRECTOR
Monica Schlaug

DESIGNERS
Monica Schlaug, Chris Taillon

A controlled and classical yet lively design brings youthful energy to the collateral graphics for a timeless art form.

Running text, such as a continuous story or synopsis, is set in two even columns.

Sections devoted to each performance open with large, dramatic photos.

Anna Castle and
Christine Schäfer sing
the title roles.

GRETEL WAKES HANSEL,
and the two find themselves in front of a gingerbread house.

ACT II

Gretel sings while Hansel picks strawberries. When they hear a cuckoo calling, they imitate the bird's call, eating strawberries all the while, and soon there are none left. In the sudden silence of the woods, the children realize that they have lost their way and grow frightened. The Sandman comes to bring them sleep by sprinkling sand on their eyes. Hansel and Gretel say their evening prayer. In a dream, they see 14 angels protecting them.

ACT III

The Dew Fairy appears to awaken the children. Gretel wakes Hansel, and the two find themselves in front of a gingerbread house. They do not notice the Witch, who decides to fatten Hansel up so she can eat him. She immobilizes him with a spell. The oven is hot, and the Witch is overjoyed at the thought of her banquet. Gretel has overheard the Witch's plan, and she breaks the spell on Hansel. When the Witch asks her to look in the oven, Gretel pretends she doesn't know how: the Witch must show her. When she does, peering into the oven, the children shove her inside and shut the door. The oven explodes, and the many gingerbread children the Witch had enchanted come back to life. Hansel and Gretel's parents appear and find their children. All express gratitude for their salvation.

Engelbert Humperdinck
HANSEL and GRETEL

PREMIERE: HOFTHEATER, WEIMAR, 1893

Originally conceived as a small-scale vocal entertainment for children, *Hansel and Gretel* outgrew its original design to become the most successful fairy-tale opera ever created. Like so many children's classics, *Hansel and Gretel* achieved greatness because it resonates with both adults and kids. The composer Engelbert Humperdinck was a protégé of the musical titan Richard Wagner, and the score of *Hansel and Gretel* is flavored with the sophisticated musical lessons he learned from his idol while maintaining a charm and a light touch that were entirely Humperdinck's own. The ancient tale of the young brother and sister who get lost in a dark forest and almost get eaten by an old witch became a classic of German literature in the famous collected stories of the Brothers Grimm. The opera acknowledges the darker features present in the story, yet presents them within a frame of grace and humor. Humperdinck's fellow composer Richard Strauss was delighted with this score from the start and conducted its world premiere. *Hansel and Gretel* has been internationally popular ever since and must be one of the very few operas that can boast equal acclaim from such diverse and demanding critics as children and musicologists.

THE CREATORS

Engelbert Humperdinck (1854–1921) was a German composer who began his career as an assistant to Richard Wagner in Bayreuth in a variety of capacities, including tutoring Wagner's son Siegfried in music and composition. Humperdinck even composed a few minutes of orchestral music for the world premiere of Wagner's *Parsifal* (1882) when extra time was needed to effect a scene change. (This music is not included in the printed score of *Parsifal* and is no longer performed.) *Hansel and Gretel* was Humperdinck's first complete opera and remains the foundation of his reputation. The world premiere of his later opera *Königskinder* took place at the Met and was one of the sensations of the company's 1910–11 season, following less than three weeks after the world premiere of Puccini's *La Fanciulla del West*. *Hansel and Gretel*, however, is the only one of Humperdinck's works to remain in the repertory. The libretto was written by his sister, Adelheid Wette (1858–1916), and is based on the famous fairy tale from the Grimms' collection. The brothers Jacob (1785–1863) and Wilhelm (1786–1859) Grimm were German academics whose groundbreaking linguistic work revolutionized the understanding of language development. Today, they are best remembered for editing and publishing collections of folk tales.

THE SETTING

In the libretto, the opera's three acts move from Hansel and Gretel's home to the dark forest to the witch's gingerbread house deep in the forest. Put another way, the drama moves from the real, through the obscure, and into the unreal and fantastical. In this production, which takes the idea of food as its dramatic focus, each act is set in a different kind of kitchen, informed by a different theatrical style: a D.H. Lawrence-inspired setting in the first, a German Expressionist one in the second, and a Theater of the Absurd mood in the third.

THE MUSIC

The score of *Hansel and Gretel* successfully combines accessible charm with subtle sophistication. Like Wagner, Humperdinck assigns musical themes to certain ideas and then transforms the themes according to new developments in the drama. Much of this development occurs in the orchestra, like the chirpy cuckoo, depicted by the winds in Act II, which becomes

---

Typography, adjusted to distinguish information, shows a counterpoint between serif and sans serif information.

Presenting different kinds of information, such as a question-and-answer format, calls for a two-column grid, with a narrower column for the questions and the wider column for the answers.

---

that Tristan is simply performing his duty. Isolde maintains that his behavior shows his lack of love for her, and asks Brangäne to prepare a death potion. Kurwenal tells the women to prepare to leave the ship, as shouts from the deck announce the sighting of land. Isolde insists that she will not accompany Tristan until he apologizes for his offenses. He appears and greets her with cool courtesy ("Herr Tristan trete nah"). When she tells him she wants satisfaction for Morold's death, Tristan offers her his sword, but she will not kill him. Instead, Isolde suggests that they make peace with a drink of friendship. He understands that she means to poison them both, but still drinks, and she does the same. Expecting death, they exchange a long look of love, then fall into each other's arms. Brangäne admits that she has in fact mixed a love potion, as sailors' voices announce the ship's arrival in Cornwall.

ACT II

In a garden outside Marke's castle, distant horns signal the king's departure on a hunting party. Isolde waits impatiently for a rendezvous with Tristan. Horrified, Brangäne warns her about spies, particularly Melot, a jealous knight whom she has noticed watching Tristan. Isolde replies that Melot is Tristan's friend and sends Brangäne off to stand watch. When Tristan appears, she welcomes him passionately. They praise the darkness that shuts out all false appearances and agree that they feel secure in the night's embrace ("O sink hernieder, Nacht der Liebe"). Brangäne's distant voice warns that it will be daylight soon ("Einsam wachend in der Nacht"), but the lovers are oblivious to any danger and compare the night to death, which will ultimately unite them. Kurwenal rushes in with a warning: the king and his followers have returned, led by Melot, who denounces the lovers. Moved

and disturbed, Marke declares that it was Tristan himself who urged him to marry and chose the bride. He does not understand how someone so dear to him could dishonor him in such a way ("Tatest Du's wirklich?"). Tristan cannot answer. He asks Isolde if she will follow him into the realm of death. When she accepts, Melot attacks Tristan, who falls wounded into Kurwenal's arms.

ACT III

Tristan lies mortally ill outside Kareol, his castle in Brittany, where he is tended by Kurwenal. A shepherd inquires about his master, and Kurwenal explains that only Isolde, with her magic arts, could save him. The shepherd agrees to play a cheerful tune on his pipe as soon as he sees a ship approaching. Hallucinating, Tristan imagines the realm of night where he will return with Isolde. He thanks Kurwenal for his devotion, then envisions Isolde's ship approaching, but the Shepherd's mournful tune signals that the sea is still empty. Tristan recalls the melody, which he heard as a child. It reminds him of the duel with Morold, and he wishes Isolde's medicine had killed him then instead of making him suffer now. The shepherd's tune finally turns cheerful. Tristan gets up from his sickbed in growing agitation and tears off his bandages, letting his wounds bleed. Isolde rushes in, and he falls, dying, in her arms. When the shepherd announces the arrival of another ship, Kurwenal assumes it carries Marke and Melot, and barricades the gate. Brangäne's voice is heard from outside, trying to calm Kurwenal, but he will not listen and stabs Melot before he is killed himself by the king's soldiers. Marke is overwhelmed with grief at the sight of the dead Tristan, while Brangäne explains to Isolde that the king has come to pardon the lovers. Isolde, transfigured, does not hear her, and with a vision of Tristan beckoning her to the world beyond ("Mild und leise"), she sinks dying upon his body.

SCALING THE HEIGHTS

Deborah Voigt and **Ben Heppner** on how they'll ascend opera's Mount Everest—the title roles of *Tristan und Isolde*—with a little help from Maestro James Levine.

Debbie, you've only sung Isolde on stage once before, several years ago. Why the long interval?

Deborah Voigt: I first sang the part in Vienna five years ago. It came along sooner than I anticipated, but the circumstances were right and I decided to go ahead and sing it. When you sing a role as difficult as Isolde, people are going to want you to sing it a lot, and I didn't want to have a lot of them booked if it didn't go well. So I didn't book anything until the performances were over. The first opportunity I had after Vienna are the Met performances.

Ben, what makes you keep coming back to Tristan?

Ben Heppner: Before it starts, it feels like I'm about to climb Mount Everest. But from the moment I step on the stage to the last note I sing it feels like only 15 minutes have gone by. There is something so engaging about this role that you don't notice anything else. It takes all of your mental, vocal, and emotional resources to sing. And I like the challenge of it.

The two of you appear together often, and you've also both worked a lot with James Levine.

DV: Maestro Levine is so in tune with singers—how we breathe and how we work emotionally. I remember I was having trouble with a particular low note, and in one performance, he just lifted up his hands at that moment, looked at me and took a breath, and gave me my entrance. The note just landed and hasn't been a problem since.
BH: He has this wonderful musicality that is so easy to work with. As for Debbie, we just love singing together and I think that is really its own reward.

This *Tristan* will be seen by hundreds of thousands of people around the globe. How does that impact your stage performance?

DV: None of us go out to sing a performance thinking that it is any less significant than another, so my performance will be the same. But when you are playing to a huge opera house, gestures tend to be bigger. For HD, some of the operatic histrionics might go by the wayside.
BH: When the opera house is filled with expectant listeners—that becomes my focus. The only thing I worry about is that it's a very strenuous role, and I'm basically soaking wet from the middle of the second act on! ∎

21. Make It Look Simple

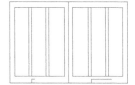

The most successful design looks simple but is subtly versatile. A design that seems open and spare can support a lot of material, especially in a book or catalog.

If the project contains both text and images, look at the proportion between the two and determine how much space is needed for each. When captions are long and contain a lot of additional information, such as credits and supplemental descriptions, distinguish the captions from the text by using different type-faces, by setting the type smaller, or by varying the amount of space between elements.

One structural solution is a three-column grid that scans like a one- or two-column design. Use two of the columns for a single text width and position the text on the right side of the page. The result is a clean look for the running text and a generous left margin for a long caption.

If the material dictates, two columns of captions can replace the single text column, allowing captions and images to sit readably on the same page. With a three-column grid, it's possible to size images to be one, two, or three columns wide or a full-page bleed.

PROJECT
Beatific Soul

CLIENT
New York Public Library/
Scala Publishers

DESIGN
Katy Homans

This book, a companion to an exhibition exploring the life, career, art, journals, and manuscripts of Jack Kerouac, features his landmark novel, *On the Road.* The three column grid allows many variations and extreme flexibility, resulting in a page that looks spacious, calm, and beatifically simple.

This simple but versatile multicolumn grid accommodates all kinds of information. The generous leading of the serif running text makes it easy to read. Captions sit in the left column and are set in a sans serif face for ultimate clarity. The page structure can easily accommodate variations in the text.

Fig. 2.8
List of women, 1962, 10.75" h.

Fig. 2.9
"Lilith." Multicolored felt pens on paper, ca. 1964, 11" x 8.5"

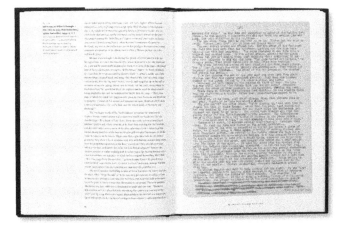

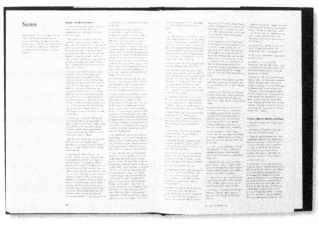

Three columns provide a strong framework for narrow art and multiple captions. On the left page of the spread, captions take the place of the running text, and a narrow image sits in the left column; the right page of the spread is reserved for text alone.

For pacing and clarity, large images occasionally have a page to themselves. Here, an image of Jack Kerouac's typewritten manuscript holds its own against the calm column of text on the left page.

For reference material, such as the notes and index sections, the grid becomes three columns.

22. Define Columns Typographically

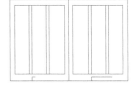

Typography can help define columns. The use of different weights and sizes can help to determine the order of information, creating a hierarchy that can be either horizontal (title, description, yield) or vertical (columns, left to right). Different type, such as a sans serif, can set off lists or information that differs from running text or instructions. Bold weights for titles or the numbers in instructions can function as alerts as well as add zest to the page. Lighter weights, possibly in a different face, can work for headnotes or subservient copy. The clearly-defined spaces can keep the range of typefaces from becoming a visual mash.

Soft and Chewy Chocolate Chip Cookies

A sugar- and butter-rich batter is the foundation for these cookie-jar classics. Just baked, they make a perfect snack on a chilly winter night — or any time. MAKES ABOUT 3 DOZEN

2¼ cups all-purpose flour
½ teaspoon baking soda
1 cup (2 sticks) unsalted butter, room temperature
½ cup granulated sugar
1 cup packed light brown sugar
1 teaspoon coarse salt
2 teaspoons pure vanilla extract
2 large eggs
2 cups semisweet or milk chocolate chips, or a combination (about 12 ounces)

1. Preheat oven to 350°F. Whisk together flour and baking soda in a bowl. Put butter and sugars in the bowl of an electric mixer fitted with the paddle attachment. Mix on medium speed until pale and fluffy, about 2 minutes. Reduce speed to low. Add salt, vanilla, and eggs; mix until well blended, about 1 minute. Mix in flour mixture. Stir in chocolate chips.

2. Drop heaping tablespoons of dough onto baking sheets lined with parchment paper, spacing 2 inches apart. Bake cookies, rotating sheets halfway through, until edges turn golden but centers are still soft, 10 to 12 minutes. Let cool on sheets on wire racks 2 minutes. Transfer cookies to wire racks; let cool completely. Cookies can be stored between layers of parchment in airtight containers at room temperature up to 1 week.

58 · soft and chewy

Peanut Butter and Jelly Bars

This version of a well-loved combination from childhood concentrates the flavors into a sweet dessert that appeals to all ages. We like strawberry jam, but feel free to substitute any flavor you prefer. MAKES ABOUT 3 DOZEN

1 cup (2 sticks) unsalted butter, room temperature, plus more for pan
3 cups all-purpose flour, plus more for pan
1½ cups sugar
2 large eggs
2½ cups smooth peanut butter
1½ teaspoons salt
1 teaspoon baking powder
1 teaspoon pure vanilla extract
1½ cups strawberry jam, or other flavor
1 cup salted peanuts (5 ounces), roughly chopped

1. Preheat oven to 350°F. Butter a 9 by 13-inch baking pan, and line the bottom with parchment paper. Butter the parchment, dust with flour, and tap out excess.

2. Place butter and sugar in the bowl of an electric mixer fitted with the paddle attachment. Beat on medium speed until fluffy, about 2 minutes. With mixer running, add eggs and peanut butter; beat until combined, about 2 minutes. Whisk together flour, salt, and baking powder. Add to the butter mixture, and beat on low speed until combined. Add vanilla.

3. Transfer two-thirds of mixture to prepared pan; spread evenly with an offset spatula. Using offset spatula, spread jam on top of peanut-butter mixture. Crumble remaining third of peanut butter mixture on top of jam. Sprinkle evenly with peanuts.

4. Bake until golden, 45 to 60 minutes, rotating halfway through. Tent loosely with foil if bars are getting too dark. Transfer to a wire rack to cool. Run knife around edges and refrigerate, 1 to 2 hours. Cut into about thirty-six bars (about 1½ by 2 inches). Cookies can be stored in airtight containers at room temperature up to 3 days.

59

Ingredients are in sans serif, and instructions are in a serif typeface. A bolder version of the sans serif is used for emphasis.

PROJECT
Martha Stewart's Cookies

CLIENT
MSL Clarkson Potter

DESIGN
Barbara deWilde

Sophisticated photography and typography accurately reflect the elegance and taste of a domestic authority.

Coconut-Cream Cheese Pinwheels

Rich cream cheese dough, coconut-cream cheese filling, and a topper of jam make these pinwheels complex—chewy on the outside, creamy in the center. Create a variety of flavors by substituting different fruit jams for the strawberry. MAKES ABOUT 2½ DOZEN

for the dough:

2 cups all-purpose flour, plus more for work surface

⅔ cup sugar

½ teaspoon baking powder

½ cup (1 stick) unsalted butter, room temperature

3 ounces cream cheese, room temperature

1 large egg

1 teaspoon pure vanilla extract

for the filling:

3 ounces cream cheese, room temperature

3 tablespoons granulated sugar

1 cup unsweetened shredded coconut

¼ cup white chocolate chips

for the glaze:

1 large egg, lightly beaten

Fine sanding sugar, for sprinkling

⅓ cup strawberry jam

1. Make dough: Whisk together flour, sugar, and baking powder in a bowl. Put butter and cream cheese into the bowl of an electric mixer fitted with the paddle attachment; mix on medium-high speed until fluffy, about 2 minutes. Mix in egg and vanilla. Reduce speed to low. Add flour mixture, and mix until just combined. Divide dough in half, and pat into disks. Wrap each piece in plastic, and refrigerate until dough is firm, 1 to 2 hours.

2. Preheat oven to 350°F. Line baking sheets with nonstick baking mats (such as Silpats).

3. Make filling: Put cream cheese and sugar into the bowl of an electric mixer fitted with the paddle attachment; mix on medium speed until fluffy. Fold in coconut and chocolate chips.

4. Remove one disk of dough from refrigerator. Roll about ⅛ inch thick on a lightly floured surface. With a fluted cookie cutter, cut into fifteen 2½-inch squares. Transfer to prepared baking sheets, spacing about 1½ inches apart. Refrigerate 15 minutes. Repeat with remaining dough.

5. Place 1 teaspoon filling in center of each square. Using a fluted pastry wheel, cut 1-inch slits diagonally from each corner toward the filling. Fold every other tip over to cover filling, forming a pinwheel. Press lightly to seal. Use the tip of your finger to make a well in the top.

6. Make glaze: Using a pastry brush, lightly brush tops of pinwheels with beaten egg. Sprinkle with sanding sugar. Bake 6 minutes. Remove and use the lightly floured handle of a wooden spoon to make the well a little deeper. Fill each well with about ⅓ teaspoon jam. Return to oven, and bake, rotating sheets halfway through, until edges are golden and cookies are slightly puffed, about 6 minutes more. Transfer sheets to wire racks; let cool 5 minutes. Transfer cookies to rack; let cool completely. Cookies can be stored in single layers in airtight containers at room temperature up to 3 days.

Elements are wittily stacked to create a sense of play. Using different faces for accents enlivens the format, so it can be fun and instructive.

23. Contain Crowding

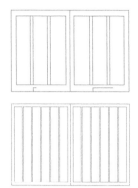

When designing multiple columns, it's not necessary to fill absolutely every inch of space. It's good to leave certain columns open. White space directs the reader's eye around the page, making it easy to pick and choose certain stories, images, or logos. Rules of varying weights help control and give punch to the information.

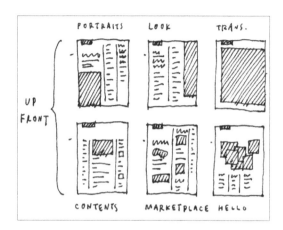

Preliminary sketches show a sense of space.

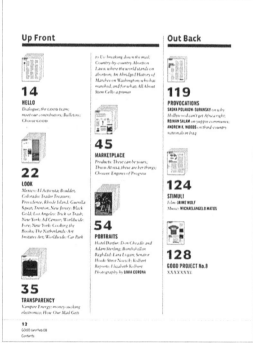

PROJECT
Good magazine issue 008

CLIENT
Good Magazine, LLC

DESIGN DIRECTION
Scott Stowell

DESIGN
Open

White space and witty, edgy design help readers cruise through a lively combination of hard-core big ideas that make the globe a better place.

Contents pages are often difficult to parse. This one gets rid of the clutter and makes it easy for readers to find their way around the magazine's offerings. The various sizes and weights of the typography give the page interest and balance. Icons at the upper right determine a format used throughout the magazine.

The page contains five levels of information, which are clear and easy to read due to tidy typography and generous space.

Rules and cleverly controlled typography set off a range of information types.

Muscular typography cascades through a spacious page opposite an equally muscular illustration.

HELLO
:dialogue

GOOD

(magazine spread with dialogue letters and masthead columns)

BIGIDEAS!

QUANTUM HIPPIES

Q

RUSSIAN DEMOCRACY

R

$$\Delta x \, \Delta p \geq \frac{\hbar}{2}$$

= whoa.

WENDY KOPP

Russian Gambit

Garry Kasparov, the Russian presidential candidate and former chess grandmaster, is trying to keep Vladimir Putin in check.

interview by
CHRISTOPHER BATEMAN

illustrations by
DARREN BOOTH

Big ideas? Big letters! Large drop caps playfully signal starts of stories and play on the words of the heading. Icons introduced in the contents page appear in a consistent position, at the upper right of the page, with only the appropriate icons in use.

24. Lower the Columns

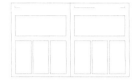

A full page of three-column text can become dense. A good way to keep the reader engaged and undaunted is to lower the columns on the page, which creates clean spreads and a feeling of movement.

Lowered text columns also enable the designer to create a clear area for lead information, such as the running head and page number, spread title, headnote, and photos.

PROJECT
Pew Prospectus 2008

CLIENT
The Pew Charitable Trusts

DESIGN
IridiumGroup

EDITOR
Marshall A. Ledger

**ASSOCIATE EDITOR/
PROJECT MANAGER**
Sandra Salmans

A nonprofit's works are presented seriously, yet elegantly.

Variation is the spice of design, so it's also good to add contrast by designing the introductory material to a wider measure. For additional texture, set the headnote in a typeface altogether different from the typeface used for rest of the material.

Culture

Change was sweeping the arts scene in 1948, with an impact that would not be fully realized for years. American painters led the way into abstract expressionism, reshaping both the visual arts and this country's influence on the art world.

Meanwhile, technology was setting the stage for revolutions in music and photography. The LP record made its debut, and the Fender electric guitar, which would define the rock 'n roll sound in the next decade and thereafter, went into mass production. Both the Polaroid Land camera, the world's first successful instant camera, and the first Nikon went on sale.

In New York, the not-for-profit Experimental Theatre, Inc., received a special Tony honoring its path-breaking work with artists such as Lee Strasberg and Bertolt Brecht. But in April it was disclosed that the theatre had run up a deficit of $20,000—a shocking amount, given that $5,000 had been the maximum allocated for each play—and in October *The New York Times* headlined, "ET Shelves Plans for Coming Year."

Apart from its miniscule budget, there is nothing dated about the travails of the Experimental Theatre. The arts still struggle with cost containment and tight funds. But if the Experimental Theatre were to open its doors today, it might benefit from the power of knowledge now available to many nonprofit arts organizations in Pennsylvania, Maryland and California—and, eventually, to those in other states as well. Technology, which would transform music and photography through inventions in 1948, is providing an important tool to groups that are seeking to streamline a grant application process that, in the past, has been all too onerous.

That tool is the Cultural Data Project, a Web-based data collection system that aggregates information about revenues, employment, volunteers, attendance, fund-raising and other areas input by cultural organizations. On a larger scale, the system also provides a picture of the assets, impact and needs of the cultural sector in a region.

The project was originally launched in Pennsylvania in 2004, the brainchild of a unique collaboration among public and private funders, including the Greater Philadelphia Cultural Alliance, the Greater Pittsburgh Arts Council, The Heinz Endowments, the Pennsylvania Council on the Arts, Pew, The Pittsburgh Foundation and the William Penn Foundation. Until then, applicants to these funding organizations had been required to provide similar information in different formats and on multiple occasions. Thanks to the Pennsylvania Cultural Data Project, hundreds of nonprofit arts and cultural organizations throughout the state can today update their information just once a year and, with the click of a computer mouse, submit it as part of their grant applications. Other foundations, such as the Philadelphia Cultural Fund, the Pennsylvania Historical and Museum Commission and the Independence Foundation, have also adopted the system.

So successful has the project been that numerous states are clamoring to adopt it. In June, with funding from multiple sources, Maryland rolled out its own in-state Cultural Data Project. The California Cultural Data Project, more than five times the size of Pennsylvania's with potentially 5,000 nonprofit cultural organizations, went online at the start of 2008, thanks to the support of more than 20 donors. Both projects are administered by Pew.

As cultural organizations in other states enter their own data, the research will become exponentially more valuable. Communities will be able to compare the effects of different approaches to supporting the arts from state to state and city to city. And the data will give cultural leaders the ability to make a fact-based case that a lively arts scene enriches a community economically as well as socially.

The Cultural Data Project is not the first initiative funded by Pew's Culture portfolio to go national or to benefit from state-of-the-art technology. For example, the system used by Philly-FunGuide, the first comprehensive, up-to-date Web calendar of the region's arts and culture events, has been successfully licensed to other cities.

In addition to the Cultural Data Project, another core effort within Pew's Culture portfolio is the Philadelphia Center for Arts and Heritage and its programs, which include Dance Advance, the Heritage Philadelphia Program, the Pew Fellowships in the Arts, the Philadelphia Exhibitions Initiative, the Philadelphia Music Project and the Philadelphia Theatre Initiative. Since the inception of the first program in 1989, these six initiatives have supported a combined total of more than 1,100 projects and provided more than $48 million in funding for the Philadelphia region's arts and heritage institutions and artists.

Through its fellowships, Pew nurtures individual artists working in a variety of performing, visual and literary disciplines, enabling them to explore new creative frontiers that the marketplace is not likely to support. The center also houses the Philadelphia Cultural Management Initiative, which helps cultural groups strengthen their organizational and financial management practices.

Almost from the time it was established, Pew was among the region's largest supporters of arts and culture. While it continues in this role, committed to fostering nonprofit groups' artistic excellence and economic stability, and to expanding public participation, Pew—like the arts themselves—has changed its approach with the times.

Marian A. Godfrey

Managing Director
Culture and Civic Initiatives

2007 Milestones

Each year we join with excellent organizations to produce work that exemplifies exactly what we mean in stating that Pew serves the public interest. On these pages, we highlight the results of some of the Pew-supported work that made a difference in 2007.

25. Shift Shapes

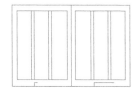

Changing the shapes of photos and drawings can enliven and enlighten a how-to story. If everything is the same size and width, the piece will be clear but dull. Instead, it's possible—and better—to vary the mix.

Handbook How-Tos

HOW TO
WASH, DRY, AND STORE LETTUCE

1. Fill a clean basin or a large bowl with cold water, and submerge the lettuce leaves completely. (For head lettuce, first discard the outer leaves; they're most likely to harbor bacteria. Chop off the end, and separate the remaining leaves.) Swish the leaves around to loosen dirt.

2. Once sediment has settled, lift out the lettuce, pour out the dirty water, and refill the bowl with clean water. Submerge the lettuce again, and continue swishing and refilling until there are no more traces of dirt or sand in the bowl. You may need to change the water 2 or 3 times.

3. Dry the lettuce in a salad spinner until no more water collects at the bottom of the bowl. Alternatively, blot the leaves between layered paper towels or clean dish towels until no water remains.

4. If you plan to store the lettuce, arrange the dry leaves in a single layer on paper towels or clean dish towels, roll up, and seal inside a plastic bag. Lettuce can be stored this way in the refrigerator for 3 to 5 days. To prevent it from browning rapidly, don't tear the leaves into smaller pieces until you're ready to use them.

SOAK AND SPIN THE LEAVES

STORE IN A TOWEL

HOW TO
IRON A BUTTON-FRONT SHIRT

For easier ironing and the best results, start with a thoroughly damp shirt. Mist the shirt with water using a spray bottle, roll it up, and keep it in a plastic bag for 15 minutes or up to a few hours. (If you can't iron the shirt sooner, refrigerate it in the bag so the shirt won't acquire a sour smell.) Most of the ironing will be on the wide end of the board. If you're right-handed, position the wide end to your left; if you're left-handed, it should be on your right.

1. Begin with the underside of the collar. Iron, gently pulling and stretching the fabric to prevent puckering. Turn the shirt over, and repeat on the other side of collar. Fold the collar along seam. Lightly press.

2. Iron the inside of the cuffs; slip a towel under the buttons to cushion them as you work. Iron the inside of the plackets and the lower inside portion of the sleeves, right above the cuffs. Iron the outside of the cuffs.

3. Drape the upper quarter of the shirt over the wide end of the board, with the collar pointing toward the narrow end of the board, and iron one half of the yoke. Reposition, and iron the other half.

4. Lay 1 sleeve flat on the board. Iron from shoulder to cuff. (If you don't want to crease the sleeve, use a sleeve board.) Turn the sleeve over, and iron the other side. Repeat with the other sleeve.

5. Drape the yoke over the wide end of the board, with the collar facing the wide end, and iron the back of the shirt.

6. Drape the left side of the front of the shirt over the board, with the collar pointing toward the wide end; iron. Repeat with the right front side, ironing around, rather than over, buttons. Let the shirt hang in a well-ventilated area until it's completely cool and dry, about 30 minutes, before hanging it in the closet.

62

PROJECT
Martha Stewart Living

CLIENT
Martha Stewart Omnimedia

DESIGN
Martha Stewart Living

CHIEF CREATIVE OFFICER
Gael Towey

Clear how-to images and finished photos sit in a strong yet flexible format.

One way to clarify text or instructions is to include how-to illustrations and a photo of the finished recipe or craft object. The images will be useful, and their varying shapes keep the page from being static.

OPPOSITE PAGE: The typography in this piece is functional and detailed; it's also exquisite without being precious. The boxed-in sidebar signals the reader to important information that's separate from the recipes.

SAUTÉED SOLE WITH LEMON
SERVES 2

Gray sole is a delicately flavored white fish. You can substitute flounder, turbot, or another type of sole.

- ½ cup flour, preferably Wondra
- 1 teaspoon coarse salt
- ½ teaspoon freshly ground pepper
- 2 gray sole fillets (6 ounces each)
- 2 tablespoons unsalted butter
- 2 tablespoons olive oil
- 2 tablespoons sliced almonds
- 1½ tablespoons chopped fresh parsley
  Finely chopped zest and juice from 1 lemon, plus wedges for garnish

1. Combine flour, salt, and pepper in a shallow bowl. Dredge fish fillets in flour mixture, coating both sides, and shake off excess.

2. Melt butter with oil in a sauté pan over medium-high heat. When butter begins to foam, add fillets. Cook until golden brown, 2 to 3 minutes per side. Transfer each fillet to a serving plate.

3. Add almonds, parsley, zest, and 2 tablespoons juice to pan. Spoon over fillets, and serve with lemon wedges.

HARICOTS VERTS
SERVES 2

- Coarse salt, to taste
- 8 ounces haricots verts
- 2 tablespoons extra-virgin olive oil
  Freshly ground pepper, to taste
- 1 bunch chives, for bundling (optional)

1. Bring a pot of salted water to a boil. Add haricots verts, and cook until bright green and just tender, 3 to 5 minutes. Drain, and pat dry. Transfer to a serving bowl.

2. Toss with oil, salt, and pepper. Tie into bundles using chives.

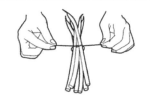

HOW TO BUNDLE GREEN BEANS

....

1. Cook haricots verts. Drain, and pat dry. Let stand until cool enough to handle.
2. Lay a chive on a work surface. Arrange 4 to 10 haricots verts in a small pile on top of chive. Carefully tie chive around bundle. Trim ends of chive if desired.

QUICK-COOKING CLASSIC Seared sole fillets glisten beneath a last-minute pan sauce made with lemon, parsley, and almonds. The resulting entrée, served with blanched haricots verts, is satisfyingly quick yet sophisticated.

26. Syncopate the Rhythm

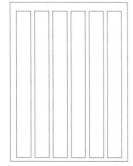

As crucial as it is to have a clean, controlled page or screen, the same elements repeated without variation can lull the reader into boredom. Avoid gridlock by having the column of text follow the shape of the art. Variation can help underline, as opposed to undermine, hard-core information.

This grid contains huge amounts of information. The staggered columns follow the shape of the trumpet and enhance an already handsome and lively listing. Typographically, the schedule is a virtuoso work of balance, rhythm, and craft.

PROJECT
Program schedule

CLIENT
Jazz at Lincoln Center

DESIGN
Bobby C. Martin Jr.

Large amounts of information are jazzed up by a sharp layout.

A columnar grid provides a clear framework for boxes, which fill a number of roles. The boxes contain the material, give a sense of dimension to the schedule by creating a plane on top of the photo, and they rhythmically move across the page.

27. Mix It Up

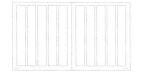

Weight. Size. Texture. Shape. Scale. Space. Colors. It's possible to combine a lot of elements for an energetic look that is varied but coherent. A firm grid can act as a base, enabling a piece containing lots of images and headlines to make room for one or two more. Weights and sizes of type, and dynamics of image sizes and shapes call for attention without sacrificing readability in the basic story.

The bold, five-column grid that appears consistently in this magazine grounds the spread and supports a variety of shapes and sizes. The page structure is strong, especially with extra space around images.

PROJECT
Metropolis magazine

CLIENT
Metropolis magazine

CREATIVE DIRECTOR
Criswell Lappin

A disciplined grid enables local work to shine. A strong multicolumn grid foundation at the base of a page provides a sturdy underpinning to a spread with a cavalcade of sizes, weights, and colors.

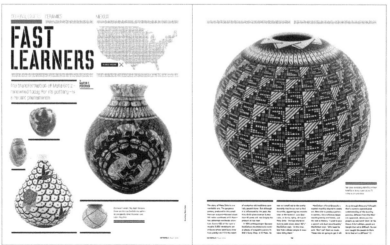

Although the typography is black with only an accent color, it adds color and texture through the dynamics of bold, stencil-like type playing off smaller sizes and weights. Thick and thin rules also add texture.

OPPOSITE PAGE: Rules become grounding elements for the rocking chair silhouettes

HANDMADE HOME

A crafts group enlists local artisans to create a one-of-a-kind dwelling

by BELINDA LANKS

AKIRA SATAKE

CERAMICS

Satake produces functional ceramic pieces—from mugs, pitchers, and bowls to decorative bizo—with a refined Japanese aesthetic.

FATIE ATKINSON

FURNITURE

Employing a steam-bending technique, Atkinson can make this chair out of any open-pored wood, including hickory, ash, and white or red oak (above).

BARBARA ZARETSKY

TEXTILES

Zaretsky creates earth-toned patterns using natural fibers, plant dyes, and textile paints.

HandMade in America has been fervently promoting craft in Western North Carolina since 1993, but this year marks the nonprofit's first foray into real estate. In a unique collaboration, the group has partnered with private developer Biltmore Farms to construct the HandMade Home, a 3,700-square-foot model in Asheville showcasing the work of 100 local craftspeople. The house, which broke ground last September, is expected to meet the green-building standards of North Carolina's Healthy Built Homes program and fetch $2.25 million when it makes its debut in October as part of the city's annual "Parade of Homes."

Founding executive director Becky Anderson hopes the project will spur other developers, architects, and homeowners to tap the region's greatest resource: the 4,500 resident artisans making everything from furniture and lighting fixtures to tableware and rugs (examples shown above). "We want to become the center of handcrafted homes," she says. "To make it easy, HandMade in America has produced director- and context information for the crafts-people in its network. But lien Brown, the project's publicist, recommends that people considering such an undertaking think smaller. "This is the first project of its kind, and it will probably be the last," Brown says. "With one hundred independent-minded artists involved, people are ready to shoot each other." ○

PEWABIC

The designs for Brookside School at Cranbrook (top), at Bloomfield Hills, and Detroit's Comerica Park stadium (above) were custom-made by the potters in house then.

MOTAWI

The Frank Lloyd Wright Collection includes Avery (left) and Coonley (below). Also shown Ventimia (above) and Amaryllis (right), an adaptation of a Louis Sullivan design.

DAVID ELLISON

Soldiering Coconity Floors, like Apollo Plaque (above) is a reinterpretation of historic details found on buildings in New York's Flatiron District.

Eastern Michigan is home to one of the most active crafts movements in the country.

MOTOR CITY GLAZE

by EVA HAGBERG

"We'd start doing these tile shows that were just tile, and we'd think, How could anyone make a living at this?" says Marcia Hovland, part of a loose-knit group of Michigan-based tile-makers, reminiscing about the good old days before the tile industry took off. "And now everyone is doing really well."

Hovland is one of the artisans who came up through Detroit's famed Pewabic Pottery—a tile factory, exhibition space, and educational facility. She studied there with David Ellison—a name that comes up again and again in conversation with these eastern-Michigan tile fiends—and realized that she could turn her painting and design background into a whole new bag of (ceramic) chips. Karim Motawi runs Motawi Tileworks out of Ann Arbor with his sister, Nawal. The company makes historically influenced pottery in line with the types of things that were produced in the earliest days of Pewabic in the 1900s. "We're literally plowing through the history books and the source books, the old catalogs," he says. "We're trying to re-create lost craft." As the official Frank Lloyd Wright licensee, it's reproducing just fine.

Motawi Tileworks operates on a relatively tiny scale—it produces 16,000 square feet of tile a year, a drop in the bucket—and so do many of its local cohorts, which is why they're so happy to know Joseph Taylor, president of the Tile Heritage Foundation, which works to raise the historic craft's profile. "They are like tile cheerleaders," Motawi says. ○

BROOKLYN'S OWN

A crafty DIY-inspired furniture movement emerges in New York's most creatively vibrant borough

ELUCIDESIGN

DANISH CHAIR

Inspired by the Scandinavian classics, this Danish chair is made of aspen and uses a hand-dimensioned frame for the back and seat.

WÜD

WÜD CHAIR

This dining-room chair designed by Corey Springer and Eric Ervin in 2005 comes in a variety of woods, including cherry (shown), walnut, and maple.

UHURU DESIGN

DK METAL ARMCHAIR

Designed by Jason Horvath, this lounge chair consists of a sandblock by two-inch steel frame and upholstered cushions available in custom colors and patterns.

CITY JOINERY

WEBBE CHAIR

This dining-room chair was designed by Jonah Zuckerman in 1997. Pictured in space walnut, it's available in a variety of woods.

SCRAPILE

PROTOTYPE I

Designed by Bart Bettencourt, the chair is made of repurposed wood scraps that were bound for a landfill. The process makes the material unique for each piece.

PAUL SAMKO

ROCKING CHAIR

The walnut rocker is composed of 16 demand pieces. Created by Samko in 2007, the chair can be customized using different types of wood or upholstery.

by EVA HAGBERG

Far from the maddening crowds of the contemporary-furniture scene, a small group of intrepid designers is sprouting like trees in Brooklyn. Aesthetically, they're all over the map. Scrapile (from Greenpoint) is known for the pun it's named after: a scrap pile of locally sourced wood that designers Bart Bettencourt and Carlos Salgado turn into a building material; each block incorporates everything from walnut to plywood and is then processed through a labor-intensive layering method. Uhuru, founded by Bill Hilgendorf and Jason Horvath, offers a line of sleek, multimaterial pieces, all of which, if viewed through a larger lens, are just as sustainable.

Those forms got started about four years ago, and they join the older guard Elucidesign, founded in 2001, and City Joinery, which set up shop in 1996. Elucidesign's Redpoint collection is a beautifully spare series of pared-down pieces; City Joinery's range and look is broader and heavier. These firms may not share a look, but they do share a sensibility shaped by their size, scale, and voluntary outsider status in the design world. "We're in this straddling position," City Joinery's Jonah Zuckerman says. "We care a lot about design, but we also care a lot about craft." Horvath brings up a similar tension: "We don't want to be this big furniture company that does production overseas, but we don't want to be just building furniture as Red Hook." He shouldn't worry too much. His company and his competitors are part of a new phenomenon—the rise of the artisan designer, Brooklyn division. ○

28. Simplify Complex Elements

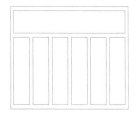
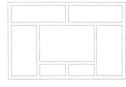

Multicolumn grids are perfect for controlling a range of no-nonsense elements within a report. A explicit plan can chunk information in a number of ways. Columns, rules, and text in different sizes, typefaces, and colors work together to convey technical information.

A bold horizontal band defined by heavy rules supports and contains headlines, authors, locations, and logos. Occasionally, bands below the headings are broken to denote space between each of the multiple columns.

Figure 2: The ICE probe is placed in the right heart for imaging during PFO closure and pulmonary vein isolation.

The ICE probe can be advanced into the inferior vena cava (IVC), enabling high quality imaging of the abdominal aorta (Figure 3).

Varying sizes and leadings distinguish research information from conclusions, which are set large. Captions, in a contrasting sans serif, tidily recap the facts. A vertical rule sets off each section of text that appears within the column, further clarifying the information.

PROJECT (ABOVE)
Poster

CLIENT
NYU Medical Center

DESIGN
Carapellucci Design

DESIGNER
Janice Carapellucci

A poster for NYU Medical Center is a textbook example of a clearly handled information hierarchy. Facts and findings are easy to read. Each type of information is differentiated, and the leading and space between elements are in perfect, readable proportions. Although chock-full of information, each section is easy to read, even for a nonphysician.

PROJECT (OPPOSITE)
Workshop Placemat for SXSW

CLIENT
smith + beta

DESIGN
Suzanne Dell'Orto

Hard-working, step-by-step instructions for makers includes different elements, icons, tips, hierarchies, a checklist, and fearlessness.

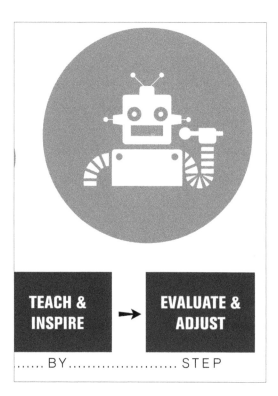

Text running from left to right across the top of the placemat explains the overarching idea. The middle zone bursts with infobits. Type dropping out of horizontal bars separates the middle zone of lists, flow diagrams, and resources.

Evaluation of the Abdominal Aorta and its Branches Using an Intravascular Echo Probe in the Inferior Vena Cava

Carol L. Chen, MD
Paul A. Tunick, MD
Lawrence Chinitz, MD

Neil Bernstein, MD
Douglas Holmes, MD
Itzhak Kronzon, MD

New York University School of Medicine New York, NY USA

NYU Medical Center

Background

Ultrasound evaluation of the abdominal aorta and its branches is usually performed transabdominally. Not infrequently, the image quality is suboptimal. Recently, an intracardiac echocardiography (ICE) probe has become commercially available (Acuson, Mountain View CA, Figure 1). These probes are usually inserted intravenously (IV) and advanced to the right heart for diagnostic and monitoring purposes during procedures such as ASD closure and pulmonary vein isolation (Figure 2). Because of the close anatomic relation between the abdominal aorta (AA) and the inferior vena cava (IVC), we hypothesized that these probes would be useful in the evaluation of the AA and its branches.

Figure 2: The ICE probe is placed in the right heart for imaging during PFO closure and pulmonary vein isolation.

The ICE probe can be advanced into the inferior vena cava (IVC), enabling high quality imaging of the abdominal aorta (Figure 3).

Figure 1: ICE probe (AcuNav, Acuson)

Figure 3: The position of the ICE probe in the IVC allows for excellent imaging and Doppler flow interrogation of the abdominal aorta and its branches (renal arteries, SMA, celiac axis) and the diagnosis of diseases such as renal artery stenosis and abdominal aortic aneurysm.

Methods

Fourteen pts who were undergoing a pulmonary vein isolation procedure participated in the study. In each pt, the ICE probe was inserted in the femoral vein and advanced to the right atrium for the evaluation of the left atrium and the pulmonary veins during the procedure. At the end of the procedure, the probe was withdrawn into the IVC.

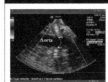

Figure 4: Two-dimensional image with color Doppler, of the abdominal aorta at the level of the right (Rt) and left (Lt) renal ostia. Note visualization of the laminar renal blood flow in the right renal artery, toward the transducer (red) and the left renal artery, away from the transducer (blue).

Results

High resolution images of the AA from the diaphragm to the AA bifurcation were easily obtained in all pts. These images allowed for the evaluation of AA size, shape, and abnormal findings, such as atherosclerotic plaques (2 pts) and a 3.2 cm AA aneurysm (1 pt). Both renal arteries were easily visualized in each pt. With the probe in the IVC, both renal arteries are parallel to the imaging plane (Figure 4), and therefore accurate measurement of renal blood flow velocity and individual renal blood flow were possible.

Calculation of renal blood flow:
The renal blood flow in each artery can be calculated using the cross-sectional area of the artery ($\pi r2$) multiplied by the velocity time integral (VTI, in cm) from the Doppler velocity tracing, multiplied by the heart rate (82 BPM in the example shown).

CSA · VTI · HR = renal blood flow/min.

Figure 5

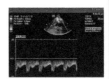

Figure 6: Pulsed Doppler of the right renal artery blood flow. The diameter of the right renal artery was 0.85 cm, and the VTI of the right renal blood flow was 0.19 meters (19 cm). Therefore the right renal blood flow was calculated as 516 cc/minute.

Figure 7: Pulsed Doppler of the left renal artery blood flow. The diameter of the left renal artery was 0.51 cm, and the VTI of the left renal blood flow was 0.2 meters (20 cm). Therefore the left renal blood flow was calculated as 334 cc/minute.

The total renal blood flow (right plus left) in this patient was therefore 850 cc/min. (average normal = 1200 cc/min).

Conclusions

High resolution ultrasound images of the AA and the renal arteries are obtainable using ICE in the IVC. The branches of the abdominal aorta can be visualized and their blood flow calculated. Renal blood flow may be calculated for each kidney using this method. This may prove to be the imaging technique of choice for intra-aortic interventions such as angioplasty of the renal arteries for renal artery stenosis, fenestration of dissecting aneurysm intimal flaps, and endovascular stenting for AA aneurysm.

Why making? *Are you a maker? We hope so.*

It is a particularly critical time to put intelligent, ethical thought into "things." Perhaps you are shaping products that move markets…or, knitting fluffy hats. Do you recognize, in an antique chair, its narrative… The hand of the artisan who reshaped a tree to offer comfort?

Have you ever optimistically pulled apart broken electronics with hope of resuscitation? Confused by new car engines? *(You are not alone.)* Since the onset of the Anthropocene Age, humans have been obsessed with things. We have allowed them to help us, crowd us, amuse us, comfort us, etc. **Joy, sustainability, curiosity and purpose** are some of the keywords for 21c making manifestos. One must have trust in invisible electronic worlds yet remember the many paths we have traveled.

Why make makers?

Since making can be manifested in so many ways—software, toys, or an epicurean meal, it is essential to recognize the elements of a making processes that transcend media.

Materials, meaning-making, and mastery come together as a guide for companies who value creative processes and courageous individuals.

" I HEAR AND I FORGET. I SEE AND I REMEMBER. I DO AND I UNDERSTAND. " —Confucius

Making Makers Who Fearlessly Make

SXSW 2015

Lori Kent, Ed. D.
Allison Kent-Smith
Catherine McGowan

10 tips

1. Know what your team makes. Know their skills.
2. Design learning experiences that engage the senses…have emotional meaning and connect to everyday work.
3. Define common terminology around making. Acknowledge team's existing knowledge.
4. Manage people so that their inner imaginations soar. *Tell them that what they know recombines as "creativity."*
5. Encourage everyone around you to have pride in their craft and continue to grow over a lifetime.
6. Design learning experiences that support multiple learning styles and configure complementary teams.
7. Making EXPLICIT a vision and your provisional goals.
8. AND…create a work (making) process that is shared and iterative.
9. Get people to connect with their inner child to lift creative blocks. Take makers to unexpected places.
10. This workshop is a beginning. Your culture, individual needs…**take a first step.**

Resources

Texts

Shopcraft as Soulcraft: An Inquiry into the Value of Work by Matthew B. Crawford
The Courage to Create by Rollo May
Spark: How Creativity Works by Julie Bernstein (Studio 360)
Makers: The New Industrial Revolution by Chris Anderson
The Craftsmen by Richard Sennett
Ten Faces of Innovation by Kelley & Littman (IDEO)

WWW

http://aeon.co/magazine/being-human/
https://dschool.stanford.edu/groups/dhandbook/
http://edge.org/
http://makerfaire.com/
http://dx.cooperhewitt.org/lesson-plans/
http://www.fixerscollective.org/
http://www.techshop.ws/

Thanks to

Strawbees, SparkFun, Sally Oettfinger, Meredith Olsen, Grace Borchers, and the s & b teacher collective.
Designed by Suzanne Dell'Orto.

 KNOW YOUR TALENT → GATHER TEAM & VISION → DESIGN & PLAN → TEACH & INSPIRE → EVALUATE & ADJUST

PROGRAM .... BUILDING .... STEP .... BY .... STEP

3 ELEMENTS OF MAKING : MATERIALS, MEANING-MAKING, & MASTERY

Materials
* Materials tell you what to do.
* "Functional fixedness" is seeing a "thing" or material as having a specific use…rethink.
* Ordinary materials can inspire, transform….

Meaning-Making
* Be a generative thinker…able to sort, filter, bifurcate, combine and expand.
* Your experience gives you an incredibly rich "well" for making.
* Develop wonder. Think too much.

Mastery
* Mastery? What do you do best?
* How can you deconstruct process to teach mastery?
* How do you support individual and team mastery?

smith&beta
www.smithandbeta.com

SXSW Evaluation Link: sxsw.feedogo.com/fdbk.do?sid=IAP36301

29. Make Do-It-Yourself Easy to Follow

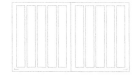

How-to instructions must be easy to follow. A clearly formatted layout can be followed (to a degree), even if it's in a language the reader doesn't understand. Clarity can be achieved by means of numbered steps and images. Choices of what to photograph as well as photos that are clear in and of themselves can be combined in a layout that is as delightful as well as easy to follow.

PROJECT
Kurashi no techo (Everyday Notebook) magazine

CLIENT
Kurashi no techo (Everyday Notebook) magazine

DESIGNERS
Shuzo Hayashi, Masaaki Kuroyanagi

A how-to article mixes Western icons—Charlie Brown and his lunch bag—with an Eastern sense of space.

PEANUTS © United Feature Syndicate, Inc.

Space can set off introductory text. A cartoon speaks to a number of cultures.

Ruled boxes set off ways to get from one bullet point to another. Each component on the page is clearly on a well-defined grid.

Numbers clarify each step of the process, with subset steps defined by small, circled numbers. Every element is organized; diagrams are so clear that a motivated craftsperson without knowledge of the language could make the item. The space and relative sizes of each component, along with handsome photos, can make the most detailed instructions seem less daunting.

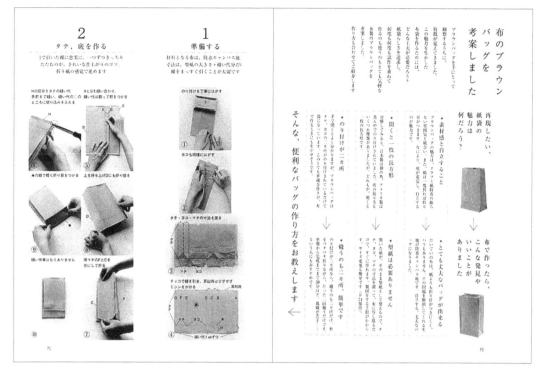

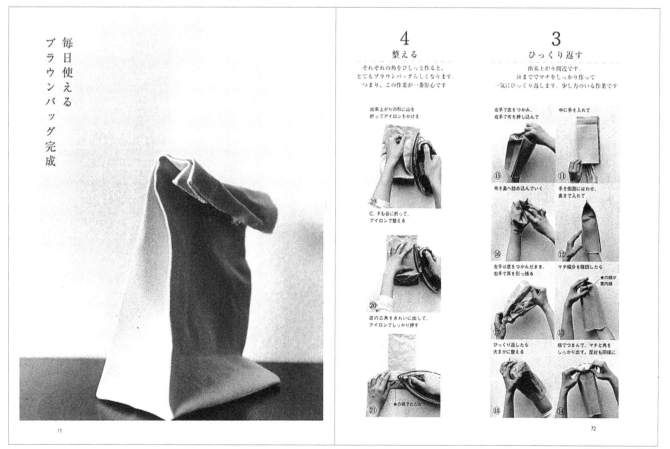

30. Know Website Basics

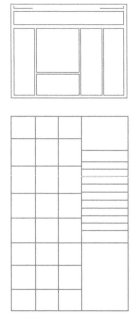

To accommodate huge amounts of information, large websites are organized using grids. Space is broken into chunks to control information. Start by reviewing any constraints. Take into account screen margins and toolbars, such as the navigational toolbar for the screen, as well as the browser. As with print, web design calls for considering anything that takes up space. In the case of many websites, items to consider include ads, videos, and a complex array of heads, subheads, bylines, lists, and links. Clear typographical choices are crucial.

SCREEN SIZES

Users have different screen sizes, so many designers define a live area, of certain pixel width and depth, that will fit readably on a small screen. Computer screen sizes have become larger over the years, but the introduction of handheld devices has resulted in the variation of screen sizes and a simpler, hierarchical formats.

PROJECT
nytimes.com

CLIENT
The New York Times

DESIGN
The New York Times

CREATIVE DIRECTOR
Tom Bodkin

The design of this site combines no-nonsense information and clear, handsome, traditional typography, enhanced by a sense of detail, a variation of sans serif complementing serif, and colors highlighting stories and time frames.

A tight structure creates a container for a navigation column, stories, images to different sizes and grid widths, ads, and videos.

According to Khoi Vinh, former design director of the *New York Times,* "units are the basic building blocks of a grid," and "columns are the groupings of units that create the visual structure of the page." Vinh notes that, ideally, a designer will "create units in multiples of three or four, with twelve as an ideal, because it is a multiple of three and four." Although not visible, such calculations give a strong underpinning to the site, which shows an extreme discipline of units and columns.

Once a designer consolidates units into columns, it's important to design additional space, or insets, to the left and right of the type, so there's a consistent alignment, whether the column contains images, type only, or type in a box.

World »

Thai Cave Rescue Will Be Murky, Desperate Ordeal, Divers Say

English City, Stunned, Tries to Make Sense of New Poisonings

Japan Executes Cult Leader Behind 1995 Sarin Gas Subway Attack

U.S. »

A Black Oregon Lawmaker Was Knocking on Doors. Someone Called the Police.

Migrant Shelters Are Becoming Makeshift Schools for Thousands of Children

Trump Administration in Chaotic Scramble to Reunify Migrant Families

Politics »

Amy McGrath Set Her Sights on the Marines and Now Congress. Her Mother Is the Reason.

Trump Assails Critics and Mocks #MeToo. What About Putin? 'He's Fine'

Brett Kavanaugh, Supreme Court Front-Runner, Once Argued Broad Grounds for Impeachment

New York »

The Rise of the Stressed-Out Urban Camper

A City Founded by Alexander Hamilton Sets the Stage for Its Next Act

Culture of Fear and Ambition Distorted Cuomo's Economic Projects

Science »

Trilobites: Never Mind the Summer Heat: Earth Is at Its Greatest Distance From the Sun

The Lost Dogs of the Americas

Rhino Embryos Made in Lab to Save Nearly Extinct Subspecies

Health »

Global Health: In a Rare Success, Paraguay Conquers Malaria

Trilobites: Lots of Successful Women Are Freezing Their Eggs. But It May Not Be About Their Careers.

Voices: When a Vegan Gets Gout

Education »

'Access to Literacy' Is Not a Constitutional Right, Judge in Detroit Rules

Colleges and State Laws Are Clamping Down on Fraternities

In the Age of Trump, Civics Courses Make a Comeback

Real Estate »

New Buildings Rise in Flood Zones

Right at Home: Buried in Paperwork

The Hunt: Trading Chelsea Clatter for Greenpoint Calm

Business Day »

U.S. Hiring Stayed Strong in June Despite Trade Strains

The Unemployment Rate Rose for the Best Possible Reason

China Strikes Back at Trump's Tariffs, but Its Consumers Worry

Technology »

Tech Giants Win a Battle Over Copyright Rules in Europe

State of the Art: Employee Uprisings Sweep Many Tech Companies. Not Twitter.

The New New World: Why Made in China 2025 Will Succeed, Despite Trump

Fashion & Style »

Modern Love: This Is What Happens When Friends Fall in Love

The Secret Price of Pets

Fashion Review: A Declaration of Independence at Valentino and Fendi

Sports »

Neymar and the Art of the Dive

Garbiñe Muguruza and Marin Cilic Join the Wimbledon Exodus

On Pro Basketball: Finally Free From LeBron's Reign, the N.B.A. East Has No Reason to Change

Obituaries »

Ed Schultz, Blunt-Spoken Political Talk-Show Host, Dies at 64

Michelle Musler, Courtside Perennial in the Garden, Is Dead at 81

Claude Lanzmann, Epic Chronicler of the Holocaust, Dies at 92

Travel »

The Getaway: Looking for a Weekend Escape? Here Are 5 Family-Friendly Options

Carry On: What W. Kamau Bell Can't Travel Without

The Rise of the Stressed-Out Urban Camper

Food »

Wines of The Times: American Rosés Without Clichés

Hungry City: A Filipino Specialty Best Paired With a Brew in the East Village

Australia Fare: Yatala Pies Has Served Nostalgia for More Than 130 Years. Arguably.

The Upshot »

The Unemployment Rate Rose for the Best Possible Reason

There Isn't Much the Fed Can Do to Ease the Pain of a Trade War

Americans Are Having Fewer Babies. They Told Us Why.

Opinion »

What Nelson Mandela Lost

'Hope Is a Powerful Weapon': Unpublished Mandela Prison Letters

We'll All Be Paying for Scott Pruitt for Ages

Arts »

If It's on 'Love Island,' Britain's Talking About It

Four Musicals on Three Continents: An Australian Company's Big Bet

The Art of Staying Cool: 10 Can't-Miss Summer Shows in New York

Movies »

Lakeith Stanfield Is Playing Us All

Review: 'Ant-Man and the Wasp' Save the World! With Jokes!

Review: 'Sorry to Bother You,' but Can I Interest You in a Wild Dystopian Satire?

Theater »

Four Musicals on Three Continents: An Australian Company's Big Bet

Review: 'The Royal Family of Broadway.' This Time in Song

Critic's Notebook: Orlando Bloom and Aidan Turner Are Drenched in Blood in London

Television »

If It's on 'Love Island,' Britain's Talking About It

'Sharp Objects,' a Mesmerizing Southern Thriller, Cuts Slow but Deep

On Comedy: A Netflix Experiment Gives Deserving Comics Their 15 Minutes

Books »

Profile: Attention, Please: Anne Tyler Has Something to Say

Books of The Times: When It Comes to Politics, Be Afraid. But Not Too Afraid.

Captain America No. 1, by Ta-Nehisi Coates, Annotated

Magazine »

Feature: Can the A.C.L.U. Become the N.R.A. for the Left?

Letter of Recommendation: Letter of Recommendation: 'The Totally Football Show With James Richardson'

Feature: Who's Afraid of the Big Bad Wolf Scientist?

Times Insider »

Outsmarted by a Smart TV? Not This Reporter.

With Our World Cup App, Fans Are Part of the Action

The Times at Gettysburg, July 1863: A Reporter's Civil War Heartbreak

Trading Chelsea Clatter for Greenpoint Calm

By JOYCE COHEN

Living on Eighth Avenue was fun, but after six years Emery Myers wanted some peace and quiet — not to mention a garden. Walls were optional.

- Search for Homes for Sale or Rent
- Mortgage Calculator

MOST EMAILED   MOST VIEWED   **RECOMMENDED FOR YOU**

1. What Can You Do About a Hammertoe?

2. Mom, I Need a Break

3. Countdown to Retirement: A Five-Year Plan

4. A Cult Show's Recipe for Success: Whiskey, Twitter and Complex Women

5. Facebook Removes a Gospel Group's Music Video

6. A Cult Show's Recipe for Success: Whiskey, Twitter and Complex Women

7. Airline Crew Have Higher Cancer Rates

8. London Mayor Allows 'Trump Baby' Blimp for President's Trip to U.K.

9. When a Vegan Gets Gout

10. Statue of Liberty Stamp Mistake to Cost Postal Service $3.5 Million

Log in to discover more articles based on what you've read.

LOG IN   REGISTER NOW

What's This? | Don't Show

31. Break It Down

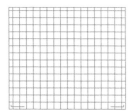

Sometimes information is a cross between a chart and a module. When presenting complex information, consider clarity, readability, space, and variation. Breaking complicated information into manageable chunks results in clearer layouts.

Use a modular grid when

• there are so many chunks of separate information that continuous reading isn't necessary or possible
• you want all material to fill a similar block of space
• you want a consistent—or nearly consistent—format
• units of information are headed by numbers or dates, with similar amounts of material

Breaking the material down also involves the typography that serves the content. Playing off size and weight against the explanatory copy helps make a page easier to follow. As mentioned in other principles, using different typefaces in a controlled way can make the difference between information that is clear but dull, and information that borders on the whimsical.

OPPOSITE PAGE: In this list of tips, there's a consistent amount of space around the copy, with the amount of copy driving the size of the box. A rule, with a weight that doesn't overshadow the material in the box, can separate each tip, resulting in a sidebar that consists of subinformation.

In any language, bullets function as an alert in a heading, and, as always, sizes and weights signal the pecking order of information.

As for the numbered items, just as size and weight help to vary the look of the typography, Arabic numbers and Kanji characters give variation and a homey spin to the helpful, if odd, information. Translation of tip 7 is "It's getting dry. When you come home from outside, try to gargle. Having a glass near the sink makes it easier."

PROJECT
Kurashi no techo (Everyday Notebook) magazine

CLIENT
Kurashi no techo (Everyday Notebook) magazine

DESIGNERS
Shuzo Hayashi, Masaaki Kuroyanagi

A feature in a how-to magazine lists tips for domestic life in a controlled fashion.

ここにならんでいる
いくつかのヒントを
ふと目についた項目を
読んでみてください。
たぶん、ああそうだったと
いうことになるでしょう

1 テーブルにコップを置くときは、静かに置くことを心がけましょう。やさしいしぐさが気持ちをやわらげます。

2 組み立て式の椅子やテーブルのネジは、意外とゆるんでいるものです。締めなおしておきましょう。

3 暮らしには笑顔が大事です。いろいろあっても、にっこり笑顔を忘れずに。

4 一年使った枕を新しいものに替えてみましょう。新しい気持ちで眠りにつけるでしょう。

5 今日こそゆるんだ水道のパッキンを取替えましょう。家中の蛇口をチェックします。

6 毎日の暮らしのなかで見て見ぬふりはやめましょう。そういう癖を身につけてはいけません。

7 空気が乾燥してきます。外から帰ったらすぐにうがいができるように、洗面所のコップをきれいにしておきましょう。

8 朝、目が覚めたら、ベッドの中で今日一日、何をするかを考えます。することがたくさんあれば、うかうかしていられず、すぐ起きるでしょう。

9 どんなことでもまずはお金を使わずにできるかを考えてみましょう。それが工夫の一歩になります。

10 言いたいことを言った後は、笑顔で接することが大事です。険悪にならないように、まわりに気を使いましょう。

11 日曜日の朝、天気が良かったら、外でご飯にしませんか。ごく簡単なお弁当を近所の公園などで食べるのです。散歩もかねて気分も変わります。

12 風邪をひいて、お風呂に入れないときは、足だけでも洗って、温めましょう。さっぱりして気分がよくなります。

13 今日は一歩ゆずってみましょう。その一歩がそのまま新しい一歩を進めるちからになるものです。

14 裁縫箱を整理しましょう。さびた針やよれた糸は処分して、新しいものに取替えます。

15 今日は粗食デーにしましょう。味噌汁にお漬物とか、ありあわせのおかずで間に合わせます。明日は今夜の分もごちそうにしましょう。

16 冷蔵庫が夏の設定になっていませんか。気温も下がったし、あけての回数も減ってきたので、調節しておきます。

17 虫歯があったら、いますぐ治しておきましょう。年末年始のお医者さんが休みのときに痛くなったら大変です。

18 手紙ばさみを買ってみましょう。とても便利なので、毎日届く郵便をさっさと片づけられます。

19 今日は一日、お年寄りのお相手をつとめましょう。お茶を飲みながら、ゆっくりと昔話を聞いてあげたり、一緒に出かけたりします。

20 毎日を心地よく過ごすには、あまりに潔癖すぎてもいけません。ようするにこれやけがれも受け入れてこそ暮らしがあるのです。人との関係も同様です。

21 きびしい肌寒さをおぼえる夜になりました。ことにお年寄りにはひざ掛けか、肩掛けを一枚、早めに用意してあげましょう。

22 しめきりの窓をあけて、敷居のゴミを払いましょう。アルミサッシの溝など、ほこりがつまっているものです。

23 洋服ダンスの防虫剤は大丈夫でしょうか。においはしていても、中身はもうなくなっていることが案外多いものです。

24 新しいチャレンジは自分で決めるものです。ひとに惑わされて後悔しないように。

25 ガス台の下やすきまを掃除しましょう。意外に汚れているものです。きれいになると気持ちよく料理ができるでしょう。

32. Leave Some Breathing Room

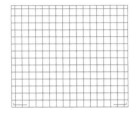

Not all modules need to be filled. A modular grid determines precise increments and lets designers plot out and manage multiple details. The modules can be invisible or visible. They can be large or small. They render a firm structure, holding type, a letter or color, or ornamentation. And they can simply support white space.

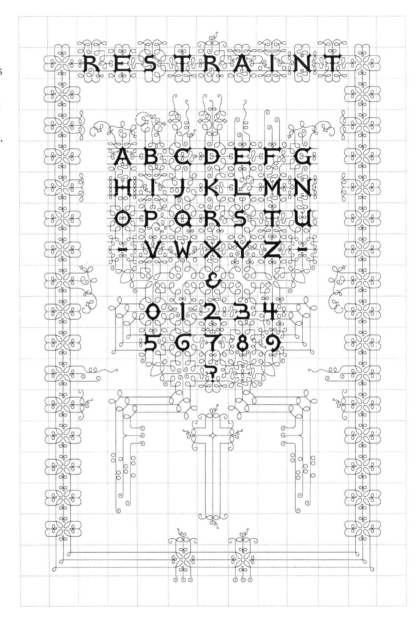

The display face is designed for use in headings or titles but not for running text. When used at small sizes, display faces become hard to read because their distinguishing features disappear.

PROJECT
Restraint Font

CLIENT
Marian Bantjes

DESIGN
Marian Bantjes, Ross Mills

Handcrafted typography brings digits to digital.

Filling modules in the center of a piece and leaving space around the edges turns the space at the outer areas into a frame.

Another approach is to use the modules as a frame, leaving space in the center. In all cases, showing restraint marks the difference between a cacophony and a symphony.

This end user license agreement shows beautiful typography, as well as the terms for using the font Restraint.

RESTRAINTS

Font Software Product License
End-User License Agreement (EULA)
(page 1 of 2)

❂ PLEASE READ ❂
Some restrictions apply to the use of this software

The 'Restraint' typeface (Font Software) and designs contained therein is protected by copyright laws and international copyright treaties, as well as other intellectual property laws and treaties. The Font Software is licensed, not sold. This license is only valid when the licensee has been listed below and this agreement is signed by a representative of Tiro Typeworks. Please retain copies of this agreement.

Whereas 'Tiro Typeworks' is represented by one or both of the following individuals:
William Ross Mills of Galiano Island, British Columbia, Canada. DBA Tiro Typeworks and
John Hudson of Gabriola Island, British Columbia, Canada. DBA Tiro Typeworks

Subject to the foregoing, Tiro Typeworks grants (hereafter the 'licensee') :
M E Tondreau
611 Broadway
Room 511
New York, NY 10012
United States

a perpetual non-exclusive license to use the Restraint Font Software with the following terms and conditions:

1. ACCEPTANCE OF TERMS
Installation and use of this Font Software constitutes acceptanceof the terms of this licence agreement.

1.1 You acknowledge that the Font Software is the intellectual property of Tiro Typeworks and/or designers represented by Tiro Typeworks and contains copyrighted material authored by Tiro Typeworks and/or designers represented by Tiro Typeworks. The term Font Software shall also include any updates, upgrades, additions, modified versions, and development copies of the Font Software licensed to you by Tiro Typeworks. The media itself is and shall remain the property of Tiro Typeworks. Expanded versions, subsets or other derivatives of this design may also exist under other names and be distributed by Tiro Typeworks or other licensed Distributors.

2. GRANT OF LICENSE.
This document grants you the following rights:

2.1 INSTALLATION AND USE.
You may install and use the Font Software on up to five computer hard drives or other storage devices and up to two physical output devices (e.g. printers, imagesetters) based at one single geographical location stipulated by the licensee (laptops may be considered 'based' at a single location). The Font Software may not be used by more than five users on a network. Extended licenses may also be purchased, in which case a new license agreement will be drafted to reflect the new conditions.

For the sole purpose of data backup, additional backup copies of the Font Software may be made.

2.2 FAIR USE.
You may use the Font Software in most personal and commercial applications. However, under this license, you may not use the font software:

a) for the creation of logos or identities (including movie titles)

b) for the creation of signage or architectural details.

c) for the creation of advertising campaigns which include-outdoor advertising (billboards, bus shelters, etc.) or television advertising, wherein the designs contained in the Font Software comprises the sole or major design element.

d) to manufacture products wherein the designs contained in the Font Software comprises the sole or major design element, including but not limited to T-shirts, jewellery, fridge magnets, greeting cards, ceramics, posters for sale, etc.

If you wish to use the Font Software for any of the above, please contact us at restraint@tiro.nu for additional licensing or royalty fees. If in doubt, ask.

2.3 MODIFICATION.
You are not allowed to without written approval granted by Tiro Typeworks:

a) modify and/or recompile the Font Software: this includes generating or re-compiling the Font Software from any font design program. (where a 'font design' program is any piece of software capable of reading and re-compiling any standard font format),

b) adapt modules, produce sub-sets or supersets or alter any internal font data thereof for your own developments,

c) put the software solutions embodied in the Font Software to any commercial use other than operating your own computer(s) or output device(s), or

d) merge, ship or embed the Font Software with other software programs.

PLEASE CONTACT TIRO TYPEWORKS OR A LICENSED DISTRIBUTOR IF THERE ARE SPECIFIC MODIFICATIONS THAT YOU REQUIRE.
We acknowledge that no typeface can solve all problems and accept that some clients may wish to have modifications made to suit their particular needs. We would be happy to help with this and no one knows better the typefaces you are licensing, so please ask first.

33. Combine Modules

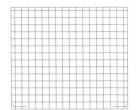

When viewed as a diagram, a modular grid can look complicated, but it's not—and it's not necessary to fill every module. Depending on the amount of information you need to fit into the space, it's possible to set up a module with a few large boxes containing images and, more importantly, key information, such as a table of contents and other kinds of indexed information.

Modules appear in the photo, with the modular Flor logo in the lower left corner.

PROJECT
Flor Catalog

CLIENT
Flor

DESIGN
The Valentine Group

Modular grids are perfect for rationing space and breaking a page into a step-by-step visual guide, as seen in this catalog for modular floor tiles.

Broken into boxes, this contents page combines easy-to-read and easy-to-view color-coded contents.

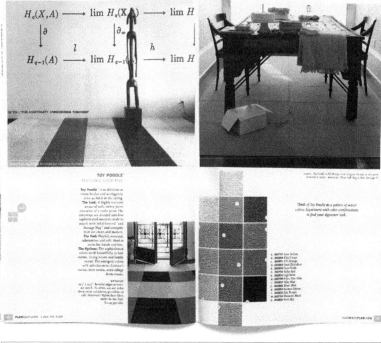

$$H_o(X,A) \longrightarrow \lim H_o(X) \longrightarrow \lim H$$
$$\downarrow \partial \qquad\qquad \downarrow \partial_\infty$$
$$H_{o-1}(A) \xrightarrow{\ l\ } \lim H_{o-1}() \xrightarrow{\ h\ } \lim H$$

Modules of color swatches play off against wittily art-directed photos and ample space.

Flor's calculator is essentially a modular chart.

ROOM FEET APPROX	7'	9'	11'	12'	13'	15'	17'	18'	20'	22'	23'	25'	27'
4'	12 TILES	16	19	21	22	26	29	30	34	37	39	42	45
5'	15	19	23	26	28	32	36	38	42	46	48	52	56
7'	21	27	32	35	38	44	50	53	58	64	67	73	78
9'	27	34	41	45	49	56	64	67	75	82	86	93	100
11'	32	41	50	55	59	68	77	82	91	100	104	113	122
12'	35	45	55	60	65	75	84	89	99	109	114	124	133
13'	38	49	59	65	70	81	91	97	107	118	123	134	144
15'	44	56	68	75	81	93	105	111	124	136	142	154	167
17'	50	64	77	84	91	105	119	126	140	154	161	175	189
18'	53	67	82	89	97	111	126	133	148	163	170	185	200
20'	58	75	91	99	107	124	140	148	165	181	189	205	222
22'	64	82	100	109	118	136	154	163	181	199	208	226	244
23'	67	86	104	114	123	142	161	170	189	208	217	236	255
25'	73	93	113	124	134	154	175	185	205	226	236	256	277 TILES

34. Make Space Count

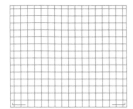

Plotting out complicated information starts with a strong grid design. Plan the proportions of each module based on the information being presented so that even potentially confusing material is clear.

Thanks to their larger format, posters are a great vehicle for nabbing attention. Headlines are best set large in order to be readable from a distance to intrigue a user to read every detail.

PROJECT
Voting by Design poster

CLIENT
Design Institute,
University of Minnesota

EDITOR/PROJECT DIRECTION
Janet Abrams

ART DIRECTION/DESIGN
Sylvia Harris

An extremely disciplined breakdown of a crucial process, this poster takes advantage of every inch of space, using a grid to control the reading experience.

OPPOSITE PAGE: Although the poster contains a lot of information, its method for breaking the experience into steps makes it easy to follow.

VOTING BY DESIGN

The century began with an electoral bang that opened everyone's eyes to the fragility of the American voting system. But, after two years of legislation, studies and equipment upgrades, major problems still exist. Why?

Voting is not just an event. It's a complex communications process that goes well beyond the casting of a vote. For example, in the 2000 presidential election, 1.5 million votes were missed because of faulty equipment, but a whopping 22 million voters didn't vote at all because of time limitations or registration errors. These and many other voting problems can be traced not just to poor equipment, but also to poor communications.

Communicating with the public is what many designers do for a living. So, seen from a communications perspective, many voting problems are really design problems. That's where you come in.

Take a look at the voting experience map below, and find all the ways you can put design to work for democracy.

A COMMUNICATIONS MAP OF THE AMERICAN VOTER'S EXPERIENCE

EDUCATION	REGISTRATION	PREPARATION	NAVIGATION	VOTING	FEEDBACK
LEARNING ABOUT VOTING RIGHTS AND DEMOCRACY	SIGNING UP TO BECOME A REGISTERED VOTER	BECOMING INFORMED AND PREPARED TO VOTE	FINDING THE WAY TO THE VOTING BOOTH	INDICATING A CHOICE IN AN ELECTION	GIVING FEEDBACK ABOUT THE VOTING EXPERIENCE
WORD-OF-MOUTH	PAPER REGISTRATION FORMS	SAVE-THE-DATE CARD	EXTERIOR STREET SIGNS	HAND-COUNTED PAPER BALLOT	CENSUS SURVEYS
HIGH SCHOOL CIVICS CLASSES	ONLINE REGISTRATION FORMS	VOTER REGISTRATION CARD	PRECINCT SIGNAGE	MACHINE-COUNTED PAPER BALLOT	EXIT POLLS
CITIZENSHIP CLASSES	MOTOR VOTER APPLICATIONS	PUBLIC SERVICE ANNOUNCEMENTS	LINE AND BOOTH IDENTITY	MECHANICAL LEVER	VOTING EXPERIENCE SURVEYS
	VOTER ROLLS	PRE-ELECTION INFO PROGRAMS	PRECINCT WORKERS	PUNCHCARD	
		CAMPAIGN LITERATURE	CAMPAIGN WORKERS	DIRECT RECORD ELECTRONIC	
		SAMPLE BALLOTS		VOTING INSTRUCTIONS	

DESIGN PROBLEM	DESIGN PROBLEM	DESIGN PROBLEM	DESIGN PROBLEM	DESIGN PROBLEM	DESIGN PROBLEM
DISAPPEARING CIVICS CLASSES	FORMS THAT ARE BARRIERS TO PARTICIPATION	TOO MUCH OR TOO LITTLE INFORMATION	GETTING TO THE BOOTH ON TIME	USER-UNFRIENDLY VOTING MACHINES	FUTURE IMPROVEMENTS LACK VOTER INPUT

DESIGN TO THE RESCUE

ALL KINDS OF DESIGNERS CAN PARTICIPATE IN VOTER REFORM. HERE'S WHO SHOULD BE ON ANY VOTING DESIGN DREAM TEAM:

GRAPHIC DESIGNERS

ENVIRONMENTAL GRAPHIC DESIGNERS

INFORMATION DESIGNERS

ARCHITECTS

INDUSTRIAL DESIGNERS

EXPERIENCE DESIGNERS

HOW YOU CAN GET INVOLVED

THERE IS WORK TO BE DONE TO IMPROVE VOTING BY DESIGN, STARTING WITH YOUR OWN COMMUNITY. HERE ARE FIVE THINGS THAT ANY DESIGNER CAN DO, TO MAKE A DIFFERENCE BEFORE THE 2004 ELECTIONS:

1. BECOME A POLLWORKER

2. FORM A VOTING DESIGN COALITION

3. WORK WITH THE POLITICAL PARTY OF YOUR CHOICE

4. CALL YOUR CONGRESSPERSON ABOUT HR 3295

5. FORM A VOTING DESIGN ADVISORY TEAM

35. Consider Organic Modules

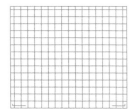

The beauty of a modular grid is that it doesn't necessarily need to be squared off. Within a consistent modular program, it's possible to vary shapes, sizes, and patterns and maintain a sense of order and delight.

Limiting the color variations and creating a palette for each page provides a sense of balance.

REGINA, TO THE TRADE; NANCY CORZINE: 212-223-8340.

ELAN, FROM $84; PINE CONE HILL: 413-496-9700.

VINTAGE FABRIC, $95; ABC CARPET & HOME: 212-473-3000.

CHINESE EMPEROR, $165; BEDFORD & CO.: 212-772-7000.

DIYA OATMEAL $265; JOHN ROBSHAW: 212-594-6006.

APPLE, $48; CARRERAS: 845-758-2200.

ETHNOA KUBA CLOTH, $265; CALYPSO HOME: 631-324-8146.

CAMINO, $195; RALPH LAUREN HOME: 888-475-7674.

19TH C. GOLD METALLIC APPLIQUE, $1350; B. VIZ: 318-766-4950.

TINA, $870; ARMANI CASA: 212-334-1271.

MODERN GOTHIC GRIFFIN, $198; MICHELE VARIAN: 212-343-0033.

DIYA AMBER, $80; JOHN ROBSHAW: 212-594-6006.

SEQUIN COVER, $83; THE CONRAN SHOP: 866-755-9079.

JACK RUSSELL, $98; L'AVENUE DES RÊVES: 212-396-9500.

ZARDOZEE, $90; ALPHA BY MILLI HOME: 212-643-8850.

STRIPES; $215; RANI ARABELLA: 561-802-9900.

112

PROJECT
House Beautiful

CLIENT
House Beautiful magazine

DESIGN
Barbara deWilde

A magazine gains new life with a crisp redesign.

Consistent and structured typography grounds each module, while the tempered, all-cap, sans serif type works as a textured rule.

SAN MARGHERITA; $245; RANI ARABELLA: 561-802-9900.

LATTICE, FROM $95; SEACLOTH: 203-422-6150.

SEABLOOM, FROM $110; OROMONO: 917-338-7568.

CORAL ON WHITE LINEN, $185; HOMENATURE: 631-287-6277.

MARYANN CHATTERTON, $498; D. KRUSE: 949-673-1302.

CHRYSANTHEMUM, $55; PINE CONE HILL: 413-496-9700.

TRANSYLVANIAN TULIP, FROM $83; AUTO: 212-229-2292.

SUZANI FLORAL, $212; MICHELE VARIAN: 212-343-0033.

IKAT, $500; D. KRUSE: 949-673-1302.

GREEK REVIVAL EMBROIDERY, $260; DRANSFIELD & ROSS: 212-741-7278.

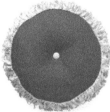

PLAID, $135; ALPANA BAWA: 212-254-1249.

WEE LOOPY FELTED, $213; THE CONRAN SHOP: 866-755-9079.

VESUVIO, $395; DRANSFIELD & ROSS: 212-741-7278.

DAVID TURNER/STUDIO D

NIZAM, $83; JOHN DERIAN DRY GOODS: 212-677-8408.

CYLINER LINEN, $195; GH INTERIORS: 888-226-8844.

LINEN, $70; ALPHA BY MILLI HOME: 212-643-8850.

KAFFE FASSETT HIBISCUS, $68; PINE CONE HILL: 413-496-9700.

113

36. Think of the Chart as a Whole

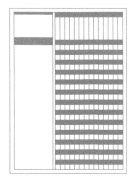

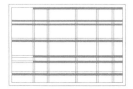

PROJECT
Timetables for
New Jersey Transit

CLIENT
New Jersey Transit

DESIGN
Two Twelve Associates

These timetables for
New Jersey Transit show that,
by simplifying and streamlin-
ing, a designer can set off
material without the separation
anxiety of too many ruled
boxes. Devices such as icons
or arrows also help the traveler
navigate through copious information. Arrows and icons may
be clichés, but, sometimes,
using a common denominator
is the best way to get the message to a mass of readers.

Creating charts, tables, and timetables is an intimidating feat dictated by numerical information.
In her book, *Thinking with Type,* Ellen Lupton advises
designers to avoid the type crime of creating what
she calls a data prison, with too many rules and boxes.
Following Lupton's advice, think of the chart, grid, or
timetable as a whole and consider how each column,
row, or field relates to the entire scheme.

Use shades of a color to help the user navigate
through dense information. Shades work whether the
job is black and white only or whether there's a budget for color. Shaded horizontal bands can be used to
set off rows of numbers, enabling users to find information. As organizational devices, frames and rules
aren't completely verboten. Rules can distinguish
particular sections and, in the case of timetables,
define specific zones of content. For more complex
projects, such as a train schedule, where a complete
system is necessary, color coding can distinguish one
rail or commuter line from another.

A grid is nothing without the information it displays, and in multiple columns, clean typography is
crucial. For directions at an airport or train station,
the way the data is typeset can make the difference
between easy travel and missed connections. Be certain to leave adequate space above and below each
line, even when there's an abundance of information.
Space will aid readability, which is the first principle of
a timetable.

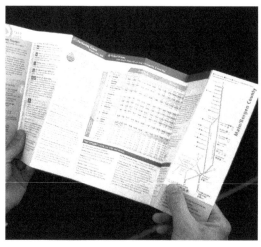

Alternating bands of color set off each stop in this timetable. Rules
are used sparingly and clearly define sets and subsets of information. Vertical rules distinguish stations from their destinations, while
horizontal rules separate major geographical zones.

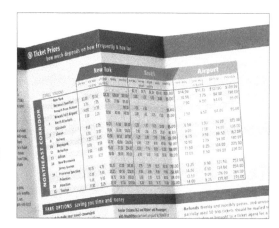

The same system that works for timetables also works for tables of
fees. Again, alternating bands of color define stations, with horizontal
and vertical rules setting off headings, such as One Way and Off-peak
Roundtrip, from the stations and fees.

Pictograms support headings in sections detailing purchasing requirements.

Arrows define express stations.

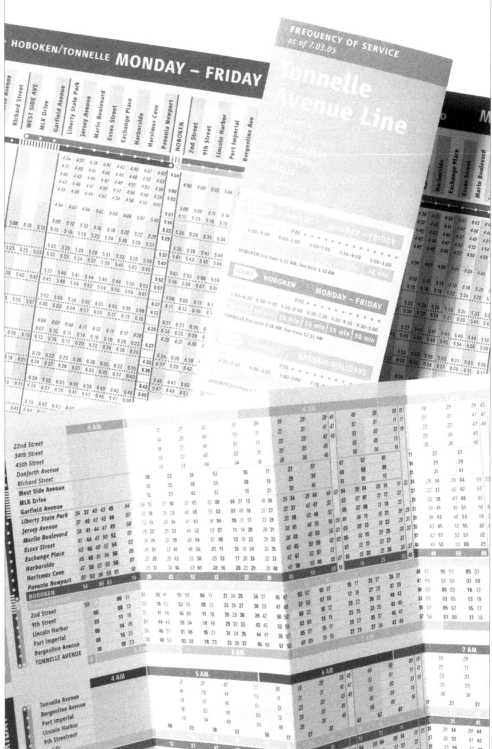

Typography is clean and no nonsense. The designers have surrounded each row and column with ample space, giving a lightness to dense information and making it easy to read. Dashes and wavy rules are used sparingly but to helpful effect. White arrows contain directionals, and black boxes with additional dropout type further clarify the day's schedule.

37. Enhance Charts

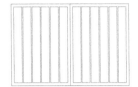

Charts and tables of necessity contain crucial information, whether it is mandated by law or a strategy to engage or persuade shareholders or investors. Such info, especially in annual reports, can sometimes be continuous droning columns of figures.

However, dynamics devised by strong graphic elements—used together with changes in size and weight can create warm rapport as much as a clear report. Even with a limited palette, sizes and shapes give the financials color and texture.

Also see pages
76–77

PROJECT
Banc Sabadell Numbers and
Annual Report 2017 (Print)

CLIENT
Banc Sabadell

DESIGN
Mario Eskenazi Studio

DESIGNERS
Mario Eskenazi,
Gemma Villegas

Numbers designed for the Banc Sabadell's Annual Reports added so successfully to the annual report that they have also been used in different promotional material (Christmas, gifts, etc.).

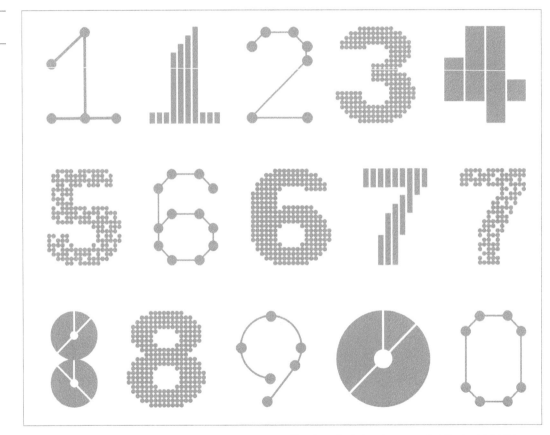

Cleverly constructed numbers are as disciplined and delightful as they are graphic.

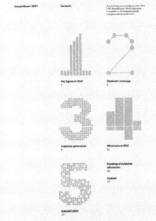

The cleverly constructed numbers grace the cover and contents and recur consistently as section numbers.

Highlighted statistics are presented in varied but controlled grids that use vertical and horizontal hierarchies as well as clearly organized heads and subheads.

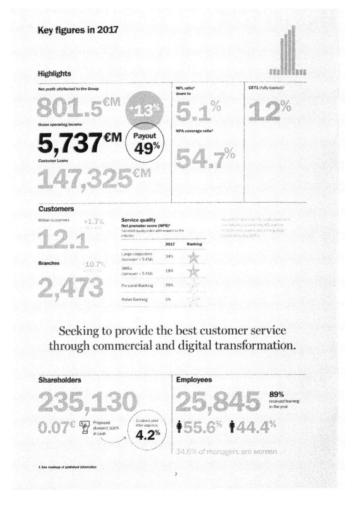

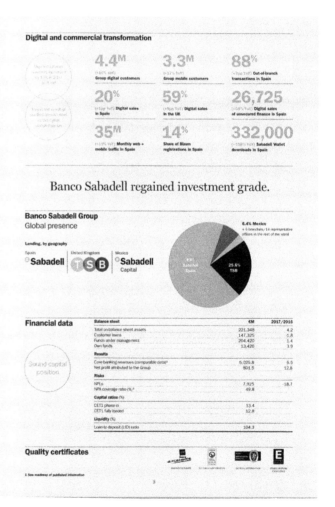

38. Deploy Joy

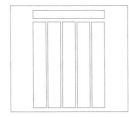

Showing consistency throughout the range of media, custom numbers provide a welcome on landing pages. Map graphics, which use some of the same patterns as the custom numbers, work well with bar charts and statistics.

Also see pages
74–75

THIS PAGE:
PROJECT
Banc Sabadell
Annual Report 2016
Desktop

CLIENT
Banc Sabadell

DESIGN
Mario Eskenazi Studio

DESIGNERS
Mario Eskenazi,
Gemma Villegas

OPPOSITE PAGE
PROJECT
Banc Sabadell
Annual Report 2016
Devices

CLIENT:
Banc Sabadell

DESIGN
Mario Eskenazi Studio

DESIGNERS
Mario Eskenazi,
Gemma Villegas

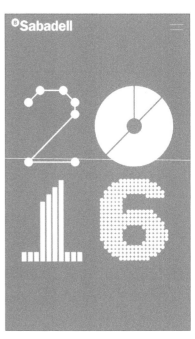

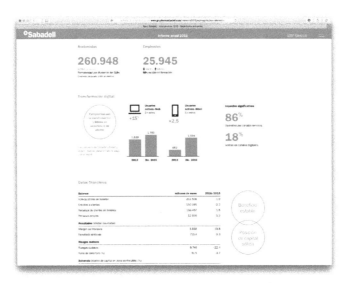

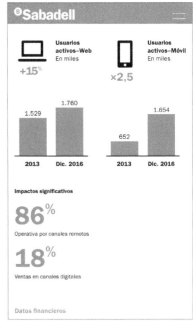

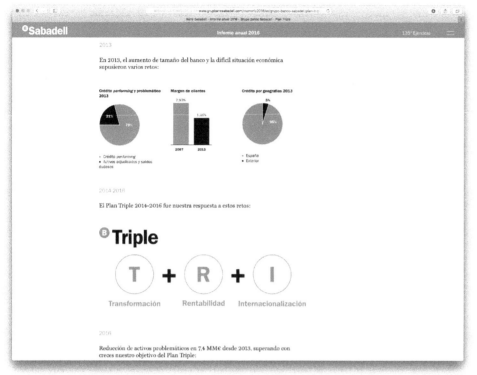

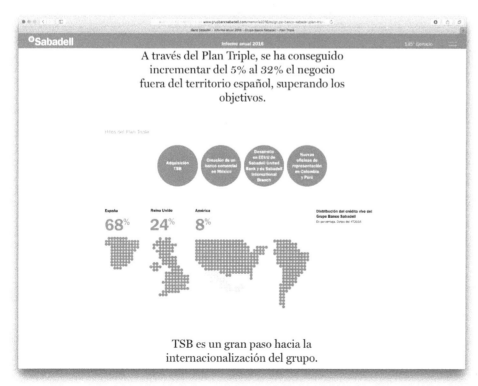

39. Use Frames Judiciously

Ideally, tabular information can be set up to avoid a boggling array of framed fields, or boxes. However, sometimes a communication involves so many discrete elements that the clearest approach to controlling data is to frame each unit.

Although it's possible to devise subscription cards that work without rules and frames and borders, different fields, as well as weights of rules and frames, cannot only impose order, but also create a layout that is reassuring in its sense of order.

PROJECT
Kurashi no techo (Everyday Notebook) magazine

CLIENT
Kurashi no techo (Everyday Notebook) magazine

DESIGNERS
Shuzo Hayashi, Masaaki Kuroyanagi

A subscription card is beautiful, as well as functional.

郵　便　は　が　き

料金受取人払郵便

新宿北局承認

4121

差出有効期間
平成21年11月
23日まで
★切手不要★

１６９−８７９０
　　　　　　１３３

東京都新宿区北新宿1-35-20

暮しの手帖社

4世紀31号アンケート係　行

ご住所　〒　　　　−

電話　　　　−　　　　−

お名前

メールアドレス　　　　　　＠

年齢　〔　　　〕歳

性別　女　／　男

ご職業〔　　　　　　　　　　　　　　　　　〕

ご希望のプレゼントに○をつけて下さい。
　□「日東紡のふきん」3枚箱入り
　□「花森安治の表紙絵ポストカード」5枚セット

いただいた個人情報は、誌面作り、当選プレゼントの発送、小社グループの商品案内等の送付に利用させていただき、厳重に管理、保管いたします。

＊ご回答は、184ページの記事一覧をご参照の上、番号でご記入下さい。
A．表紙の印象はいかがですか〔　　　〕
　　ご意見：

B．面白かった記事を3つ、挙げて下さい〔　　〕〔　　〕〔　　〕
C．役に立った記事を3つ、挙げて下さい〔　　〕〔　　〕〔　　〕
D．興味がなかった、あるいは面白くなかった記事を3つ、挙げて下さい
　　　　　　　　　　　　　　　　〔　　〕〔　　〕〔　　〕
E．今号を何でお知りになりましたか〔　　　〕
　　その他：
F．小誌と併読している雑誌を教えて下さい
G．小誌を買った書店を教えて下さい〔　　　　〕区市町村
H．小誌へのご要望、ご意見などございましたらご記入下さい

◎ご協力、ありがとうございました。

THIS PAGE AND OPPOSITE PAGE: These subscription cards pay attention to the weight of the rules. Heavier weights set off certain kinds of material and call attention to the most important text or headline. Varying weights provide balance and emphasis and offset supplementary material.

払 込 取 扱 票

| 02 | 東京 | | 通常払込料金 加入者負担 |

口座番号 00190-7 45321

金額 6300

加入者名 株式会社　暮しの手帖社

通信欄

「暮しの手帖」の定期購読を

20＿＿＿年＿＿＿号より1年間（6冊）申し込みます

※プレゼントされる場合、送付先が異なる場合はご送付先を下欄へ記入下さい。

〒□□□-□□□□
ご住所
ご氏名　tel

払込人住所氏名
（郵便番号）
（電話番号）　－　　－
（ＦＡＸ　－　　－　）

受付局日附印

裏面の注意事項をお読みください。　（私製承認東第43990号）
これより下部には何も記入しないでください。

各票の※印欄は、払込人において記載してください。

切り取らないで郵便局にお出しください。

記載事項を訂正した場合は、その箇所に訂正印を押してください。

払 込 金 受 領 証

口座番号 00190-7 45321

加入者名 株式会社　暮しの手帖社

金額 6300

払込人住所氏名

受付局日附印

料金　特殊取扱

払 込 取 扱 票

| 02 | 東京 | | 通常払込料金 加入者負担 |

口座番号 00170-1 59128

金額

加入者名 株式会社　グリーンショップ

通信欄

※プレゼントされる場合、送付先が異なる場合はご送付先を下欄へ記入下さい。

〒□□□-□□□□
ご住所
ご氏名　tel

払込人住所氏名
（郵便番号）
（電話番号）　－　　－
（ＦＡＸ　－　　－　）

受付局日附印

裏面の注意事項をお読みください。　（私製承認東第44327号）
これより下部には何も記入しないでください。

各票の※印欄は、払込人において記載してください。

切り取らないで郵便局にお出しください。

記載事項を訂正した場合は、その箇所に訂正印を押してください。

払 込 金 受 領 証

口座番号 00170-1 59128

加入者名 株式会社　グリーンショップ

金額 59128

払込人住所氏名

受付局日附印

料金　特殊取扱

40. Think Outside the Rectangle

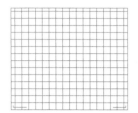

Grids can be set up to organize unconventional shapes, breaking space into discreet areas. A circle can be bisected horizontally and vertically to create quadrants, or cut radially to make pie shapes.

On one side, images bleed off and create a contrast between facts and illustrations. Typography is simple, with bold headlines echoing the logo and calling attention to the headline and URL. The horizontal lines on the subway car echo the lines in the text area.

NAME:

NEW YORK TRANSIT MUSEUM

Think About It....

When New York City's first subway opened on October 27, 1904, there were about 9 miles of track. Today the subway system has expanded to 26 times that size. About how many miles of track are there in today's system?

Most stations on the first subway line had tiles with a symbol, such as a ferry, lighthouse, or beaver. These tiles were nice decoration, but they also served an important purpose. Why do you think these symbols were helpful to subway passengers?

When subway service began in 1904, the fare was five cents per adult passenger. How much is the fare today? Over time, subway fare and the cost of a slice of pizza have been about the same. Is this true today?

Today's subway system uses a fleet of 6,200 passenger cars. The average length of each car is 62 feet. If all of those subway cars were put together as one super-long train, about how many miles long would that train be? (Hint: There are 5,280 feet in a mile.)

Redbird subway cars, which were first built for the 1964 World's Fair, were used in New York City until 2003. Then many of them were tipped into the Atlantic Ocean to create artificial reefs. A reef makes a good habitat for ocean life—and it is a good way to recycle old subway cars! Can you think of other ways that mass transit helps the environment?

To check your answers and learn more about New York City's subway system, visit our website: **www.transitmuseumeducation.org**. You'll also find special activities, fun games, and more!

© New York Transit Museum, 2007
The New York Transit Museum's programs are made possible, in part, with public funds from the New York State Council on the Arts, a state agency. All photographs are from the New York Transit Museum Collection.

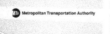
Metropolitan Transportation Authority

PROJECT
Circle Book education tool, New York Transit Museum

CLIENT
New York Transit Museum

PROJECT DEVELOPERS
Lynette Morse and Virgil Talaid, Education Department

DESIGN
Carapellucci Design

DESIGNER
Janice Carapellucci

This educational volvelle combines education, information, and activity—and, like its subject, it moves!

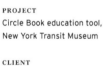

On the other side, heavy rules cleverly contain instructions and areas for notations. The blue and red colors are the actual colors used for the A, C, E, and 1, 2, 3 trains in New York City.

41. Get Attention with Color

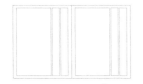

Whether its grid is unvarying or versatile, a publication benefits greatly from strong color to highlight sections, stories, or set off text. Pages with color backgrounds set against white pages or pages of lighter colors vary the pacing and keep interest and attention. Sidebar or subsidiary text in a different color is a way to set off different information without using rules or frames.

The first and second issues of a magazine launched by The Wing, a work and community space for women, boldly and colorfully informs their audience that women are on their way.

PROJECT
No Man's Land

CLIENT
The Wing

DESIGN
Pentagram

CREATIVE DIRECTION
Emily Oberman

PARTNER
Emily Oberman

SENIOR DESIGNER
Christina Hogan

DESIGNER
Elizabeth Goodspeed

DESIGNER
Joey Petrillo

PROJECT MANAGER
Anna Meixler

Color pages, backgrounds and type make a strong publication make an even stronger statement.

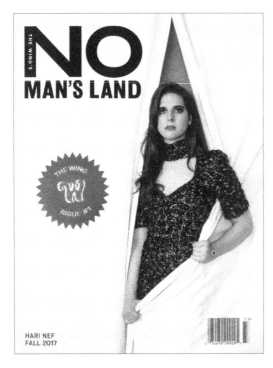

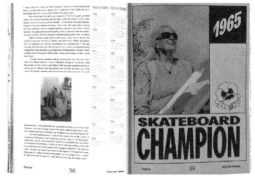

ABOVE: Color in story openers provides excitement and varies pacing.

BELOW, LEFT: Spreads with color backgrounds shake things up. BELOW, RIGHT, DETAIL: Timeline text in color and in different column widths is a clear counterpoint to running text.

McGee had seen and done a lot in her post-skate career. She worked on a fishing boat owned a topless bar got divorced raised her kids ran a trading post with her second husband. At 72, when life tends to slow down for most people McGee is ready for her next adventure

It was a little too chilly for Patti McGee in the air-conditioned skate shop, so she stood by a glass door, soaking in the California sun, presiding over the conversation like a knowing elder.

She munched on a lettuce-wrapped In-N-Out burger (protein style), her blonde hair catching the light, while the shop's owner, Matt Gaudio, told me the story of how McGee, 72, became the brand ambassador for his local skateboard team. Nearly 50 years after winning the first women's national skateboarding championship title in Santa Monica, McGee's likeness is the calling card of Gaudio's Silly Girls Skateboards, a small Fullerton-area girls' skateboarding team with 13 riders.

Behind McGee, displayed in a tall trophy case, was a Barbie doll styled to look just like her or, rather, who she was in 1965: shoeless, hair in a beehive, and doing a handstand on a skateboard. That was the year she became the first woman to win a national skateboarding competition and became a professional skateboarder. McGee made a career out of the sport before Tony Hawk and Rodney Mullen were

WOMEN SKATING THROUGH HISTORY

1963
Wendy Bearer Bull and her brother Danny become the first professionally endorsed skateboarders to be sponsored by Makaha Skateboard Club.

1965
Patti McGee appears on the cover of LIFE magazine in May 14 1965. She goes on to become the first Women's National Skateboard champion.

Laurie Turner becomes the 1965 National Girls' Champion.

1975
Peggy Oki, the only woman on the legendary Zephyr skateboard

1997
The first issue of the Villa Villa Cola zine debuts, created by Tiffany and Nicole Morgan, two skateboarding sisters. It uses humor to encourage girls to skateboard and offers advice on how to overcome being intimidated by men in the field. Other zines, Bruisers and 50-50: Skateboarding and Gender, soon follow.

1999
Elissa Steamer is the first woman to appear in Tony Hawk's skateboarding video game series.

2001
Jen O'Brien becomes the first girl to skate at

42. Control Your Palette

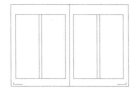

A controlled palette with only gold and black on the cover distinguishes this cover from others in the market. Thoughtful cropping makes the image more intriguing than the full frame and alludes to a life cut short.

PROJECT
King, a special edition issue commemorating the fiftieth anniversary of the assassination of Martin Luther King Jr.

CLIENT
The Atlantic

CREATIVE DIRECTOR
Paul Spella

ART DIRECTOR
David Somerville

DESIGN FIRM
OCD | Original Champions of Design

DESIGNER
Bobby C. Martin Jr.
Jennifer Kinon

Strong black-and-white pages, bold display typography that refers to history, and a limited palette with only an accent of green for the type, heightens drama throughout the piece.

A lthough many colors can arrest attention, an overabundance of colors can overwhelm the overall message. A controlled palette maintains focus on a sober or sobering subject.

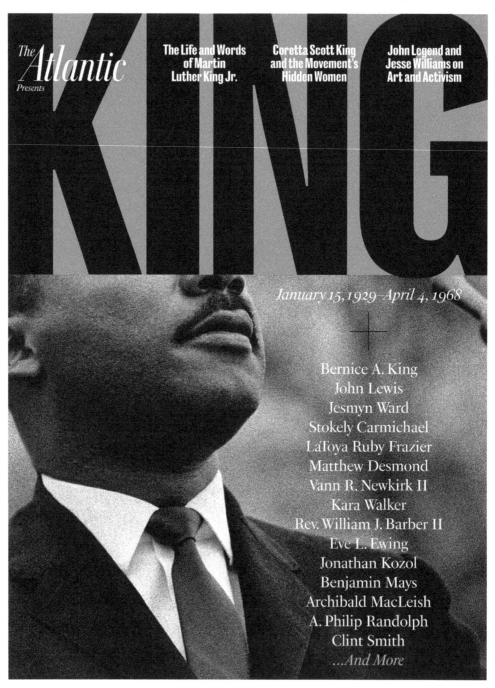

The Atlantic Presents

KING

The Life and Words of Martin Luther King Jr.

Coretta Scott King and the Movement's Hidden Women

John Legend and Jesse Williams on Art and Activism

January 15, 1929–April 4, 1968

Bernice A. King
John Lewis
Jesmyn Ward
Stokely Carmichael
LaToya Ruby Frazier
Matthew Desmond
Vann R. Newkirk II
Kara Walker
Rev. William J. Barber II
Eve L. Ewing
Jonathan Kozol
Benjamin Mays
Archibald MacLeish
A. Philip Randolph
Clint Smith
...And More

Designers occasionally use the phrase "design and the movie metaphor." Laid one on top of the other, these spreads show the filmic use of "The Negro Is Your Brother," the headline *The Atlantic* magazine used in 1963 when it published Martin Luther King Jr.'s "Letter from Birmingham Jail."
The green headline is the equivalent of a visual voiceover.

Space, black type, and an accent of green make certain to draw the reader's attention to the essay as a whole and to crucial statements.

Although this principle features color and control thereof, these spreads also embody many other aspects of working with a grid. Note the use of space, especially on the essay opening. See, too, how the caption does not fill the entire text width but instead uses a different grid module. The space allows the caption to echo the meditative image of Martin Luther King Jr.

43. Let the Color Be the Information

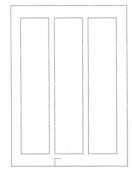

When there's a solid structure—as there often is in magazines—sometimes it's good to simply take a break, keep the typography simple, and let the color, especially in a gorgeous photo, take center stage (and sometimes center layout).

THIS PAGE AND OPPOSITE PAGE: Although it's tempting to use color to the maximum in a full-color project, using a limited amount of color— black, for instance—to offset highly saturated images allows the reader to focus on the point of the image. Too much visual competition is counterproductive.

PROJECT
House Beautiful

CLIENT
House Beautiful magazine

DESIGN
Barbara deWilde

A lush and smartly art-directed image shines without competition from other elements in the layout.

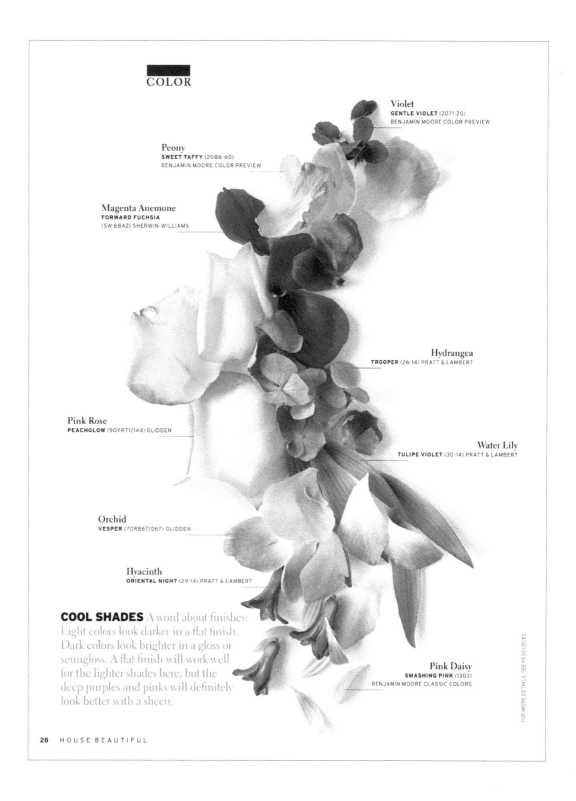

Violet
GENTLE VIOLET (2071-20)
BENJAMIN MOORE COLOR PREVIEW

Peony
SWEET TAFFY (2086-60)
BENJAMIN MOORE COLOR PREVIEW

Magenta Anemone
FORWARD FUCHSIA
(SW 6842) SHERWIN-WILLIAMS

Hydrangea
TROOPER (26-14) PRATT & LAMBERT

Pink Rose
PEACHGLOW (90YR71/144) GLIDDEN

Water Lily
TULIPE VIOLET (30-14) PRATT & LAMBERT

Orchid
VESPER (70RB67/067) GLIDDEN

Hyacinth
ORIENTAL NIGHT (29-14) PRATT & LAMBERT

COOL SHADES A word about finishes:
Light colors look darker in a flat finish.
Dark colors look brighter in a gloss or
semigloss. A flat finish will work well
for the lighter shades here, but the
deep purples and pinks will definitely
look better with a sheen.

Pink Daisy
SMASHING PINK (1303)
BENJAMIN MOORE CLASSIC COLORS

FOR MORE DETAILS, SEE RESOURCES

44. Marry Color and Typography

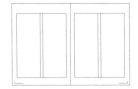

In a full-color instructional book, it's often wise to control color so that the instructions themselves aren't upstaged by the other elements on the page. However, wise color choices in a controlled palette can make typography stand out.

Section openers have lavishly colored bleed photos. Bold typography holds its own against the rich color.

An introductory spread follows each full-bleed photo. In contrast to the bold sans serif of the opener, introductory material set in serif typography drops out of the flagship color.

PROJECT
Italian Grill

CLIENT
HarperCollins

DESIGN
Memo Productions, NY

ART DIRECTORS
Lisa Eaton,
Douglas Riccardi

Grids underpin a cookbook by a chef with an outsized personality. This cookbook employs saturated, bold color and unabashedly hefty typography. Each chapter, which uses a palette with slight variations on a master color, is as handsome as the last.

THREE BOTTOM IMAGES ON THIS PAGE AND OPPOSITE PAGE: Colors vary within the palette for each section and complement the full-color photography.

FISH AND **SHELLFISH**

In Italy, cooking fish is all about freshness and simplicity— as I've said before, the philosophy of Italian fish cookery can be summed up in three words: *Leave it alone.* Complicated sauces and techniques are not part of the repertoire, and, in fact, Italians almost never serve any sauce at all with fish, other than an excellent olive oil. Lemon may sometimes appear, but even that is often considered beside the point. The one exception is *salsa verde*, the fragrant green herb sauce, which may sometimes accompany a fish with character enough to stand up to it, such as a whole grilled branzino (see page 126).

Few Italians would consider cooking anything other than local fish, whether from a mountain stream or the ocean, and I urge you to think in the same way: find a good fish market, and remember that what is freshest is best. If the specific fish called for in your recipe is not available—or doesn't look pristine and glistening—the fishmonger can help you choose another option. I include suggestions for substitutions in many of the recipes. If you are able to get fresh king mackerel for Mackerel "in Scapece" with Amalfi Lemon Salad, you will have the best mackerel dish you've ever tasted; if you can't find it, make the recipe with very fresh bluefish, or move on to another one. Most of the other fish recipes in this chapter, such as Monkfish in Prosciutto with Pesto Fregola and Swordfish Involtini Sicilian-Style, call for widely available varieties. But you'll want to be sure

to get the best tuna available—sushi-quality, that is—for Tuna Like Fiorentina, and you really should use wild salmon for the Salmon in Cartoccio with Asparagus, Citrus, and Mint.

Cooking shellfish on the grill is easy, and the recipes in this chapter use several different techniques for achieving simple perfection. Clams in Cartoccio are wrapped in a foil package and allowed to steam in their fragrant juices. The shrimp in Shrimp Rosemary Spiedini alla Romagnola are threaded onto rosemary skewers, which impart their herbal fragrance and look sexy besides. I love cooking shellfish (and cephalopods) on a piastra, a flat griddle or stone placed on the hot grill (see page 000 for more on the subject), because it gives them a great sear and char, as in Sea Scallops alla Caprese or Marinated Calamari with Chickpeas, Olive Pesto, and Oranges.

Thinking globally while buying locally is especially important when you are buying fish. Some "trendy" fish have been overharvested to the point of extinction, and we now know that there can be problems with farmed fish as well, like salmon. The Monterey Bay Aquarium, at www.montereybayaquarium.com, maintains an up-to-date list of species that are being overfished in the United States and in the rest of the world. It's an invaluable resource, and I urge you to consult it when writing your shopping list, as I do both at home and at the restaurants.

MARINATED CALAMARI

WITH CHICKPEAS, OLIVE PESTO, AND ORANGES

SERVES 6

CALAMARI

3 pounds cleaned calamari (tubes and tentacles)

¼ cup extra-virgin olive oil

Grated zest and juice of 1 lemon

4 garlic cloves, thinly sliced

2 tablespoons chopped fresh mint

2 tablespoons hot red pepper flakes

2 tablespoons freshly ground black pepper

CHICKPEAS

Two 15-ounce cans chickpeas, drained and rinsed, or 3½ cups cooked chickpeas

½ cup extra-virgin olive oil

¼ cup red wine vinegar

4 scallions, thinly sliced

4 garlic cloves, thinly sliced

¼ cup mustard seeds

Kosher salt and freshly ground black pepper

OLIVE PESTO

¼ cup extra-virgin olive oil

Grated zest and juice of 1 orange

½ cup black olive paste

4 jalapeños, finely chopped

12 fresh basil leaves, cut into chiffonade (thin slivers)

3 oranges

2 tablespoons chopped fresh mint

CUT THE CALAMARI BODIES crosswise in half if large. Split the groups of tentacles into 2 pieces each.

Combine the olive oil, lemon zest and juice, garlic, mint, red pepper flakes, and black pepper in a large bowl. Toss in the calamari and stir well to coat. Refrigerate for 30 minutes, or until everything else is ready.

Put the chickpeas in a medium bowl, add the oil, vinegar, scallions, garlic, and mustard seeds, and stir to mix well. Season with salt and pepper and set aside.

93

45. Contain and Clarify with Color

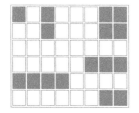

Consistent in size and within an overall grid, tightly plotted yet flexible color modules can support playful variations of both text and images, as shown in this program calendar. Boxes and color can provide an overall system and structure and can also control information clearly. When listing a lot of specific details, a grid that combines color modules can set off dates and information from other kinds of text, such as URLs, calls to action, or banners with the main title of the piece.

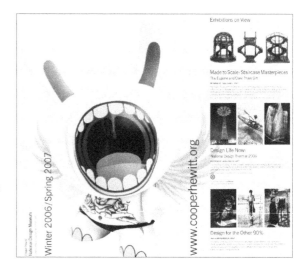

PROJECT
Program calendar

CLIENT
Smithsonian, Cooper-Hewitt, National Design Museum

DESIGN
Tsang Seymour Design, Inc.

DESIGN DIRECTOR
Patrick Seymour

ART DIRECTOR
Laura Howell

This system for seasonal program calendars supports a uniform message. It also allows dynamic variations of colors and images.

Synopses of the lead exhibits and their dates complement exuberantly large and unfettered images on the reverse side of the program calendar, setting up visual tension and compression.

Varied image sizes and the occasional silhouette adhere to, but also pop out of, the framework of the color boxes.

First, define the size of your overall area, breaking it into equal squares. Then take into account an overall outside margin. Use squares as single boxes, doubled (or even tripled) horizontally or vertically, or stacked. Paying attention to the information to be contained, the modules can be color-coded by date, month, price, event, or whatever is appropriate for the project. When designing with hardworking information, the color should communicate and enlighten the message.

Modules also support photos and illustrations. As with text, an image can fit into one module, two vertical modules, two or four horizontal modules, or four stacked modules. In short, the color boxes allow a range of variation, while maintaining control and integrity. To add further interest, play against the grid of the boxes by silhouetting the occasional image, giving further rhythm and visual space to a lively program.

Within the structural support from a cavalcade of colors, information can exist in its own space. Color modules can support a readable hierarchy of information with small type sizes, as well as larger headlines and bolder information. Varied type sizes and weights along with upper- and lowercase type make it easy for the reader to scan dates, events, times, and descriptions. Large headlines in the multimodule boxes add rhythm and surprise, as well as a consistency among similar kinds of copy, such as marketing lines, the client or museum, calls to action, and contact information.

A double-sided project, or a project on a spread, can also take advantage of the modular format, by following, but also interrupting, clearly defined areas.

OPPOSITE: Months are color coded to clearly chart the passage of time. Each event has a module to itself.

GRIDS AT WORK | 91

46. Emphasize Info with Color Typography

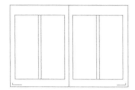

Too much color can be busy and confusing. However, the right amount of color provides a guide to help the reader recognize priorities. A pronounced hierarchy of headings can be easy to follow if aided by accents in color.

PROJECT
Croissant magazine

CLIENT
Croissant magazine

DESIGNER
Seiko Baba

ILLUSTRATION
Yohimi Obata

Color subtly sets off type, adding clarity and zest to magazine spreads. This particular magazine is a MOOK, a special edition published by *Croissant* editors. The title is *Mukashi nagara no kurashi no chie*, which roughly means "time-honored wisdom of living."

白玉すいとん

あり合わせの根菜と一緒に白玉団子を煮込んだ手軽な汁料理。「主食もおかずも一度に食べられる。撮影など仕事の合間の昼食としても活躍した汁ものです。祖母もよく準備の手を休めて食べていました」。すいとんと言えばうどん粉が王道だが、阿部さんはより手軽な白玉粉を好んで使った。豆腐を練り込んだ白玉は、もちもちと柔らかな食感。

材料 4人分
大根6cm 人参1/3本 ごぼう10cm
しめじ1/3房 まいたけ1/3房 油揚げ
1枚 三つ葉8本 煮干し10本 薄口
醤油大さじ2 豆腐約1/6丁 白玉粉約
1/3カップ
作り方
1 煮干しは頭と内臓を取り、鍋などで乾煎りしてから、水につけておく。(約6カップ、分量外)
2 人参、大根は皮をむいて薄めのイチョウ切り、ごぼうは皮をたわしなどでよくこそいで洗い、薄く斜めに切って水にさらしておく。
3 油揚げは熱湯をかけ、油抜きして食べやすい大きさに切り、しめじ、まいたけは小房に分けておく。
4 1に2を加え火にかけ、ひと煮立ちし

たら3も加え、薄口醤油を半量入れてしばらく煮る。
5 白玉粉に豆腐を混ぜ(写真)、みみたぶくらいの柔らかさにして形を整え、熱湯に入れて浮き上がってくるまで茹でたのち冷水に取る。
6 4に5を加え、ひと煮立ちしたら、残りの薄口醤油を加え味を調えて、ざく切りにした三つ葉を加える。

Setting one character larger and in color calls attention to a particular heading.

じゃが芋団子

じゃがいもひとつでできる、定番のおやつ。

材料 4人分
作り方

薩摩芋もち

冷めてもおいしい、さつまいも入りのおもち。

材料 4人分
作り方

皮も香ばしく揚げて、トッピングに使う。

茄子の胡麻煮

材料 4人分
作り方

だしに使う煮干しも、立派なメインに。

煮干しとごぼうの立田揚げ

材料 4人分
作り方

017　クウネル

暮らしの絵本 016

Here, color sets off one piece of information from another. Clear differentiation is especially useful and important for instructions. In this cookbook spread, subheads are in color. The numbers in the recipe instructions are also in red to set them apart from the text.

The weight, size, or shade of a different color for the Q Questions provides texture and visual interest.

お付き合い編　人付き合いを潤滑にする言葉づかい。

Q 知人からセールスの勧誘を受けました。うまく困るには、どう言えばいいですか？

Q 近所の主婦の中傷合戦に、巻き込まれ、私の名前も。どうすればいいですか？

Q 親しい人との食事、きょうは自分が支払いたい。どう言えばいいですか？

Q 待ち合わせ場所に、現れなかった友人に、ひとこと文句を言いたいのですが。

Q グループのある人に会場の手配を頼みたい。上手に、お願いする方法はありますか？

Q お中元やお歳暮を、お断りしたいのですが、相手に失礼にならない言い方はありますか？

095　クウネル

暮らしのABC 094

47. Enliven Calendar Modules with Color

Using color in a calendar makes it easier to separate specific elements, such as days of the week. The information both stands out and works with the overall spread. Colors can also complement the palette of the photo.

For situations where it's important that the dates are featured but not obscured, chose colors or shades that are muted and and do not upstage the material. Desaturated colors (colors with more gray) work best if type is surprinting, that is printed on top of the color.

PROJECT
Calendar of events

CLIENT
New York City Center

DESIGN
Andrew Jerabek

Photos and palettes work together to determine shades for calendar boxes.

A rich background and astounding movement play against the controlled calendar in complementary colors.

Box colors present such a delicate and distinctive palette that they complement instead of compete with a beautifully art-directed photo.

Autumnal colors support a spread containing a dramatic photo with accents of saffron.

48. Code with Color

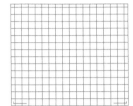

Coding information by color can help viewers quickly find the information they need. A scan of a color key, in conjunction with icons, quickly communicates far more information than words or colors alone.

Depending on the client or material, the colors can be muted or bright. Saturated colors—colors with less gray—immediately command attention.

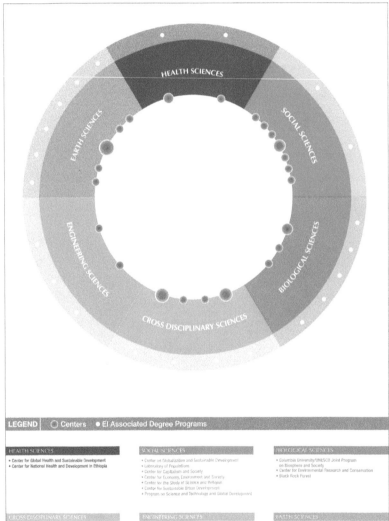

By design, each discipline includes a number of research centers and associated degree programs. Each discipline has an assigned color system.

PROJECT
Identity program

CLIENT
Earth Institute at
Columbia University

DESIGN
Mark Inglis

CREATIVE DIRECTOR
Mark Inglis

Color codes differentiate a suite of six scientific disciplines for the Earth Institute at Columbia University.

Icons also tie into the color system.

WATER
ENERGY
URBANIZATION

HAZARDS
HEALTH
POVERTY

FOOD ECOLOGY & NUTRITION
ECOSYSTEMS
CLIMATE & SOCIETY

The colors work with icons, color bands, or type.

| Water | Energy | Urbanization | Hazards | Health | Poverty | Food, Ecology & Nutrition | Ecosystems | Climate & Society |

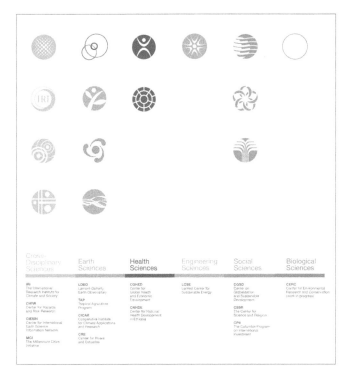

| Cross-Disciplinary Sciences | Earth Sciences | Health Sciences | Engineering Sciences | Social Sciences | Biological Sciences |

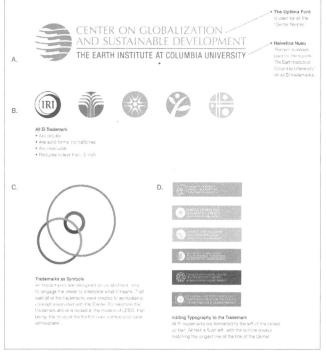

49. Separate Items with Color

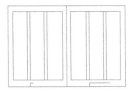

Columns with horizontal and vertical containing rules are perfectly clear and legitimate ways to separate components, but shades of different colors can add extra pizazz and interest and differentiate the voices of various contributors. Dropout type, i.e., type that is white reversed out of the background color, works to even greater effect.

Also see pages
100–101

DROPPING OUT

Dropout type is dramatic. But be aware that using dropout type for a lot of small text can easily lose clarity, especially with a serif font. Sans serifs may hold up better. On screens, type dropping out of black can be even trickier to read, so it may be necessary to go bigger and bolder.

> *AT SPOTCO, WE BEGIN WORK-*ing on a show by understanding its Event. I didn't invent this phrase—it was loaned to me by producer Margo Lion. But what I came to understand it as is quite simply the reason you see a show. Or even more simply, the reason you tell someone else to see a show. It can be straightforward,

The sample above shows the reproduction size.

PROJECT
Broadway;
From Rent to Revolution

CLIENT
Drew Hodges, author;
Rizzoli, publisher

CREATIVE DIRECTOR
Drew Hodges

DESIGN
Naomi Mizusaki

Recollections of different collaborators with Spotco, Broadway's most illustrious agency, are spotlighted in different colors.

Each color signals a contribution from a different collaborator. The text for the page finale, the black box, is not by or about a person but rather "The Event," an essential element of the agency's philosophy.

1987 | ACT ONE

DREW HODGES
FOUNDER AND CHIEF EXECUTIVE OFFICER

WE OPEN ON A YOUNG design firm called Spot Design. It was named for a dog the landlord said we couldn't have. So I named the office as my pet.

After attending art school at School of Visual Arts in New York City, I had left working for my college mentor Paula Scher and began freelancing solo out of my apartment. I was working in the kitchen of my loft, across from the now-defunct flea markets on 26th Street and Sixth Avenue. This is the same kitchen where producers Barry and Fran Weissler came to see the early designs for *Chicago*—but I get ahead of myself. Ultimately, we were five designers and one part-time bookkeeper doing entertainment and rock 'n' roll work. We were young and laughed a lot. Ten years later, we had been privileged to work with Swatch Watch, MTV, Nickelodeon, the launch of Comedy Central and *The Daily Show*, as well as record work for Sony Music, Atlantic Records, and Geffen/DreamWorks records, where our most notable projects were album packages for downtown diva Lisa Loeb and iron-lunged Aerosmith. We grew adept at strategy, design, and collaboration with many downtown artists, illustrators, and photographers,—all people we would come to take full advantage of as we began our theater work. I went to the theater—it was a New York City joy for me. I had gone since early high school, riding the train to the city. But I never dreamed I would get any nearer than second-acting *Dreamgirls* from the mezzanine.

Two bold incidents happened to change that. First, Tom Viola and Rodger McFarlane were heroes of mine for the work they did through what was to become Broadway Cares/Equity Fights AIDS. A friend and art director from Sony Music named Mark Burdett

was assigned to work with Spot ad for the Grammy Awards pro the prime position of the back was Martin Luther King Jr. Da clients were all away. So we mo doing yet another ad filled with minis of the labels and latest St release with hollow congratula a waste of a great opportunity. posited that Sony could be the record company to take a stanc AIDS by making a donation an ing a red ribbon to the back of issue of the program. And to pi idea, we called Rodger and Tor offices to help us fulfill it. The was theirs after all. Remarkabl were working on the holiday ar answered the phone. They agree and the rest is history. I believe the first awards ceremony to pu script the concern over AIDS, a friendships were formed. Later year, Tom and Rodger called. T an ad due in three days for thei show, *The Destiny of Me*, Larry sequel to *The Normal Heart*. W them a design based on a photc right hand—I guess we felt it s personal—and they loved it. Th our first theater poster.

But it would have been a sho career without the second even years later, we had just finishe the Aerosmith album for Geffe Sloane, David Geffen's star crea director, called and asked us to with the producers of *Rent*—G would be releasing the album. meeting with the ad agency in and got the assignment and a t the hottest show in town a wee had opened Off-Broadway. Wit year, we would have designed *Chicago*, and Jeffrey Seller sat in a mall in Miami to ask if we thought about starting an ad ag seemed a big risk—but it also s like a world where you could ac meet the people doing the crea you were assigned to promote. began to try and figure out just ad agency worked anyway.

8

BRIAN BERK
[CO]-FOUNDER AND CHIEF OPERATING [OF]FICER / CHIEF FINANCIAL OFFICER

[T]HE SPRING OF 1997, [...] designing the successful ad cam[...]s for *Rent* and *Chicago*, we decided [...]empt to open a theatrical ad [...]y. The first question was: What [...] we need to be able to pull this [...] or starters, we would need equip[...] office space, a staff, and most [...]tantly, clients.

[...]e equipment was easy. In order to [...]pfront costs down, we could [...]a few computers and a fax [...]ine. From there, we could scrape [...]til we had some clients.

[...]ice space: The design studio was [...]ntly housed in Drew's apartment. [...]ew that for potential clients to [...]der hiring us, we would need to be [...] theater district, and we would [...]to have a large conference room for [...]eekly ad meetings. I set out to look [...]ce. One space was located in 1600 [...]way. The building was fairly [...]own (and we would later learn it [...] mouse problem), but it did have a [...]and interesting history. It was built [...] very early 1900s as a Studebaker [...]y and showroom. In the 1920s, it [...]onverted to offices and at one point [...]d the original offices of Columbia [...]res, Universal Pictures, and Max [...]her Studios, creator of Betty Boop. [...]seemed a fitting place for a theatri[...]l agency. By 1997, the building held [...]bination of offices and screening [...]s. (It has since been torn down.) [...]pace we looked at consisted of two [...]offices, a big bullpen area for our [...]ners, and one large conference [...]with the most amazing view of [...]s Square. We actually found a [...]graph of a movie executive sitting [...] desk in the room that would [...]ually become our conference room. [...] the same wood paneling and [...]w with the view. However, the [...]kin rug, which is seen on the floor [...] photo, is long gone. The space had [...]cter. We had to furnish it on the [...]. We hired a set decorator friend to [...]he office circa 1940s, so all the used [...]furniture we purchased would look

like a very conscious design choice. We moved to the space in June 1997.

Staff: We already had a creative director (Drew), four graphic designers, an office manager, and me. I handled finance, administration, and facilities. We needed someone to head account services, an assistant account executive and a graphic production artist to produce all the ads. We'd hire a writer once we had some clients. For the production artist, we knew just who to hire: Mary Littell. She had worked for us before and was great. The person to head account services was harder to find. We needed someone who had worked at an ad agency before and understood media. From what Drew learned, one of the most respected account managers in the industry was Jim Edwards, or as was said by several producers, "He is the least hated." He had worked at two of the existing theatrical ad agencies. But would Jim join a startup? He was game and joined our team. Jim walked in the door on July 21, 1997. Mary was at her desk working on dot gain so she would be ready if we were ever hired to place an ad. Now, all we needed were some clients.

JIM EDWARDS
CO-FOUNDER AND FORMER CHIEF OPERATING OFFICER

OF DREW, BRIAN, MARY, BOB Guglielmo, Karen Hermelin, and Jesse Wann, I was the only one who had worked at an ad agency before. Little things like a copy machine that can make more than one copy every thirty seconds was not part of our infrastructure. I started on a Monday, and the pitch for *The Diary of Anne Frank* was that Friday. We didn't have any clients so that entire week was all about the pitch. Thursday night we were there late and inadvertently got locked in the office (how that is even possible still strikes me as odd). We couldn't reach anyone who had a key so we had to call the fire department to let us out. They did—and were adorable too.

Once we had a show, we became a legitimate advertising agency, which led to David Mamet's *The Old Neighborhood*, John Leguizamo's *Freak*, and Joanna Murray-Smith's *Honour* within months of being open for business.

Since SpotCo was a brand-new company, we had no credit with any of our vendors. The *New York Times* made us jump through so many hoops about establishing a relationship with them. I think we had to have a letter from the producers of *Anne Frank* saying they were hiring us as their ad agency. When it came time to reserve our first *Times* ad, about a month had passed since all those rules were handed down. Back then, you

simply called the *Times* reservation desk and reserved the space. That's what I had been doing for years so I did it again, inadvertently forgetting that the ad needed to be paid for well in advance. I knew everyone there so they accepted my reservation without question. The ad ran. No one said anything. The bill came about a month later, and we paid it. About two months in, the *Times* noticed that we were sliding under their rules but since we were paying our bills and were current, they granted us credit. By that first Christmas, we had established credit everywhere, which was and is a big deal. Not many new companies can make that kind of claim.

In the first eighteen months of SpotCo, I never worked harder in my life. The hours were long (I gained a lot of weight during that time—do not put this in the book), and it wasn't easy, but we also saw direct results from all the hard work. The work was good, and people noticed what we were doing—and we were making money! The Christmas party of 1998 was particularly memorable. That day, we had just released the full-page ad for *The Blue Room*, which was pretty provocative because all we ran was the photo and a quote about how hot the ticket was. It was a big deal for us and kind of heady. The party was at some restaurant, and Brian had secured a private room. There were only three tables of ten, and we shared our Secret Santa gifts. Everyone was really into it and every time someone opened a gift, Amelia Heape would shout, "Feel the *love*, people! Feel the *love*!" Indeed.

TOM GREENWALD
CO-FOUNDER AND CHIEF STRATEGY OFFICER

WHAT AM I, NUTS? IT WAS early 1998. I had a good job, an amazing wife, three adorable kids under five years old, and a modest but nice house in Connecticut. In other words, I was settling in nicely to the 9 to 7, suburban commuting life. But I kept hearing about this guy Drew Hodges. First I heard about him through my friend Jeffrey Seller, who had worked with Drew on the designs for *Rent*. Then I heard about him through my friend David Stone, who was just about to start working with him on *The Diary of Anne Frank*. Then, I realized, they're talking about the tall guy who talked a lot and had barreled his way through meetings at Grey Advertising (where I worked at the time) while designing the artwork for *Chicago*. So when Jim Edwards called me and said, "Hey, I'm joining up with this guy Drew and we're turning his design shop into an ad agency and did you want to meet him." I had to think about it. No way was I going to give up my job security, right? The odds of any theatrical

ad agency surviving at all were miniscule, much less one with . . . wait, let me add them up . . . one client. And besides, I'd probably have to take a cut in pay. Only an insane person would consider it. "Sure," I told Jim. "Set it up."

So I went in to talk to Drew, and after about eighteen seconds, I'd made up my mind. When Drew asked if I had any questions, I had only one. "Where do I sign?" I joined SpotCo as the head (only) copywriter, head (only) broadcast director, and head (only) proofreader. On the downside, we were a very lean department. On the upside, I never had any problems with my staff.

Now here we are, almost eighteen years later. My wife is still amazing, my three kids are still adorable (although no longer under five), and my house is still modest but nice (although we redid the TV room). I never did settle in to that 9 to 7 job, though. Instead, I decided to take a chance, a flyer, and a crazy ride—and it's worked out pretty well. So yeah, I guess I was a little nuts. But it turns out craziness has its perks.

50. Attain Color Using Weight, Size, and Shape

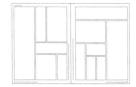

Sometimes, to reduce the barrage of elements, designers choose to print in black and white or in as few colors as possible. Other times, there are budget restrictions that dictate the use of one color. Whether with limited colors or one color only, it's possible to achieve color and texture through means of typeface, type size, and font, as well as how much of the page grid image elements inhabit.

A versatile grid supports many widths and sizes, and taking advantage of all of the options creates variation and fascination. Space, which is in effect a graphic element, also provides power and contrast.

TINTS

If the specifications—or the design preference—calls for one color or only a few colors, an option is to work with tints, i.e. pecentages of a color. A 10% bleed black background can easily support text that surprints in 100% of the color. The darker the screen, the less readable type in 100% of a color (depending on type size or paper). An option when using a dark screen is to knock out the type. Throughout *Layout Essentials*, sidebars like this one are a 70% tint of black on a white background.

Also see pages
98–99, 112–113

PROJECT
King, a special edition issue commemorating the fiftieth anniversary of the assassination of Martin Luther King Jr.

CLIENT
The Atlantic

CREATIVE DIRECTOR
Paul Spella

ART DIRECTOR
David Somerville

DESIGN FIRM
OCD | Original Champions of Design

DESIGNERS
Bobby C. Martin Jr.,
Jennifer Kinon

Varied typefaces in varying sizes and dramatic use of size and space create an epically successful special edition.

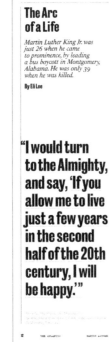

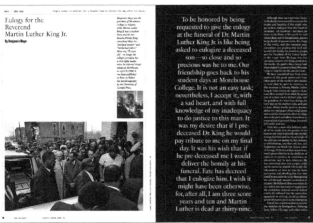

OPPOSITE PAGE: A masterpiece of presenting historical photos, quotes, and reports, the spread uses many aspects of its versatile grid to achieve texture. The three different typefaces work together to both evoke the 1960s and give a fresh face to clearly organized sections where sizes vary but timeline dates are consistent.

THIS PAGE, ABOVE: Four section openers set a dramatic pace with size, not color.

THIS PAGE, BELOW: The eulogy for the Reverend Martin Luther King Jr. is respectful but dynamic. Limiting color, enhancing passages by dropping type out of the background, spotlighting certain text by setting it in larger, wider, and narrower widths and in varying weights, and leaving parts of the grid unused, makes space as eloquent as the essays and images.

51. Separate Signage into Sections

Designing signs is a specific design challenge that requires logic, organization, and consistency. A grid system for the graphics applied to a sign system—especially designs that wrap around kiosks—can accommodate

- levels of information that are searched in sequence—choice 1, choice 2, and so on
- secondary choices that are still important, such as which language to read
- tertiary information that answers basic questions and needs, such as gate information at an airport, restroom designations, and where to get something to eat
- a host of complex options that arise in the course of following signs: for example, a user realizing he has to retrace steps.

Because the user must also be able to see the signs and read them easily, even while walking or driving, the type should be readable, with a clear hierarchy, and the colors should flag attention without obscuring the message.

Shown for use on pylons, the main signs and graphic plates form bands of information.

PROJECT
Identity and Signage

CLIENT
The Peter and Paul Fortress, St. Petersburg, Russia

ART DIRECTION
Anton Ginzburg

DESIGN
Studio RADIA

A presentation for the identity of the Peter and Paul Fortress in St. Petersburg, Russia, shows how people can find their way in both English and Russian. Parts of the project have been completed.

Details of the graphic plates show the many kinds of information the designers had to present and specify.

The text for a sign mounted on a pylon is set in clear, classic typography with a nod to the history of the city.

The blue panels are temporary banners, printed digitally and mounted on pylons, to announce changeable events. The photo panel shows the format of posters for such events.

52. Systematize Using Bands

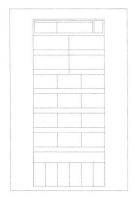

A clear way to separate information is to use a horizontal hierarchy. Information can also be organized in bands and exist as part of the navigational system. Such a hierarchy applies to devices as well as to the main site.

ABOVE AND OPPOSITE: Horizontal bands provide a framework, with the navigation bar in the top band. Making a choice in the navigation bar leads to a cascade of additional horizontally organzied information.

PROJECT
Jewish Online Museum Website

CLIENT
Jewish Online Museum

BRANDING/FRONT-END DEVELOPMENT
Threaded

WIREFRAMING
Lushai

WEB DEVELOPMENT
Ghost Street
Reactive

The website for the Jewish Online Museum—the first of its kind not only in New Zealand but internationally—was designed to be an engaging and educational resource for a wide range of visitors and to act primarily as a repository and accessible resource for the Jewish community in New Zealand.

THE IMPORTANCE OF CODERS

Often the front-end designer is not the back-end coder. This may seem incredibly obvious, yet clients often assume a designer can do it all. A good coder is sometimes hard to find. For the Jewish Online Museum site, the designers and Lushi, the company that did the wireframes, worked together through a series of workshops to develop dynamic wireframes designed to suit the needs of JoM's users. The workshops covered user interaction and responsive translation to mobile devices.

FAR RIGHT: Devices maintain consistency with the website, even when breaking the bands with other shapes to signify recollections.

53. Define Horizontal Areas Using Space

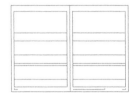

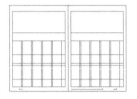

Adequate space on a text page provides order and a sense of balance. By using a larger amount of space, it's possible to separate introductory materials, such as headings and text, from more explanatory copy, such as captions or step-by-step information. The discrete areas help the reader navigate the page.

PROJECT
Kurashi no techo (Everyday Notebook) magazine

CLIENT
Kurashi no techo (Everyday Notebook) magazine

DESIGNERS
Shuzo Hayashi, Masaaki Kuroyanagi

In pages or spreads with a bounty of images and information, a horizontal hierarchy can demarcate headings and then levels of steps, giving a sense of order and calm and making it easy to parse the information.

Space clearly sets off text from images and defines pockets of information.

実際に和紙を
折ってみましょう
4種類の作り方です

折形と
日本のしきたり

折形は、室町時代に始まった、武家に伝わる礼法と伝えられます。折形をはじめとする日本のしきたりの数々は、本来の意味や由来は今に伝わっていなかったり、暮らしの中に今も続いて今に伝わったものの、と折形デザイン研究所の山口信博さんはおっしゃいます。結婚のお祝いには水引をかけたご祝儀を贈る、お正月に門松を飾るなど、民俗学者の折口信夫は「生活の古典」と呼びました。

【……】私どもの生活は、造形の目的のついで私自身、いわば心ともに思われた様式が、由来不明なる「為来り」によって、純粋にせられることが多い。その多くは、家庭生活の便性に、しなやかな力を与える。赤い花を挿てた後の心持ちのすがすがしさを考えてみればよい。……】『古代研究　祭りの発生』（古代生活の研究）中公クラシックスより

     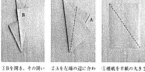

松飾り

年玉包み

屠蘇散包み

箸包み

------ は手前に折る折り目、　は後に折り返す折り目、——— は山を示します。

63　　　　62

A well-considered horizontal organization breaks introductory
material into zones. Images and captions marching across the spread
create a horizontal flow, while enabling each image-and-caption
combination to be a clear and easy-to-read step in the
article's instructions.

54. Illuminate Timelines

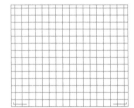

It's wise to think of a timeline as more than a functional piece of information. A timeline can also represent a person's life or an era, so the design needs to reflect the content.

PROJECT
Influence map

CLIENT
Marian Bantjes

DESIGNER AND ILLUSTRATOR
Marian Bantjes

In Marian Bantjes's illustration of influences and artistic vocabulary, craft and detail are paramount. Lessons learned from influences, such as movement, flow, and ornamentation are all in evidence. Bantjes's ten years as a book designer have informed her considerable typographical talent.

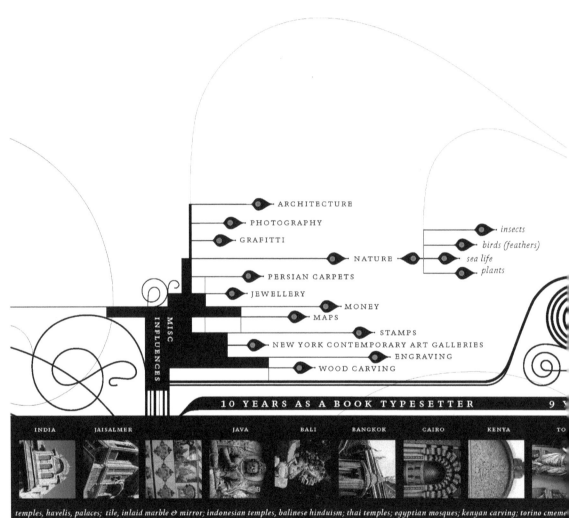

Lyricism stems not only from the curved lines of the illustrations but also from the weights of the rules. The letterspacing of the small caps creates texture and lightness. The ampersand is beautiful, and, although the piece is a knockout of movement, carefully controlled alignments play off the curves.

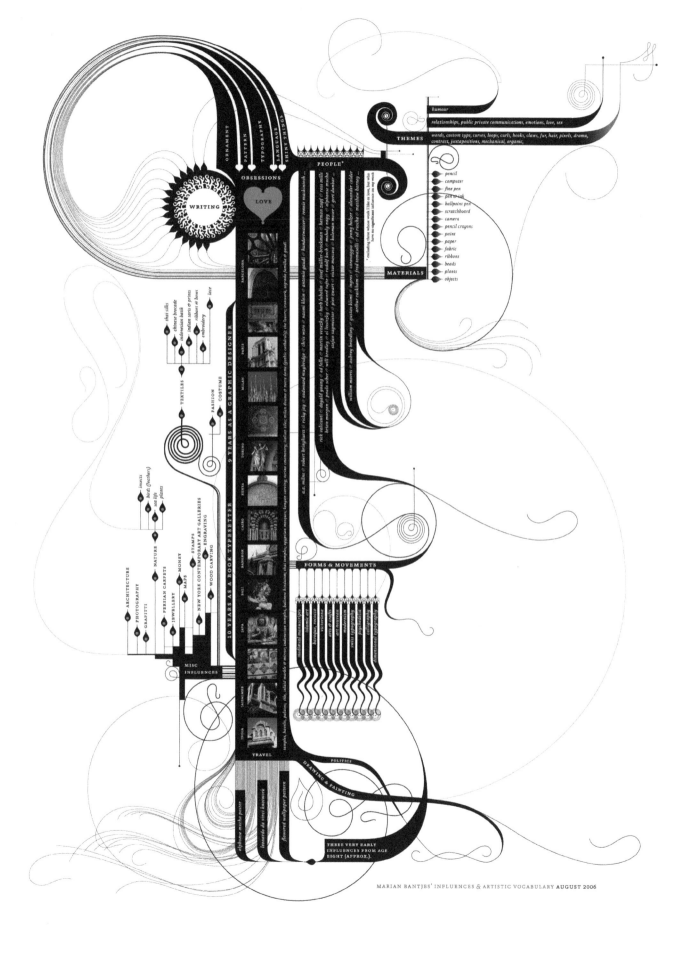

MARIAN BANTJES' INFLUENCES & ARTISTIC VOCABULARY **AUGUST 2006**

55. Use the Nav Bar as a Flag

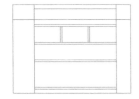

One strong way to segregate items is to simply divide the available space. A clear horizontal bar can function as a flag, a way of calling attention to the top story or information. Furthermore, using a color at the top of the bar offers the option of dropping the information out of the headline, creating a happy tension of negative versus positive, light versus dark, and dominant versus subservient.

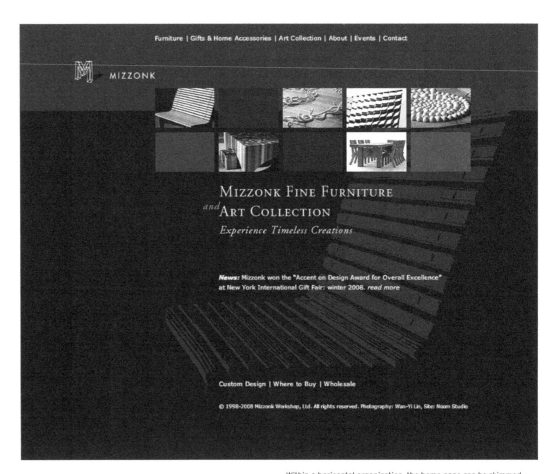

Within a horizontal organization, the home page can be skimmed from top to bottom.

PROJECT
www.mizzonk.com

CLIENT
Mizzonk Workshop

DESIGN
Punyapol "Noom" Kittayarak

Lean, low lines characterize a site for a custom furniture business based in Vancouver, British Columbia.

On subscreens, the navigation bar remains as a strong horizontal guide.

Not all elements are sized or set to the same depth. When text dips below the base of the image, it creates a lyrical flow.

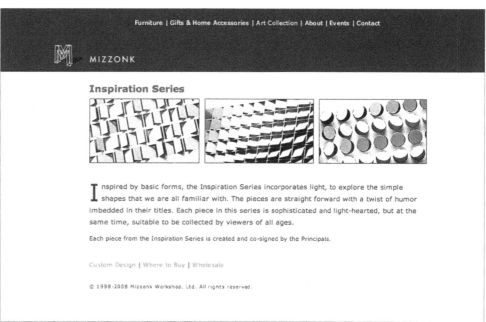

56. Be Both Clear and Playful

There's no confusion about what this label means. Everything is clear in two languages and two colors, and is designed in a system that organizes all the statistics you need to know (0%!). This lucid use of a grid is as lighthearted as it is playful (and keeps the user from becoming light-headed).

Also see pages
100–101

PROJECT
Identity and packaging for
Free Damm Alcohol-Free Beer

CLIENT
Cervezas Damm, Barcelona

DESIGN
Mario Eskenazi Studio

DESIGNERS
Mario Eskenazi,
Marc Ferrer Vives

A delightful package with organizing rules and a great amount of free spirit.

OPPOSITE PAGE, BOTH PHOTOS:
The label could work as a poster, even without the bottle. The press sheet (ABOVE) forms a modular grid of its own. The label is two only colors, yet there is a lot of power and punch thanks to type size, faces, and dropout white type.

THIS PAGE, BOTH PHOTOS:
The identity works as design and functions on the package. It is premium-quality branding.

57. Flip It

Type can work simultaneously on horizontal and vertical axes. Large type functions as a container to hold the rest of the information in the piece. The width of each name can be manipulated by clever use of tracking and varied type sizes, widths, and weights.

PROJECT
Theater ad for *Cyrano de Bergerac*

CLIENT
Susan Bristow, Lead Producer

DESIGN
SpotCo

CREATIVE DIRECTOR
Gail Anderson

DESIGNER
Frank Gargiulo

ILLUSTRATOR
Edel Rodriguez

This ad emphasizes the most memorable part of a title, avoiding a lot of text that might easily be ignored in favor of one punchy name with the surname in a smaller size.

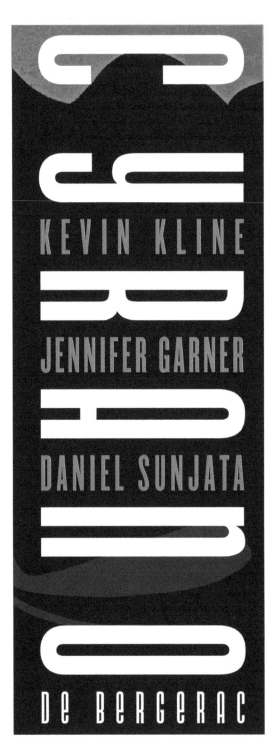

THIS PAGE AND OPPOSITE PAGE:
A tidy arrangement and a limited palette doesn't necessarily result in a static piece. Arresting, bold type forms a central column of information. The designers featured the star of the performance by marrying a brilliant illustrated profile with showstopping typography.

10 WEEKS ONLY

CYRANO

KEVIN KLINE

JENNIFER GARNER

DANIEL SUNJATA

DE BERGERAC

BY EDMOND ROSTAND

TRANSLATED AND ADAPTED BY
ANTHONY BURGESS

DIRECTED BY DAVID LEVEAUX

KEVIN KLINE · JENNIFER GARNER · DANIEL SUNJATA in CYRANO DE BERGERAC by EDMOND ROSTAND Translated and Adapted by ANTHONY BURGESS Also Starring MAX BAKER · EUAN MORTON · CHRIS SARANDON
JOHN DOUGLAS THOMPSON · CONCETTA TOMEI · STEPHEN BALANTZIAN · TOM BLOOM · KEITH ERIC CHAPPELLE · MACINTYRE DIXON · DAVIS DUFFIELD · AMEFIKA EL-AMIN · PETER JAY FERNANDEZ · KATE GUYTON · GINIFER
KING · CARMAN LACIVITA · PITER MAREK · LUCAS PAPAELIAS · FRED ROSE · LEENYA RIDEOUT · THOMAS SCHALL · DANIEL STEWART SHERMAN · ALEXANDER SOVRONSKY · BAYLEN THOMAS · NANCE WILLIAMSON
Set Design by TOM PYE Costume Design by GREGORY GALE Lighting Design by DON HOLDER Sound Design by DAVID VAN TIEGHEM Hair Design by TOM WATSON Casting by JV MERCANTI Technical Supervision HUDSON THEATRICAL
ASSOCIATES Press Representation BARLOW-HARTMAN Production Stage Manager MARYBETH ABEL General Management THE CHARLOTTE WILCOX COMPANY Directed by DAVID LEVEAUX

TICKETMASTER.COM or 212-307-4100/800-755-4000
GROUP SALES 212-840-3890 · ≥N≤ RICHARD RODGERS THEATRE, 226 WEST 46TH STREET

GOLD CARD EVENTS PREFERRED SEATING

800-NOW-AMEX
BROADWAY.YAHOO.COM

58. Keep It Clean

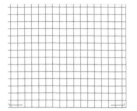

Atypeface designed on a grid and for use on a grid will, by nature, be fresh and clean. Even so, the letterforms can have fun around the curves as well as numerous other applications.

PROJECT
Cervezas Victoria
Typography

CLIENT
Cervezas Victoria (Damm)

DESIGN
Mario Eskenazi Studio

DESIGNERS
Mario Eskenazi,
Dani Rubio,
Marc Ferrer Vives

This alphabet, designed in 2017–2018 to be applied as ceramic tiles for an exhibition at the Victoria brewery in Málaga, Spain, celebrating the 90th anniversary, is also used for promotional items and advertising campaigns.

This alphabet for Victoria beer celebrates not only the brew's 90th anniversary but also its return to the city of Malaga, Spain, after twenty years away from the region. "Malaguena y exquisita" means "Malagan and Exquisite."

MALAGUEÑA
Y EXQUISITA

MAL
AGA

90 AÑ
OS

59. Play with the Grid

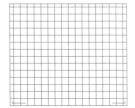

As with jazz, typography can be syncopated. Even within a tight and well-considered grid, it's possible to have a typographic jam session by varying widths, weights, and positions. The next step is to see what happens when you turn everything on its side.

Thanks to the dynamics of small sans serif type against a larger line, the type has a strong sense of movement. On its side and surprinting two layered silhouettes, the type really swings.

PROJECT
Ads and promos

CLIENT
Jazz at Lincoln Center

DESIGN
JALC Design Department

DESIGNER
BOBBY C. MARTIN JR.

The look of Jazz at Lincoln Center is bright, disciplined, and full of energy. The design is clean, Swiss, but syncopated— and very cool.

White dropout type in boxes of different sizes and depth makes a sharp and rhythmic counterpoint against smartly cropped images.

60. Involve the Viewer

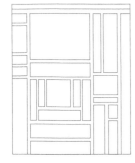

Sometimes a grid has to go off the grid. Type sizes, shapes, and weights can convey message about a culture, either locally or globally, intriguing the reader and acting as a call to action.

You can't solve the climate crisis alone.
But if we all work together, we can.

Join today.

PROJECT
Alliance for Climate Protection advertisement

CLIENT
WeCanDoSolveIt.org

DESIGN
The Martin Agency; Collins

DESIGNERS
The Martin Agency: Mike Hughes, Sean Riley, Raymond McKinney, Ty Harper; Collins: Brian Collins, John Moon, Michael Pangilinan

This ad for an environmental initiative takes advantage of bold typography to make a point.

The choice of words and type sizes might (or might not) be specifically statistically chosen. Larger type sizes shout for attention, while smaller sizes and weights act as visual glue. The bright green color is the obvious and perfect choice for an ad calling for climate protection.

61. Master Tight Spaces

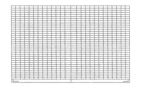

With a well-conceived grid, small margins can work. When images are aligned cleanly on obvious gridlines and when space and typography are carefully controlled, small outside margins can be part of a carefully crafted concept. The skill and order of a well-balanced page can act as a foil for narrow margins, bringing an edge to a controlled layout.

That said, when starting out, leave a margin for error. Margins are tricky for beginners and seasoned practitioners alike. Setting up a grid with few or many variables involves balance and skill, as well as trial and error. Most traditional offset printers and trade publishers wince at margins that are too small. Tiny outside margins leave little room for bounce, a slight movement of the roll of paper as it speeds through the press. For that reason, publication designers often make sure to leave generous outside margins.

PROJECT
étapes: magazine

CLIENT
Pyramyd/*étapes:* magazine

DESIGN
Anna Tunick

The clean grid of this French design magazine presents such an effective sense of order that small margins are part of a plan to fit in as much information as possible.

A balanced page with absolutely clear alignments shows the flexibility of the grid. All elements are aligned, yet the large type gives a sense of movement. Space within the spread contrasts successfully with the small outside margins. The typography is also balanced, with numerous weights, sizes, faces, and colors working harmoniously together.

j'ai vu le moment où l'on allait inaugurer le bâtiment sans mon travail. **pourquoi?** parce que l'on ne parvenait pas à s'accorder sur sa dénomination exacte: "sculpture typographique" ou "enseigne"?

62. Use Devices to Help Make Your Point

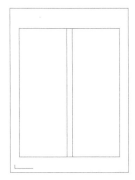

Some subject matter involves a great degree of detail, depth, and complication. When there's a wealth of information to fit into a finite amount of space, use devices to highlight points.

Such devices can include the use of space to form a masthead and color (and color-coded) sidebars, bulleted lists, icons to call attention to specific heads, and color for headings and crucial text.

A complete system of icons appears at the head of each display. The icons for relevant issues are highlighted and used as beacons for each paragraph.

PROJECT
Materials and Displays
for a Public Event

CLIENT
Earth Institute at
Columbia University

CREATIVE DIRECTOR
Mark Inglis

DESIGN
Sunghee Kim

These complex and detailed education displays employ an integrated system of icons and colors, which are used to signal issues discussed in each section or paragraph. Varied graphic devices, such as icons, headings, titles, text, images, and graphs, set off sections and make the information experience easy to navigate, while adhering to the ideal goals of space, texture, color, organization, white versus dark space, and readable type. Where a variety of educational tools are employed, clean alignments can make the difference between edifying and losing the user.

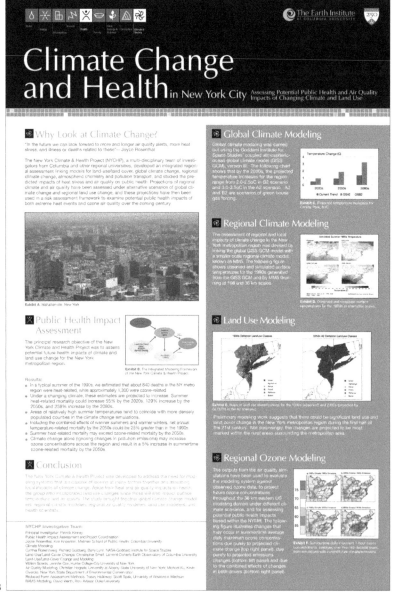

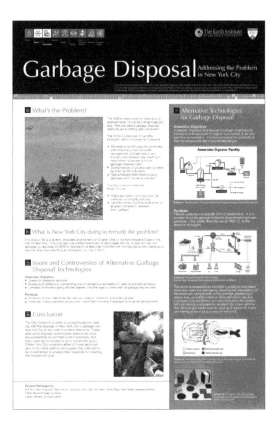

The overall display format is carefully integrated, using a consistent black band that acts as a masthead throughout all displays. The black band contains and controls information such as the system of icons, the logos for Columbia University and the institute within the university, the heading, and the subheads.

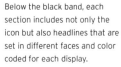

Below the black band, each section includes not only the icon but also headlines that are set in different faces and color coded for each display.

Typography is clear. Bullet points break down the information. Conclusions are always highlighted in the signature color of the scientific discipline driving the display.

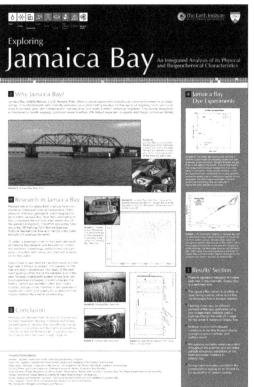

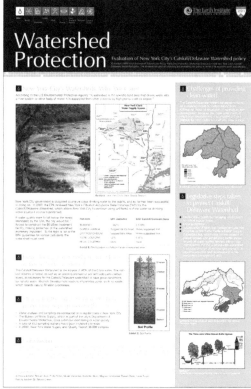

Sidebars, also color coded for each system, set off information categories such as Experiments and Research.

63. Give It a Break

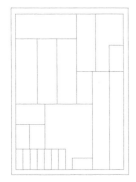

What do you do with immense numbers of stories, images, charts, cartoons, statistics, rants, and rambles? Throw everything into the overall loose structure—then, break it up.

OPPOSITE PAGE: The creator and design maven of a broadsheet newspaper created to give city residents a tactile sense of life in a crowded city notes that his paper does not use a grid. Even so, the designers certainly understand and work with grid systems.

PROJECT
Civilization

CLIENT
Richard Turley

EDITORS/DESIGNERS/WRITERS
Richard Turley,
Lucas Mascatello,
Mia Kerin,
with other contributors,

A self-published newspaper reflecting life in New York, New York, is as dense with musings, facts and factoids as the metropolis itself. When starting the publication in 2018, the creator deliberately chose a Victorian technology to deliver news to a world dazed by digital.

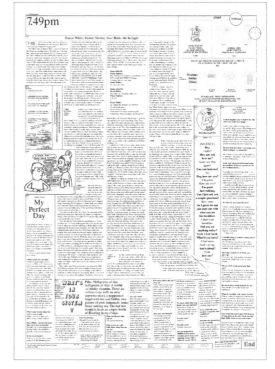

Swiss system meets concrete poetry, as shown in this detail at reproduction size.

Darcie Wilder

Cover story: We used to pass this park all the time on the bus, Dead Dog Park. There was a sign and everything. They were trying to up the number of Manhattan parks so they walked looking for squares of grass that could technically be parks. They ran out of names by the time they got to 168th and saw a dead dog and now it's Dead Dog Park, there's a sign and everything.

Father, Mother, God, Bathe Me In Light

○ 2018
HELL'S KITCHEN
1PM
15 NOTIFICATIONS

So I wake up in bed underneath a 25 pound weighted blanket that I just wanted the heaviest thing to put me out and the first thing I touch and look at is this blazing screen, and my eyes are still opening and they're making shapes adjusting to the light, I'm scrolling and looking for my dog and just scrolling and putting on the same podcasts as every morning before and trying to go back to sleep and failing. And then I'm using the new body wash that smells like pears and it's still so cold out, and I just found out my shower curtain was in the wrong place, years of making daily puddles on the floor, except who showers daily, more of a weekly puddle. I just got a new toothbrush that zaps me every thirty seconds, all I do is make it touch my teeth, moving around to a different tooth. My teeth were so soft they were stinging me when I brushed, a shooting pain up my gums. I'm trying to figure out what. I'm trying to. Every morning I can't fall back asleep but can't stay awake doing the things I want to do.

It's not that it's especially bad but that it just keeps never getting better, and I wake up around 1pm today so the kids at the high school next door are on their way home.

Two recognizable character actors are talking on a bench, I'm throwing a tennis ball with a chihuahua mix and some puppy named Lemon comes up trying to steal it and does for a second. It's the kind of weather that could be fall but is March and taking it's time and even when it finally gets good enough to walk it'll be too hot, too much, too heavy, and I'll be wearing sleeves even when I shouldn't.

App goes off PUSH notification - assault 5 blocks away. Last night, suspicious package. Tonight a car'll jump the curb and a manhole a few miles away will blow off, like I used to imagine happening when I stood on them. The helicopter in the East River, I was a few blocks away. Repeated footage over and over, New York 1 in doctor's office, this is footage of people dying. This is the last moments of five peoples' lives.

Taking her off-leash even though she could die. But everyone, all the time. Aren't we all just trying to keep ourselves alive? It's crazy, they should teach kids about uncarysms earlier. But she's too scared of the curb, too scared of cars, too scared of the brushing whizzing noises to ever go near. Sometimes I worry she'll start chasing a rat, kill a rat with her bare paws and I'll have her, covered in blood, to clean up. My friend's dog killed a rat before they had time to stop her. Rats on 43rd run next to the parking lot

bricks, behind the trees, burrowing deep. I used to sit on the wooden benches with Chiquita till my stomach settled. Also the horniness sit there sometimes and you never know about bedbugs. My stomach itches. Peeling, flaking.

Why do croissants always stain the bag? So many greasy patches and they just soak through and I ate a croissant every day, I don't even like them. I guess I crave them when I go without but those bagels from the carts, you know they're either stale or not boiled, they're just straight up bread cut in a circle, they've got to be. Once I saw a delivery guy wipe out, spill all of them on Amsterdam Ave, scattered. Straight up on the pavement. Cart guy picked them up, dusted them maybe a little bit, sold them all day. Like when this girl in high school bought cart coffee, milk and sugar - I only dad sugar then, and now I do nothing - and it started splitting out the seams of the cup. In her hand, dribbles and then you know it was just all going to pour out. So then the guy's like, doing that hand motion like c'mere, come on, and he takes it from her and says like, they had gotten wet and he let them dry and tried to use them. Soggy cups.

A few weeks ago the G wasn't running and I was stranded at that PS 1 station. I ended up walking over that bridge to Greenpoint thinking I was going to be late because I was the only one that had to deal with it and I walked into the room and no one was there. It was one of those moments where the sun was setting, sky was some color maybe pink or even red, the water was making it colder and I was listening to that Jimmy Eat World song that sounds like a stomach ache when you're on the subway home with too much energy and not enough, and you're just turning everything, everything is about to bloom, it's a fade out that just fades into something else, I was the only one on the bridge taking a video and we were all going against the wind from the exhaust of the cars.

Coco comes when I call and I force the slimy tennis ball out her mouth. She's stripped it bald, tearing out neon green fuzz. I gnawed my teeth down to bits over the years and now they fit like puzzle pieces This week I couldn't find her paperwork and had one of those spiraling meltdowns, started praying to anyone or no one or something or whatever, and then thought that I had to convince myself I'd never find it because you only get what you want when you don't want it anymore. Found it in a pile of loose papers in the closet.

○ 4PM
TIMES SQUARE

I walk on 42nd by my old office, the corporate office in a huge tower I used to walk there every morning during the Polar Vortex. When I was only wearing skirts and the same torn tights every day, and had to buy new tights

and change before any of the bosses saw me. The wind would whip against my legs and my thighs got this stinging feeling, I wore Doc Marten dress shoes that gave me blisters and read the internet all day. Sometimes I had busy days, making coffee, ordering from Staples, time sheets. I remember phases by the lunches, brief stint doing halal but then the weeks I only craved guacamole, mushrooms, chicken strips. I would order Lenny's egg wraps and dunk them in a tiny tub of Tabasco hot sauce just to feel anything, just so bored and craving anything, and the salt would rush into my, my eyes watered, my tongue hung out of my mouth. I used to drink as much water as I could as fast as possible, Poland Spring after Poland Spring, out of boredom. Then I'd google "water poisoning."

She came from LA, surrendered 10/26/2016, up for adoption for nine months until I found her. The time I spent in LA is a blur. I can't remember if I worked in retail for 3 weeks, 6 weeks, or 3 months. They checked my bag going in and out so I left it in my car and had to pay $20 for a parking spot. Parked next to a matte'd out black sedan and dissociated after work circling the aisles of Target till I drove home.

They tore down the gas station on 44th and now it's a pit. Nearly empty, construction equipment moves around piles of dirt and drills in the middle of the day when I'm checking DMs. It says "Seen." But he hasn't written back and the real read receipts don't have periods but should, to imply that it's the end of the conversation. When did we stop using periods? I don't. The drill goes on and on so I got the blackout curtains and wake up in the single digit afternoon hours, after I wake up around 5 or 6 and look at my phone to avoid evil spirits. A ghost can't get you if you're looking at a screen, so I spent hours and hours staring at my phone in my bedroom, which used to be grandma's bedroom, where I cried and wept next to her bed when they said I should say goodbye to her for the last time. She laid there, and dead bodies look different in every stage, from dying to dead to been dead to on display.

So I light a lot of sage and whisper to myself and say the same non-denominational prayer my uncle told me when I was sleeping on the floor in LA, too scared to sleep in my own room alone, I closed my eyes and a thing, I don't know, something, gripped my throat and cut off my breath and I couldn't speak, couldn't breathe, couldn't, and so now I reflexively repeat "Father Mother God Bathe Me In Light" and ignored the God part for years, and forgot I was saying it for brief stretches of time, the times when I was doing molly on weeknights and coming down when the sun was coming up and sitting in a rocking chair waiting while they met the guy and got more, doing more and

feeling dead or dying and scared of all of it suddenly. I forgot the words but they came back, and now when I close my eyes to say FUCK I accidentally feel myself with them, repeating them over and over like a lotion that absorbed all it can and now it's just swimming on top of pores, it's just too much, like everything I want is always over the surface trying to get in but there's no room, there's no space, we're all just waiting for it to combine, to infuse, to germinate and it never does anything but stick the surface.

I'm trying to come up with a way where I do what I need. I walk down the West Side Highway, I miss when it was April and May and June, the exhaust would mix with the humidity for something so unpleasant and rank but in that way where you destroy something, you keep on flossing too hard and keep touching a cut, you keep stinging yourself. Walk all the way down listening to headphones so much the soles of your foot hitting the pavement reverb up, bouncing up into your ears against the headphones. Taking selfies on West Street, whatever it's called. Walk until you reach the cobblestones. Up until a certain point and on weekends it's so crowded and I can't leave my house. In high school I rode my bike down Sixth Ave. on the fourth of July listening to the cracks of fireworks and avoiding it all, street so clear. Bike rides every month, Critical Mass, used to bike up the highway outnumbering the cars. I gave up when there were too many white bikes, ghost bikes, memorials of hits and dead people. I got hit once or twice.

Remember that guy I got in the cyber fight with? The twitter feud shit thing a few weeks ago? He was biking in Central Park and his handlebars shook. apparently, and he wiped out lost control and his face slid across the pavement.

There was this time right before I kept stealing stuff - but only from Whole Foods and Barnes and Noble - where, for a whole year, I wore these fake glasses. And I never talk about it but a whole year, and no one ever said anything when I stopped wearing them except Carla, but they were $8 glasses from St. Marks

I like the hot when the diner booths stick to the backs of your thighs and it hurts to move. It stings to stand up. Sometimes they don't even have AC, or maybe they all got AC now. Last time I was at Waverly Diner this guy flashed a blade, maybe just a scissor but still a metal edge, between his cotton glove and the glass window, maybe it's plastic? Flashed a blade while we ate omelets and we told the waitress and she said, "What do you want me to do about it?" He crossed the street, approaching the NYPD van, seemed like he was trying to get arrested. The van revved up, engine on, and pulled out into traffic, ignoring him. And I thought I knew rejection.

We used to come here in the mornings before we both got fired. I asked Dad to tell me about the scar again. Leaving Waverly Diner, where I cried in front of Steve that time in 2010. He tells me about Stuytown again, growing up on 15th and 1st, and climbing that metal fence in the 60s. A group of adults watched him throw himself over and catch his skin on the spike, sliced open, huge scar running down. He tells me about the crying girl in the amputation ward, who just lost her arm. I've never heard this part of the story but each time I find something else new out it's like, yeah.

○ 2017
9AM
MARCH, APRIL,
MAY, JUNE

It takes me awhile to get out of bed and I finally make coffee, Cafe Bustelo, from the grinds too small. too many of them, and the french press mesh, pushing down the plunger it always flies up, it splashes every day but today burns my fingers, grazes my hand and the counter is filled with puddles of grime and grinds that stay there for weeks, maybe just short of a month, because I feel guilty buying paper towels but it's more that I feel better avoiding tasks, evading errands.

○ 2014
MALT LIQUOR,
COCAINE,
RED WINE

I started to worry about myself when the grocery store employee, the guy stocking the milk, asked if I was OK. I thought I could just keep circling, no phone service just listening to music, and that no one would bother me but sometimes it's like, the city buffer gives out, it wears down like a rubber sneaker sole, and I end up touching the floor, the cement ground, the bottom, end up having a conversation with someone.

○ 2007
ALEX
QUEENS

There was that time ... ran out of the bookstore because I casually mentioned I made out with Alex - who I think moved to Portland and had a kid? And writes books on anarchist theory? He was living in Queens and no one else was really there, and his Greek landlady would give him liquor and he just

○ 2018
CONTAMINANTS
DETECTED IN
NEW YORK CITY
DRINKING
WATER

For the latest quarter covered by the US Environmental Protection Agency
(July 2017 - September 2017)

CONTAMINANTS DETECTED ABOVE HEALTH GUIDELINES:

• BROMODICHLOROMETHANE
Cancer forming

• CHLOROFORM
Cancer forming

• CHROMIUM (HEXAVALENT)
Cancer forming

• DICHLOROACETIC ACID
Cancer forming

• TOTAL TRIHALOMETHANES (TTHM5)
Cancer forming

• TRICHLOROACETIC ACID
Cancer forming

• OTHER DETECECTED CONTAMINANTS
• Chlorate
• Chromium (total)
• Haloacetic acids (HAA5)
• Monochloroacetic acid
• Nitrate
• Nitrate and nitrite
• Strontium

From October 2014 to September 2017 this water utility was in VIOLATION of health-based drinking water standards.

Source: ewg.org

SNEAKERS SEEN AT HOME DEPOT IN BED STUY.

NIKE	AIR JORDAN 1	RED/BLACK
ROCHE	RUN	RED
NEW BALANCE		BLACK
NIKE	AIRMAX 180	WHITE
REDBOX	CLASSICS	WHITE
NEW BALANCE	(UNKNOWN)	GREY
ADIDAS	(UNKNOWN)	ORANGE
REEBOK'S	(UNKNOWN)	BLACK
NEW BALANCE	(UNKNOWN)	BLACK
CONVERSE	HI	ORANGE
NIKE	PEGASUS	GREY
SAUCONY	(UNKNOWN)	GREY
NIKE	AIR MAX LOW	BLACK
PUMA HI	(UNKNOWN)	BLUE
NIKE	HUARACHE	ORANGE
CHAMPION	(UNKNOWN)	BLACK

BUSKER
WEST 4TH SUBWAY
SAT, MARCH 17, 2018
11.45PM

I'll tell y'all, first of all, you guys is looking all sad. You guys don't know what sad is. You don't know the half. I'm more than sad, I'm dismayed. Have a wonderful night y'all, this song is for us.

[inaudible 00:00:21]

This happened to me the other day, too, exactly what happened to me.

[inaudible 00:00:27] do you [inaudible 00:00:31]

[inaudible 00:00:32] especially with [inaudible 00:00:34]

(singing)

@CivilizationNYC

MOSTLY BELOW 99TH,
USUALLY ABOVE DELANCEY
WEAR US - 15

THE WEEK

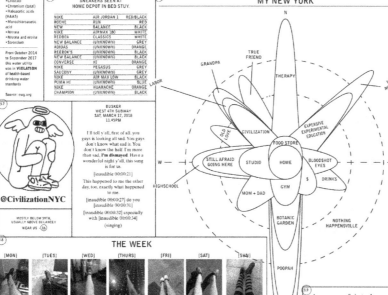

[MON]	[TUES]	[WED]	[THURS]	[FRI]	[SAT]	[SUN]
SLEPT IN A HOODIE LAST NIGHT. HAD A NIGHTMARE.	I HAVEN'T OPENED MY I-D INBOX IN 3 YEARS BECAUSE I'D RATHER NOT DEAL WITH THE SPAM	YOUR HAND CURLED INTO A FIST RESTING ON MY BACK AS YOU SLEEP	BRAN FLAKES, HALF A BOWL OF CAULIFLOWER SOUR 2 CIGARETTES, VEGAN NOODLES, HALF AN EASTER EGG, ANOTHER NIGHTMARE	MUSICIANS THAT ARE TOO YOUNG FOR ME: 1. YUNG LEAN 2. POST MALONE 3. LIL PEEP RIP 4. LIL XAN	SCRAMBLED EGGS, ALMOND MILK, FLAT WHITE EXTRA BREAD ROLLS	WOKE UP AT 4AM COULDN'T MOVE, PANIC ATTACK OR AGGRESSIVE INDIGESTION DEPENDS WHO U ASK

MY NEW YORK

N

GRANDPA · TRUE FRIEND · THERAPY · WANING NOSTALGIA · OLD LOVE · CIVILIZATION · EXPENSIVE EXPERIMENTAL EDUCATION · STILL AFRAID GOING HERE · STUDIO · FOOD STORE · HOME · BLOODSHOT EYES · HIGHSCHOOL · GYM · DRINKS · MOM + DAD · BOTANIC GARDEN · NOTHING HAPPENSVILLE · POOPAH · WATER · LABOR

W — E
S

A woman fainted on my train today and I just stood and watched. Everyone mobbed her and I was worried about being late.

EMILY SEGAL

CLOSE YOUR EYES. THINK ABOUT HOME. DESCRIBE WHAT YOU SEE

"The living room of my mom and step dad's apartment on 91st Street. Oriental rug from my great grandpa, kitschy drippy orange and green glass vases from the 60s, a colossal plant that holds the spirit of my step dad's late mother Evelyn, heavy wrought iron coffee table my parents had made from a bank grate in Philadelphia when they were still in their 20s. Squeaking and squawking cars and sirens from Amsterdam Avenue, coming in from the street."

How many pillows do you sleep on?
Two.

Are you a thief?
Unfortunately I am no longer a thief, at least as far as physical objects are concerned. As a teen I was a consistent, if not terribly ambitious, shoplifter – bent on amassing the sum total of makeup available at a constellation of local CVS's and Duane Reades. I got caught taking a straightening iron (particularly unnecessary, because I have straight hair) one afternoon when I was fourteen.

I remember planning the heist during English class that afternoon. The manager told me she would call my mother, and I looked withering, "my mother is dead" Then, once they threatened to call my school (something I found humiliating beyond measure).

I recanted and revealed my mother was still alive. Once she arrived to pick me up they told her I'd said she was dead, which she said she thought was pretty ingenious, given the circumstances I was in though the age difference. For years later I limited my shoplifting to the costume jewelry at Top Shop – it was kind of my stealing methadone. Eventually I gave that up, too.

To whom are you indebted?
Literally all of my friends (spiritually, not financially).

Changing the names to protect the guilty, what's the worst thing anyone's ever done to you?
Besides a couple gnarly heartbreaks and more-or-less typical divorced-family trauma - the worst things have been creative or collaborative betrayals... like when former collaborators had gone behind my back to talk trash or change an artwork, or bosses made announcements about me to large groups without talking to me first. I'm a Scorpio, obsessed with my work and horrified by loyalty transgressions!

Favorite soup?
Vichyssoise

Favorite scent?
Hinoki; Musty Basements

How do you deal with guilt?
I FaceTime my best friends Alexa and Rachel repeatedly until one of them tells me it's all right, or I write about it, or I psychically bury it!

If you could relive one moment in your life what would it be?
Toss up between a particular lecture and a particular fuck – both experiences of "flow" (blech)

Where do you sit on the many-worlds interpretation of quantum mechanics and the probability of infinite variants of every single moment in time?
Staunchly "pro"

Starsign?
Scorpio, Aries Rising, Leo Moon (<— Profoundly 'onchill' combination)

How long do you sleep for?
Eight hours Sleep is the greatest determining factor in my sometimes disturbingly volatile mood landscape.

Tell me about the last time someone held your hand?
My long lost friend Elizabeth, dragging me through the streets of Hollywood to pluck an orange off the tree in someone's backyard!

Have you got your dues?
Not even close ○

— EMILY SEGAL IS A STRATEGIST & FOUNDER OF K-HOLE/NEMESIS

stood in his doorway and maybe, looking back ten years, I should've left? Was that a social cue? It's like, weird with social cues because I have enough of my own brain telling me I'm a piece of shit and that I should just go, that like, I'm fighting that enough that I think normal things are social cues to leave and then I end up missing the real social cues because I'm talking myself down from the imagined stuff, you know?

○ 2014
IPHONE 5
RED WINE,
WHISKEY,
VODKA, WEED

There was that cat, on my way home when I was in Sunset Park, the year before my bag was locked up When I was on my way home I saw a orange cat, infested and dirty, those huge black splotches of grime, and I kept petting it, talking to it, calling it a rat. My little orange rat. I thought it'd bite me eventually and I didn't want to deal with the paperwork so I kept walking. An hour and a half home on a yellow line train but no one calls them that but that's what they are. On the way home a guy told me, he was like, 60s maybe? That I should be a teacher. That I'm a "nice girl." It was the same subway station where I called that ambulance the last day of high school. She was nodding out on a bench, poisoned, and the cop asked her why her birth year was scratched out. Ended up going to Methodist and getting an IV and then I took a $60 cab ride home. The air is different at the top

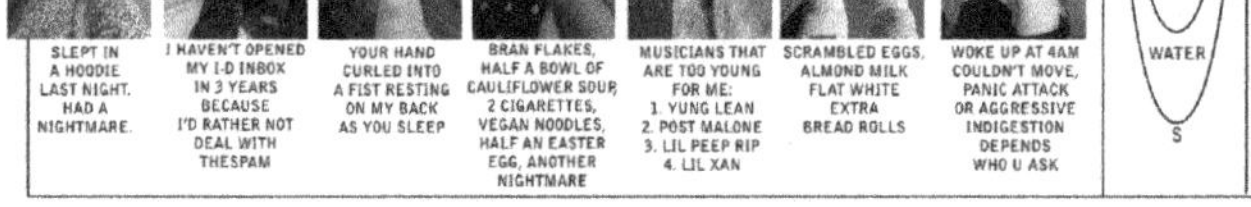

CONT PAGE 16

64. Balance Dense Material

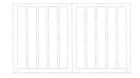

Some types of communications call for a balancing act. Length is often of paramount importance in newsletters, especially for nonprofit organizations. The need to fit everything into a predetermined number of pages (often four or eight) imposes strictures, which in turn help to determine structure.

PROJECT
Newsletter

CLIENT
Cathedral Church of
St. John the Divine

DESIGN DIRECTION
Pentagram

DESIGN
Carapellucci Design

A newsletter for a nonprofit organization is a hymn to the versatility of a five-column grid.

On this page, the outside column is a utility area, listing credits, services, contact information, and directions. Separated from the outside column by a vertical rule, the remaining columns contain an essay. Art and a quote quietly interrupt the meditative essay.

The grid structure appears consistently on the back page, which doubles as a mailer.

Events Calendar

The Cathedral Church of Saint John the Divine
1047 Amsterdam Avenue
New York, NY 10025
212 316-7540
www.stjohndivine.org

December

12th Annual Crafts Fair

Installations

The Cathedral Christmas Concert

Let My People Go: A Service of Liberation

January

New Year's Day Eucharist

Mosaic Workshop

Someone to Watch Over Me: Spotlight on Saints

Spotlight Tours: Diversity United: Spotlight on the Chapels of Tongues

Children's Programs: Medieval Arts Children's Workshop

February

Ash Wednesday

Paper Making Workshop

Paul Winter's 28th Annual Solstice Concerts

"Fool's Mass"

Spotlight Tour: Signs and Symbols: Spotlight on Symbolism

Children's Programs: Camels & Kings: Celebrating the Epiphany

Kids' Cathedral

Arches Everywhere!: A Children's Architecture Workshop

Services

Christmas Eve Eucharist

Early Music New York

Christmas Day Eucharist

Annual New Year's Eve Concert for Peace

General Information

Highlight Tours

Vertical Tours

New Year's Eve Eucharist

Spotlight Tours: On Common Ground: Spotlight on Faith Traditions

Brilliant Walls of Light: Spotlight on Cathedral Windows

Ongoing

Children's Programs

Medieval Arts Children's Workshop

A Season of Lights: A Winter Solstice Celebration

Medieval Scribes: A Children's Illumination and Bookmaking Workshop

Medieval Birthday Parties

Winter 2007/2008

Griswold Appointed Canon

Junior League Honors Brock

Henry L. King to Receive Diocesan Lawyers' Award

Blessing of the Bicycles Rolls Into Cathedral on May 12

Temporary Play Area Opens on the Pulpit Green

Key Roof Work Finished

The events calendar takes advantage of the grid, subdividing the columns for the days of the week into varying widths, depending on the material. Rules as dividers, thick rules as containers for type, screens for sidebars, and large headings bring variation and texture to the information.

Articles and their headings can fill one, two, or three columns. Images fill every parameter of the column widths, with a vignette giving organic relief to a disciplined structure.

65. Combine Density with Dynamism

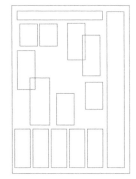

Sometimes the main goal of a project is to include everything readably. For directories, glossaries, or indexes, the best way to start is to figure out how things fit.

THIS PAGE: A clear nameplate with horizontal organization withstands a lot of good visual trouble on the first page of a protest zine.

OPPOSITE PAGE: The zine's columns are unregimented and peppered with a question and answer feature in separate, skittishly placed boxes.

PROJECT
Good Trouble

CLIENT
Ron Stanley

DESIGNER
Richard Turley

A broadsheet that puts the "pro in protest" skews what most likely was a clean plan and moves it off the grid.

NON WORLDWIDE is a group of African or diaspora musicians and artists. Their tagline is EXORCISE THE LANGUAGE OF DOMINATION. And they're here to shatter every illusion.

JUST SAY NON!

Even by the platform-agnostic standards of today, NON's activities are dizzying. They're a label, releasing stunning, radical music by musicians from Cape Town to Egypt to Virginia to Brixton. They're also magazine publishers who organise talks that run into all-night raves, who have opened a NON-branded range of travel merchandise in a duty-free store in downtown New York. Yet their ambitions go beyond these: NON is a borderless country open to all, a dissident political faction and a tight group of creative idealists.

Though the collective is sprawling and dozens of artists have released through their compilations and EPs, the core group is three DJ-producers-artists – the South African Angel-Ho, the Belgian-Congolese Nkisi, and Nigerian-American CHINO.

AMOBI. After a series of incredible mixes and mixtapes, Amobi has just released his debut album proper – the epic, collision, is double album Paradiso. It's an epic, complex, urgent, thrilling album, themed around an apocalyptic Edgar Allan Poe poem, and a radio station that flickers through moments of hellishness and total beauty. Kind of what life in America feels like right now.

"I like the chaos, throwing different variables in there, letting the chips fall where they may, shattering and breaking the canon in a way," Chino told us over Korean food in Berlin. "The depth and scale of the narrative is wider and deeper than one thinkpiece. The idea of NON is a constant rejection of definition. We're going to tell it ourselves."

RIGHT NOW

Your album is called Paradiso. Are you optimistic?
This time we're in has been growing. Trump is a benchmark, but a certain politicised feeling has been festering for time, with people like Black Lives Matter, the LGBTQ rights community, immigration, terrorism, home-grown terrorism and the way information is disseminated online; it's all come to a head. It's like a boiling point.

Sometimes I think like the whole thing has to burn down in order for new life to be birthed. I say that optimistically. I'm not talking about masses dying – I don't want that – but destruction causes creation. It's always darkest before the dawn: in my life, the good things have happened directly after the bad.

I feel good about the future, about the youth, the spirituality in youth, the love. I think that the good will triumph. You can strengthen and pressure each other through productive measures. I'm all about shattering illusions, and the more you shatter, the better.

CHRIST

Your album is soaked in Christian allusion. Why is this so important today?
In times of strife which feel very dark, people go to faith to reconcile with what's going on, and [communicate] with something that's larger than themselves. Sometimes Christianity is represented like this fluffy thing, but the bible is super dark. It's gothic as hell. There's a mystery in those words. I'm just more malleable with data than some people are.

I identify as a follower of Christ, but I also identify as a queer body. That's often seen as a contradiction in the world, but the way I think about it, is it's about queering time and space. I really feel like The Bible did that.

Jesus entered time and space in a body that was queer, because only a queer body can transcend time and space, and change it in physical space. I believe that the body of Christ is here with us now and is changing who we are and our hearts. There's a sacred Blood that unites us together in that way, but that bond becomes more than just me, which connects me to other people, which is The Body. I know – it's a lot.

There's a certain magic element of faith that's important. A leap into that magic, I think, can change hearts. I put that into my music, and it's something that brings me closer to NON artists. Two become one. Transindividuation was something I was thinking about heavily on this album.

Q&A: RICHARD CABRAL

Born in the mid-80s into a family of East LA gang members, RICHARD CABRAL did his first time aged 13, going back to jail every year until he was 25. His longest stint, for attempted murder, was his last. On getting out, he left the gang he had grown up in. With the help of Christian organisation Homeboys Industries, he began mentoring those still caught up in gang life and prison, and embarked on a new career as an actor. He secured an Emmy nomination for his portrayal of Hector Tontz, a former gang member struggling to go straight, in the excellent ABC series American Crime, now in its third season.

"People see me how they see me, and that's all they see," Cabral's character says at one point. And Cabral's own story is one of identity and acceptance – of how the marks of a tough, violent past impact the present. But his story is also one of of how hard history can be held close, and how loyalty – to himself, as well as his fellow former gang members – can allow radical honesty to help others. "I witnessed guns, and violence, and everything people growing up there witness," he says, as we speak for an hour about prison reform, power and acting. "I finally came home at 25. And then it turned to what it is now."

GOOD TROUBLE: Tell us about life in LA.
Richard Cabral: I'm a second-generation Mexican-American, raised by my mom in East Los Angeles. I grew up in a metropolis of just Mexicans. The inner cities of Los Angeles have been riddled with guns and drugs since the beginning – it was poor, and law enforcement just didn't care. I was born in 1983, when the crack epidemic hit. So, I guess you could say I was a product of that energy, that time, and that sickness. Gangs, murder, mass incarceration.

LA historian Mike Davies said this escalation of gang violence from the 80s onwards is the result of deindustrialization. You have places where jobs were disappearing, so people were hanging around instead of working. And this coincides with the arrival of crack...

It was like these two forces that coincided at the same time. Boom. In the south side and in East LA, you have these cities which are all industrial. Right along the LA River, it's all factories and warehouses. So, you those kids with the mind to work, but all you have are drugs. The knowledge now is methamphetamine, and has been for the last 15 years. And while it's not as visible as the crack epidemic, it's taken its toll on the communities. The craziness of the stories, mothers killing babies and shit, all that has to do with drugs. The drugs really fucked things up.

One thing I heard about solving gang violence was that only warriors can end the war. Yeah, that's a good one. For sure, for sure. To talk about the war, you have to know the war. To talk about death, you have to know death. There's a normality to it. It's the philosophy of a warrior, or a man in the army. It's not abnormal to know you might die, because there's a gang of other motherfuckers that might die with you. They all get it: we talk about death, and we talk about jail. The first time I went to jail as a kid, I looked around and thought 'Oh! There's hundreds of others like me.' I remember being young and seeing my uncle go to prison. My uncle has been a gang member since before I was born. You look outside and see gang members. You know the violence and craziness it carries, but you know they're not bad people... They're people.

What was the thing that turned it round?
The truth was I didn't want to spend my life in prison. I spent a year in jail. I had a whole year to think. And through my prayers or whatever, I got five years. But for that whole fucking year, you're thinking you might never come home.

What is the effect of all these years getting handed down by the state on the various communities affected?
You fuck up the community by having kids grow up without their fathers and mothers. You destroy the community. My best friend was 15 when he got life. Fifteen! California gives you life.

Why do you not hide from the past you had?
If I don't stand behind it, and say this is what made me, I cannot be inspiration. I cannot go into prisons and talk to people. Embracing it has been the most powerful thing.

Was getting the Emmy nomination for your acting a validation?
Yeah, but a validation I wasn't seeking. I'm happy now. I was in a cell eight years ago. Now I'm out and working and seeing my kids. But it was a surprise, because I just concentrate on the work, and this just meant people recognised the work.

What are your feelings about Trump?
Well, during Obama's reign, he deported more than any other president in history, so we've always been in the shit in a way! But when the threat becomes real evident, it makes people united. If I let someone piss me off, I've given them power. This Too. Will. Pass. As a prison reformer, we're in a good place. In California, laws are getting passed, and we just need to push on.
CHARLIE ROBIN JONES
Photography by James Mooney

THE NATION

You've issued passports to concert attendees in the past. Is NON a nation?
Yes it is. It's a nation, it's a platform, it's an identification. We use the word NON because NON is everything and nothing. It's not limited to one thing. We can do anything. We can work with scientists, non-profit organisations, dancers, mathematicians, publications, designers. We can reflect our interests without things getting watered down. We have artists all over the world, and I believe in multi-citizenship – to a NON citizen can be also be a citizen of the UK, or Nigeria, or the US, but NON citizenship augments the citizenship of the location, where they are able to utilise that citizenship for creative intervention in their community, online, and the world.

I love that quote, "Work as if you are living in the early days of a better nation."

I love that too. NON is very nascent. I'm very concerned about giving ourselves space to develop. It's like a garden. Say there's water in the garden. If people hoard the water, the garden suffers. The power of the garden is in diversity. It's important to have that multiplicity of voices. The water is data. And the garden is the systems and infrastructures we work in.

AIRPORTS

You work a lot with air travel – you released an album called Airport Music For Black Folk, and opened a duty free-style shop of NON-branded travel accessories in New York. What's behind this?
I always come back to airports because of what they represent to me. It's a liminal space between cities and countries, and it's a trans space, where we literally are preparing to change our bodies, inside and out, by getting on a plane. It's a very democratic space, but there's so much class things. There's so many codes of society and ideology that's brought to surface this really transparent way. It's almost like a no space. It's like someone took white infinity and made a building out of it. I'm very drawn to that in a very tactile way.

My parents are from Nigeria, and oftentimes Nigeria is on the list of countries for Americans not to visit. So, sometimes I've been questioned and searched heavily, as have other NON artists. I've also had really good experience at airports. I love to people watch. There's multiple things going on: migrants, workers, amazing-looking dogs, the richest people in the country. There's a lot of spontaneity. But spontaneity in this formal way. When statements are isolated in a way, sometimes very mundane actions are way more powerful, because there's some much space around them. Airports are a very "NON" space.

It's between countries, but it's also the only place you can literally point at what a country is. It's a man with a gun saying "You can enter, and you can't." Everything else is scenery. You can really tell a lot from a country by its airport.

DIASPORA

For many of the global south, long-distance air journeys are an integral part of life – not a luxury, as in the global north. This may be an obvious point, but it blows my mind.
The diaspora has given people of the global south this fluidity. This, I think, changes how we create. The ability for our creativity to cross cultures, and also have enough being to assimilate to where we are. People of the diaspora learn to speak in many languages and touch on countries they're in and where they're from. It forces you to think in a way that's multi-levelled, very abstract, and highly conceptual. It's a trans idea.

You've said before that you make music to reject passivity. If you're a migrant, you took the most incredibly active step a person can. Take a lot of guts.
Heavy guts. And urgency. And you can see that urgency, in the work and the conversations. Like, they have so much life. Because you have to have that life – and light, because it can get super dark. And you have to do it together, because your take your family and culture and identity to survive, if you fail a little bit, you have at least that. There's this double consciousness.

MONEY

You're a corporation, rather than non-profit. You had the Duty Free shop, work with Red Bull, and set up Buy-Black Friday. How does money fit in?
I always go back to Robin Hood, man. Steal from the rich to give to the poor. Divide it as equally as we can. We believe in walking in the building and saying "We here. We don't believe in everything you believe, but: We. Are. Here. You need us, we don't need you." We're not playing around, we're smart, you know. Infiltrate and subvert culture in whatever ways we see fit.

It's more honest to operate in these spheres and to politick in them, than go back into the echo chamber and only be around voices that agree with me. Nah. We need a multiplicity of voices, and we deserve to be heard.
CHARLIE ROBIN JONES
Photography by Johny Utterback,
Live photography by Brian Whar

"INSTRUCTIONS FOR NON-CITIZENS"

1 — Volunteer at an organization which benefits the quality of life of marginalized people.
2 — Feed your friends. Share your resources with one another.
3 — Spread the message of The Non State.

'VIOLENCE = NO CHANGE'

CALLIGRAPHY

Over the last few months, artist TAUBA AUERBACH has written out the word 'Persevere' thousands and thousands of times.

A series of posters and public installations are now aiming to raise money and awareness for organizations including the Committee to Protect Journalists and GEMS (Girls Education and Mentoring Services).

"My favorite exercise in Daniel T Ames' Compendium of Practical and Ornamental Penmanship shows the word persevere written in lowercase script. Each letter is surrounded by a loop, similar to the a in the @ symbol. The loops are all the same but the letters are different, so the exercise teaches you to maintain a rhythm amidst otherwise varying circumstances."

"Calligraphy has become the activity during which I reflect on what's happening in the world, what's at stake, and what I'm willing to do about it. Maybe I've just needed

something to do with my hands while I think. Until now, my politics have manifest mostly in quotidian, domestic choices like being vegan, composting and riding a bike. Feel free to roll your eyes. I support a few organizations. Big deal. I've always spoken my mind, but probably too politely. Besides, all of these choices are luxuries, and none of them registers as a sacrifice because they actually make my life more enjoyable. They are also, clearly, not sufficient."

"While doing calligraphy I've listened to a lot of speeches made by activists and philosophers. I've asked myself frequently if revolutionary change can take place without violence, and I've heard many sound arguments for why it cannot. Nonetheless, I remain certain that violence = no change, and that it is a doomed methodology for achieving it. In my view, violent means not only don't justify but also don't result in peaceful ends because the notion of an "end" is flawed. Now is the end.

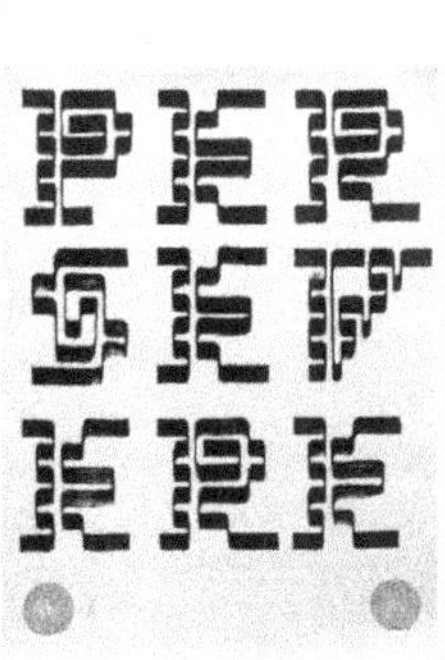

Every moment is the end. Civilization will always be in a state of becoming, so how we become what we want to be is what we are."

"Over the last few months, I've probably written the word persevere thousands times and in of hundreds ways. I've needed the time to think about what I can truly offer, about what a real contribution might be. I have some ideas, but I don't yet know if any of them are any good. In the meantime, I'm offering these drawings to support and thank some of the people I've held in my mind as I've written the word."
TAUBA AUERBACH

Persevere posters are available from diagonalpress.com for $25. 100% of profits benefit the Committee to Protect Journalists, GEMS (Girls Education and Mentoring Services), Chinese American Planning Council, and PLSE (Philadelphia Lawyers for Social Equity)

CLOSING SHOT

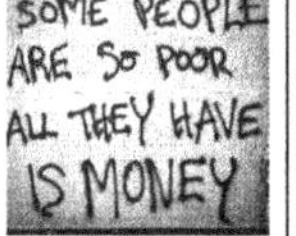

SOME PEOPLE ARE SO POOR ALL THEY HAVE IS MONEY

MARTIN SKAUEN

SAVED BY A MASSIVE GI's PAINTING

66. Guide Your Reader

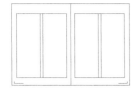

Even the most compelling piece benefits from a design that leads the eye through the material. Rules, drop caps, bold headlines, and different (although controlled) weights and colors can break up the grayness of many pages of running text and help the reader find various points of interest—and resting points—along the way. Judiciously sized and placed images further enhance the reading experience.

PROJECT
Upfront

CLIENT
The New York Times and Scholastic

DESIGN DIRECTION
Judith Christ-Lafond

ART DIRECTION
Anna Tunick

The crisp design of this magazine helps fulfill its mission to engage its teen readers with news of the world and to regard them as "seriously and straightforwardly as they regard themselves."

Large drop caps, bold subheads, and strong pull quotes provide color, texture, and interest, while an illustration surprinting a photo adds texture and depth. The pages are full but seem spacious.

Rules containing dropout type enhance elements, such as decks (similar to taglines) and pull quotes. A bold rule containing a caption leads the eye to an intriguing image.

EMROZ KHAN IS HAVING A BAD DAY

Which is not unusual,
and helps explain why
Pakistan's youth are tinder
for Islamic extremism.

International

E mroz Khan destroys for a living. He dismantles car engines, slicing them open with a sledgehammer, tearing out pistons, and throwing the metal entrails into a pile that will be sold for scrap. His hands and arms are stained a rich black, like fresh asphalt, and ribboned with scars.

He is 21 and has been doing this sort of work for 10 years, 12 hours a day, 6 days a week, earning $1.25 a day. Emroz rolls up his sleeve and puts my finger along a bulge on his forearm; it feels as hard as iron. It is iron, a stretch of pipe

he drove into his body by mistake. He cannot afford to pay a doctor to take it out.

"We work like donkeys," Emroz says, a few paces from the tiny shop where he works in Peshawar, a city in northwest Pakistan. "That's what our life is like. It is the life of animals."

Javaid Khan watches with apprehension. Javaid, who is 17, began chopping up engines four months ago when he left school because he could no longer pay the fees. Javaid wishes he could be one of the clean-cut medical sales reps he sees at the nearby hospital. "I do not have the education," he acknowledges. "It makes me sad to think about it." —

By Peter Maass

AT WORK: Emroz Khan, center, chops engines into scrap for $1.25 a day.

I f you want to understand why young Muslim men line up to be suicide bombers, you would do well to stroll down Cinema Road, where Emroz and Javaid work. You would hear the chanting call to prayer, the shouts of peddlers selling braised bananas, the groan of buses so overloaded that passengers ride on the roofs, and the cries of mutilated beggars pleading for a few cents. And all around, you would notice young men for whom life is abuse. The population of Peshawar (pronounced puh-SHAH-wuhr) reflects the population of Pakistan as a whole—63 percent are under the age of 25.

Most of these young men are not burning effigies of President George W. Bush or fighting Pakistani riot police. Their anger is only loosely expressed, often because they are struggling to survive and cannot afford the luxury of taking an afternoon off to join a demonstration.

They believe, or can be led to believe, that America is to blame for their misery. Many are adrift, cut off from their social foundations. Perhaps they moved to the city from dying villages, or were driven there by war or famine. There is no going back for them, yet in the city there is not much going forward; the movement tends to be downward. As they fall, they grab hold of whatever they can, and sometimes it is the violent ideas of religious extremists.

AN ANCIENT CITY PLAGUED BY WAR

P eshawar, once conquered by Alexander the Great and Genghis Khan, is one of the oldest cities in Asia. The city has long been the gateway to Afghanistan—a designation that became a curse 22 years ago when Afghanistan entered an era of warfare that has yet to end. Nearly half of Peshawar's 2 million inhabitants are Afghan refugees, most of them living in squalid camps. The local economy revolves around the smuggling of guns and ammunition, of VCRs and TVs, of heroin and hashish.

Aziz ul Rahman is a product of Peshawar. He is 18 and works in the mornings at a tire shop. In the afternoons, he studies the Koran at a madrassa, or religious school. The

one he attends is of the extreme variety, as most are these days. I meet him at a protest organized by a pro-Taliban religious party.

"The American leaders are very cruel to Muslims, so that is why I am taking part in the demonstration today," he says politely. What he means is that America supports Israel, which is seen in the Muslim world as oppressing Palestinians, and supports certain Arab regimes, such as the one in Saudi Arabia, which are regarded as corrupt and oppressive.

In the background, a speaker is railing against Pakistan's military government, which supports the U.S. anti-terror campaign. "The generals are stupid," the speaker shouts. Then, like a rock star inviting crowd participation, he calls out, "Generals!" and the crowd roars back, "Stupid!" They are quick learners.

Aziz did not fall into religious extremism by choice; his preferred path, of becoming an engineer, was closed off by poverty. This is common in Pakistan. Poor families do their best to send a son to school, but in the end they cannot manage. The son will get a backbreaking job or maybe keep the donkey's life at bay by enrolling at a madrassa, most of which offer free tuition, room and board. That's where they learn to think it's honorable to blow yourself up amid a crowd of non-Muslims and that the greatest glory in life is to die in a holy war.

1,000 BRICKS A DAY, SIX DAYS A WEEK

O n the outskirts of Peshawar is Dabaray Ghara, an expanse of pits in which several thousand men, mostly Afghan refugees, make bricks. This labor, literally backbreaking, pays next to nothing and takes place outdoors, no matter how hot or cold.

Bakhtiar Khan began working in the pits when he was 10. He is now 25 or 26. He isn't sure, because nobody keeps close track. He works from 5 in the morning until 5 in the afternoon, making 1,000 bricks a day, six days a week, earning a few dollars a week. He is thin, wears no shirt or shoes, and he cannot believe a foreigner is asking about his life.

"Life is cruel," Bakhtiar says. "You can see for yourself. You wear nice clothes and are healthy. But look at us. We have no clothes to wear, and we are not healthy. Your question is amazing."

The youths at Dabaray Ghara are illiterate, and the world of politics is beyond their grasp. They can be led to rally behind any person or idea that promises to improve their lot. "I don't know about politics, but for our problems, I blame the world community," Bakhtiar says. "All humans should be equal, but we are not. . . . We arrived from Afghanistan 15 years ago. Since then I blame America.

PETER MAASS is the author of Love Thy Neighbor: A Story of War, his memoir of the conflict in Bosnia. Copyright 2001 Peter Maass.

'WORK OR PLAY: Children scoop up ash at a Peshawar brick kiln.

CHILD LABOR: This 7-year-old works at a brick factory outside Peshawar. About 3.3 million Pakistanis under 14 work full-time.

The youths at Dabaray Ghara are illiterate, and the world of politics is beyond their grasp. They can be led to rally behind any person or idea that promises to improve their lot.

because it used to support us, but now it leaves us in a place like this. So if someone is fighting a jihad against America, I would support them. But if America is willing to help us, we support that, too."

VIDEO GAMES & A FARAWAY FATHER

I hsan u Din is enrolled at a civil engineering college in Peshawar. Ihsan, 18, speaks good English, and he has the ultimate luxury in Pakistan—pocket money, which is why I ran into him at a video parlor. Compared with Emroz and the brick makers and most youths here, Ihsan has it good. But there's a catch. Pakistan is one of the poorest countries in the world. Even with a degree, it's very hard to get an

engineering job. You need connections and money. Ihsan's family doesn't have enough of either.

"It is a game of money," he explains. "Even if you are a good engineer, you will not get a positive response when you apply, unless you pay. This has been the truth for 20 years."

The second catch is this: Ihsan's father is staying in the United Arab Emirates, where he works as a taxi driver earning infinitely more than he could in Pakistan. He sends money back to his family so that his children can eat well and go to school, but he doesn't earn enough to buy a plane ticket home.

"I have not seen my father for eight years," Ihsan says. "Is that right? He sends pictures and calls. But we don't want

---

The strong structure of the page format is enlivened by a smartly chosen photo and white boxes that break into the image.

Color, caps, rules, and boxes pull the reader to the text start. Typographic elements work well together and lead to a touching photo.

67. Pace Yourself

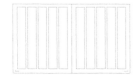

Layout is storytelling, especially in a highly illustrated work with multiple pages. Many projects, especially book chapters or feature articles in magazines, involve devising layouts for multiple pages or screens.

Opening spreads provide opportunities for full-bleed layouts. This spread dramatically sets the scene for what follows, much as titles set the tone for a film.

PROJECT
Portrait of an Eden

CLIENT
Feirabend

DESIGN
Rebecca Rose

A book detailing the growth and history of an area employs varied spreads to guide the reader through time.

Varying type sizes, shapes, columns, images, and colors from one page or spread to the next guides the flow of the story and provides drama.

Opposite
Gertrude leaning against a coconut palm in Lummus Park wearing a playsuit, 1938. A hedge of Milkweed in the background connecting the length of Lummus Park from South Shore to 14th Place. Lummus Park was donated to the City in 1912 by the Lummus Brothers Ocean Beach Realty Company.

A Bermuda grass lawn was introduced bonded with the Hope that its aggressive root system would supply strong under-ground runners to hold the sandy soil in place. Coconut palms were planted as well. A movie theatre of sort and a sense of safety. Finally a fish from exotic tidewater was mounted. From 1912 to 1917 the Lummus Brothers spent $40,000 to create and maintain Lummus Park for the people of Miami Beach.

Left
Barbara June Oka poses by the Shower of Gold Cassia fistula, late 1940s. Her tight grip reflects the smooth harvest times, points of movement and growth; the elbow and knee are natural structures.

Healing Plant

Miami Beach of the Orient
Master Kenneth Oka 1912 and Miami Beach's glad occasion in Pelleoben-Evenholen's festival mirrored People's to People. Peoples and institutes the city difference between Miami Beach and America's peoples. They being joined carousel and administrative publicity for Miami BAZIN.

in visibility vision for his educational work in foreign relations, Oka rang out the annual Residents People Award in New York City from United Nations Ambassador of service 1950s with Gertrude beside. He brush white splendored he and carefree visiting all of the new Japanese stands in the Miami Beach of the Orient.

Ink drawing by Gertrude Oka, c. 1950.

68. Create an Oasis

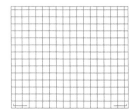

T o present a sense of authority and focus attention, less is indeed more. Space allows the viewer to concentrate.

Also see pages
138–139

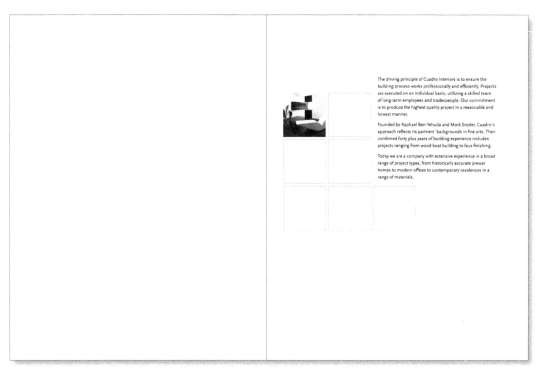

A modular motif introduces the piece.

PROJECT
Cuadro Interiors
capabilities book

CLIENTW
Cuadro Interiors

DESIGN
Jacqueline Thaw Design

DESIGNER
Jacqueline Thaw

PRIMARY PHOTOGRAPHERS
Elizabeth Felicella,
Andrew Zuckerman

Founded on a modular grid, a capabilities brochure for an interior design firm is stripped down to focus on the featured homes and offices.

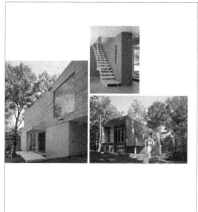

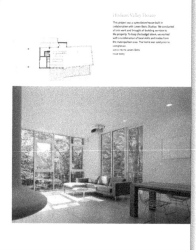

An oasis of white affords the reader an opportunity to linger over every aspect of the images and information.

69. Let the Images Breathe

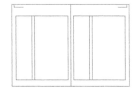

Aspare page will quickly direct the focus on the photo or illustration being featured. Viewers can take in the main attraction without distraction.

MAKING SPACE

As always, the content of a piece leads the designer in apportioning space for text or images. If the text refers to specific photos, art, or diagrams, it's clearest to the reader if the image appears near the reference. Flipping forward or backward through a piece to compare text is counterproductive.

Scale of images counts, too. Enlarging a piece of art to feature a detail lends energy to a spread. As for getting attention, image surrounded by white space tends to draw in the viewer more than images that are grouped with many other elements.

Also see pages
136–137

PROJECT
Mazaar Bazaar: Design and Visual Culture in Pakistan

CLIENT
Oxford University Press, Karachi, with Prince Claus Funds Library, The Hague

DESIGN
Saima Zaidi

A history of design in Pakistan employs a strict grid to hold a trove of Pakistani design artifacts, with ample resting space built in.

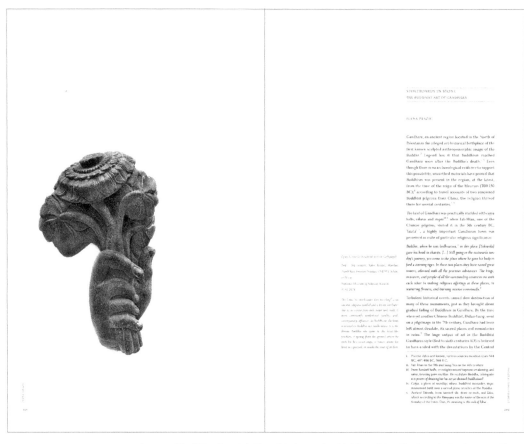

An essay, titled "Storyboards in Stone," features a hand holding a lotus; it's given plenty of room and is balanced by captions, an essay, and footnotes on the opposite page.

Packaging for hair oil is paired with a portrait, with plenty of room for review.

Paintings and patterns, one from the back of a truck, create a colorfully textured layout.

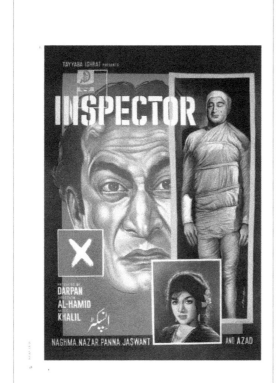

A strong image opens an essay.

70. Map It Out by Hand

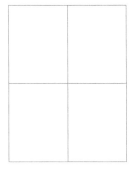

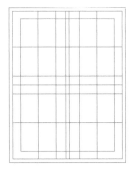

Sketching gives form to ideas and helps to plan the layout of a publication or page. Initial sketches may look more like scribbles than recognizable elements, but they can give form to an overall plan or concept. When including one or more images within a larger concept, it's a good idea to organize templates and a grid to plot how various elements in a piece of art fit and work together.

Roughing out an idea and a template can save a lot of work. Few people have time to repeat steps. Plotting is vital, whether a layout includes type, images, or hand-drawn combinations of both.

This sketch shows both thinking and planning processes and a method of organizing the multiple images contained in the overall piece of art.

PROJECT
McSweeney's 23

CLIENT
McSweeney's

DESIGN
Andrea Dezsö

MANAGING EDITOR
Eli Horowitz

In this jacket for *McSweeney's 23*, artist Andrea Dezsö's hand-drawn, mirrored, and repeated pattern unifies work created in various media. Pencil drawings, hand embroidery, photographs of handmade three-dimensional shadow puppets, and egg tempera paintings coexist easily within the strong framework. For this project, Dezsö used the computer only for scanning and compositing.

ABOVE AND BELOW: With the big picture taken care of and mapped out, each separate piece can be designed.

The project is about pattern and planning, as well as wrangling cover art for many different books within one large book jacket.

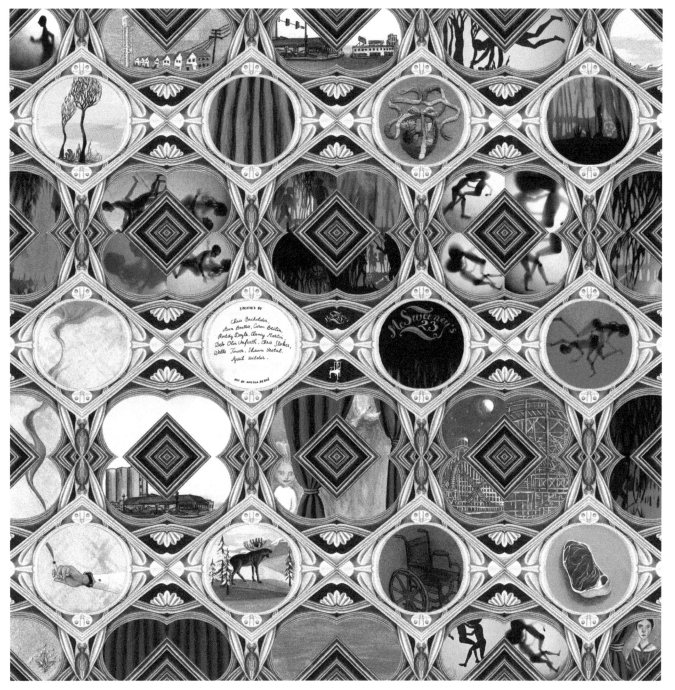

Frames within frames contain illustrations for ten front and back covers, one for each of the stories included in *McSweeney's 23.* All ten covers are further combined in a wraparound jacket that unfolds into a full-size poster suitable for display. The hand-drawn visual framework is such a successful unifying element that separate pieces of art fit together into an even-greater whole.

71. Wrangle Anarchy with Hierarchy

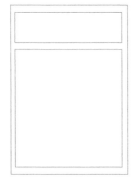

A consistent, simple band enables navigation through the steps of composting data.

Dealing with too much data can be complicated and messy. A simple horizontal band with clear explanations and instructions can wrangle the overwhelming into the comprehensible.

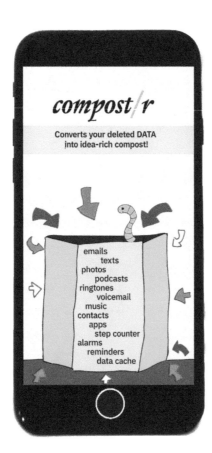

PROJECT
compost/r

CLIENT
Dopodomani

DESIGN
Suzanne Dell'Orto

ILLUSTRATOR
Nina Lawson

An app that echoes composting in the physical realm, *compost/r* wrangles a phone's deleted data into poems, patterns, ringtones, and music.

Composting!

Composting!

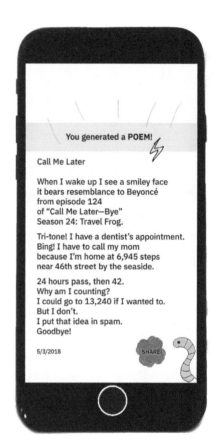

You generated a POEM!

Call Me Later

When I wake up I see a smiley face
it bears resemblance to Beyoncé
from episode 124
of "Call Me Later—Bye"
Season 24: Travel Frog.

Tri-tone! I have a dentist's appointment.
Bing! I have to call my mom
because I'm home at 6,945 steps
near 46th street by the seaside.

24 hours pass, then 42.
Why am I counting?
I could go to 13,240 if I wanted to.
But I don't.
I put that idea in spam.
Goodbye!

5/3/2018

SHARE!

72. Use Organizing Principles

Also see page
27

PROJECTS
Some Fun, I'm Special, and
American Nerd

CLIENT
Simon & Schuster, Inc.
Scribner, an imprint of Simon
& Schuster

Some Fun
ART DIRECTOR
John Fulbrook
DESIGNER
Jason Heuer

I'm Special
ART DIRECTOR
Jackie Seow
DESIGNER
Jason Heuer

American Nerd
ART DIRECTOR
John Fulbrook
DESIGNER
Jason Heuer
PHOTO ILLUSTRATIONS
Shasti O'Leary Soundat

Three book jackets show
three uses of grids in varying
degrees of rigorousness.

D esigners use the
basic principles of
grids even when they are
used instinctively instead
of strictly. Some designs
are clearly planned on
a grid. Others are more
optical. Still other
designs have only the
hint of an underpinning.

Some Fun uses a strict grid
and then breaks it for the title,
which is . . . some fun.

American Nerd uses an optical grid—as opposed to a mathematical grid—that galleries use, as shown on the clever back-to-front concept and photo.

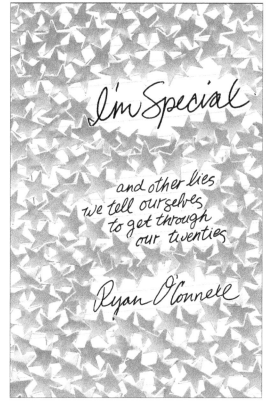

I'm Special is so special that it throws the grid out in favor of an organic feel, with a hint of blue-lined paper to accentuate its nongrid organic aspects.

OPTICAL GRIDS: INSTINCTUAL RATHER THAN MATHEMATICAL

The designer of these jackets thinks artists naturally use the grid and the golden ratio in addition to purposefully applying them. Like many designers, Jason Heuer uses an optical (instinctual rather than mathematical) grid when designing and applies a mathematical grid to clean and line up design elements at the end.

73. Maintain Fluidity

Awell-structured design has solid underpinnings, even when a framework is not immediately noticeable.

PROJECT
Magazine illustration

CLIENT
Print magazine

DESIGN
Marian Bantjes

Pages created for a design magazine have a hand in a return to the craft of detailed typography.

"I work with visual alignment. I can get pretty fanatical about this, making sure there's some structure in the piece. I'll align things with parts of imagery or strong verticals in headlines, and I'll fuss and fiddle a lot to make sure it works out. I'm also fanatical about logical structure, hierarchy of information and consistency. I believe that design and typography are like a well-tailored suit: the average person may not specifically notice the hand-sewn buttons (kerning); the tailored darts (perfect alignment); or the fine fabric (perfect type size) . . . they only know instinctively that it looks like a million bucks."

THIS PAGE AND OPPOSITE PAGE: Marian Bantjes pays formal attention to typographic details, such as justified paragraphs, with consistent letter- and word spacing and typefaces from a particular time period that look all the fresher for her sharp eye. What really makes the page sing, though, is her illustrative, calligraphic wit.

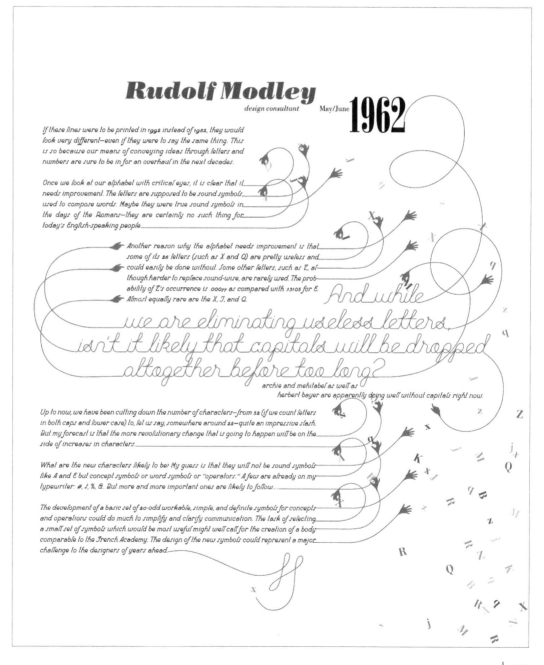

74. Plan for Interruptions

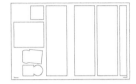

Planning is one of the foremost principles of design. Formats are plans. Grids are plans. Interruptions can be a major part of the plan, and typography can be part of a very clear plan for interruptions. By determining what name or feature is worth setting larger or bolder, what needs a color, and whether a drop cap is helpful or necessary, a designer makes decisions about what can be considered typographical interruptions.

Varying image sizes can also provide controlled interruptions, giving energy and excitement to a piece or spread.

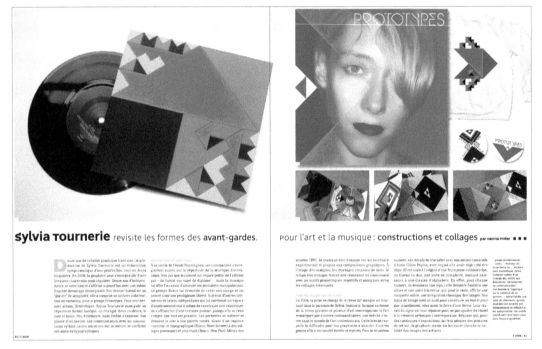

Large, colorful images play against a clean grid.

PROJECT
étapes: magazine

CLIENT
Pyramyd/*étapes:* magazine

DESIGN
Anna Tunick

Spreads from the French magazine, *étapes,* show how a large image, a silhouette, or large amounts of white space can keep a spread or story from feeling mechanical.

– Pochette du maxi-vinyle
"novo screen" pour
le groupe aosco, 2002.
– Pochette co pour santi
will, album "H.E.L.L.", 2005
– Pochette de "fastback"
maxi-vinyle pour aodex
(pour le label client 2000t1,
utilisation d'une typo
originale, la copland)
– Pochette co pour
experience, album
"hémisphère gauche", 2004.

ses "gimmicks"

À l'incontournable – et douloureuse – question sur l'auto-
définition de son style, Sylvia Tournerie évoque deux éléments signifiants. L'école s'étant équipée d'ordinateurs à
la fin de ses études et le recours à la photocopieuse étant
également plus facile, cela a entraîné un style repérable,
économique, un jeu de découpes. *Mon travail est marqué
par des grosses masses noires avec des couleurs primaires.*
Difficile de ne pas faire allusion à l'empreinte de Cieslewicz. Sylvia Tournerie a étudié à l'ESAG-Penninghen au
temps où Roman Cieslewicz y enseignait[3]. Il fut son maître
de thèse. De lui, elle se souvient d'un rire qu'il eut, durant
un stage, alors qu'il manipulait des formes et concevait un
hors-série pour *Le Monde*. Cette excitation, cette légèreté,
qui ne s'essouffle pas malgré les années, cette ouverture
d'esprit face aux étudiants, n'excluant pas la sévérité, sont
les "outils" qu'il lui légua. L'attitude de Cieslewicz, entre
détachement et jouissance personnelle d'une affirmation,
semble être une aspiration, comme un moteur pour la graphiste. Son style se forgea aussi en raison des contraintes
financières qu'elle subit. Les labels n'ayant pas de budgets
pour une production photo, jugeant que ses propres photos ne peuvent se suffire à elles-mêmes, elle transforme
celles qu'elle reçoit ou qu'elle prend en paysages. Ainsi, ses
photos sont-elles plus à l'aise avec l'esprit décalé provoqué
par les collages. Dans ces conditions naît le mémorable et
si furtive identité de *Point éphémère*, où elle transforme en
une toile de Jouy, *les acteurs de la musique*.

émergence

Sylvia Tournerie ne compose que sur ordinateur, et parle
de la légèreté de l'outil, puisque, au propre comme au figuré,
les données ne pèsent rien. Sur son Mac, un dossier vrac
regroupe ses premières sessions de travail peu organisées,
*une étape de vidage, suite à ma rencontre avec le comman-
ditaire*. Dans un état presque hypnotique, où l'important est
de se laisser aller; elle façonne une matière formelle abs-
traite. Elle la pétrit jusqu'au moment où se manifeste la
première émotion, cette émotion, qu'elle peut perdre en
cours de route, mais qu'elle *n'a de cesse de faire vivre, de
conserver jusqu'au bout du projet*. Tout est dans le doigté et
dans ces ressentis impalpables. Sylvia Tournerie parle avec
sensibilité, avec intelligence de cette étape de travail, capi-
tale, qu'elle interroge douloureusement aussi. Elle évoque son
incapacité à décrypter ses convictions. Cette étape est de
l'ordre de l'émotion, *J'ai rarement une idée avant de faire les
choses*. Ainsi, l'objet graphique émerge-t-il de son façon-
nage. *Je justifie les formes une fois qu'elles sont là.* Pendant
longtemps, il lui fut difficile d'assumer cette prétendue gra-
tuité, aujourd'hui, Sylvia Tournerie se dit plus sereine face
à sa façon de composer[4]. Ses formes ne sont pas le fruit du

www.andreacrews.com

[Project mené à la Tête of
one day, 2006] avec la
participation de Leslie
david, 2006). Au recto, les
mannequins présentant
la collection de la saison et
des motifs géométriques
auréolaient chaque modèle
et accentuaient leurs
postures irrévérencieuses,
au recto, le processus
de travail d'andrea crews
se révèle dans un vaste
désordre recuité. La styliste
élabore ses pièces uniques
à partir d'habits récupérés
et recyclés.

hasard, avec l'expérience, toutes relèvent d'un choix. Sylvia Tournerie agit dans la traduction – le graphisme avec
ses composants parle de l'âme directement de la même
manière que la musique parle avec ses notes et ses gammes
–, elle n'est pas sur le territoire des intentions. Ses identi-
tés visuelles ne sont pas des chartes, mais des pulsations,
des vibrations, concentrées ou fragmentées.

Peu d'affiches, pas de théâtre, ni d'identité institution-
nelle (excepté sa participation avec Gilles Popian à l'identité du CNAP é : 126), pas de gros chantiers, ni de régularité
(cette situation qu'on retrouve chez d'autres de ses
contemporains devrait inciter les commanditaires à défier
ces graphistes sur ces terrains balisés). Pourtant, les
gammes de Tournerie marquent leur empreinte dans le

Silhouetted shapes and cleverly chosen art bring energy to a well-ordered spread.

75. Be Dramatic

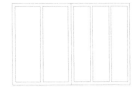

Cropping creates drama. Showing an image as it was originally photographed can tell the story, but cropping that same image makes a particular point, gives a point of view, and generates fear or excitement. A crop can also change what a photo communicates, directing the eye to one particular aspect of the shot and eliminating superfluous information.

CHECK FOR RESTRICTIONS

Be aware of restrictions on cropping some images. Many photographers, stock houses, and museums have strict regulations about how a piece of art can be reproduced. Some images, especially of famous paintings or sculptures, are inviolable.

OPPOSITE PAGE: The book jacket sets the format of callouts in circles (spotlight). Collages can dilute impact, but the cropping of all the images makes the art a showstopper.

THIS PAGE: RIGHT The callouts in circles add movement to the gritty photos designed on a grid.

PROJECT
Broadway:
From Rent to Revolution

CLIENT
Drew Hodges, author;
Rizzoli, publisher

CREATIVE DIRECTOR
Drew Hodges

DESIGN
Naomi Mizusaki

Energy, shapes, cropping and great typography add to the drama of a book designed with a clear grid but with All. That. Jazz.

ON BROADWAY

FROM RENT TO REVOLUTION

DREW HODGES

INTRODUCTION BY
DAVID SEDARIS

FOREWORD BY
CHIP KIDD

RIZZOLI
NEW YORK

76. Cut It Out

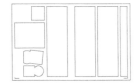

S ilhouettes can keep a spread from feeling too regimented or blocky.

For layout purposes, a silhouette, also abbreviated to "silo," is an image from which the background has been eliminated. A silo can be an organic shape such as a leaf or a more regular shape such as a circle. The more fluid shapes of a silhouette add greater movement to a spread.

PROJECT
Croissant magazine

ART DIRECTOR
Seiko Baba

DESIGNER
Yuko Takanashi

This spread from a Japanese craft magazine reveals how a story that epitomizes discipline and organization benefits from silhouetted shapes. This particular magazine is a MOOK, a special edition published by *Croissant* editors. The title is *Mukashi nagara no kurashi no chie*, which roughly means "time-honored wisdom of living."

Vertical and horizontal rules clearly define areas containing headlines, introductions, and information. The instructional aspects of these pages are successful, but they are enlivened by the organic shapes of the silhouettes.

Rules create an additional
grid within the magazine grid.
Alignments are clear and clean.
Varying shapes lend a sense of
movement to the disciplined
and hierarchical spreads.

77. Let Culture Rule

It is possible to have a strong and clear framework with copious amounts of visual oxygen and yet maintain aspects that differentiate a project, not to mention educate the viewer or reader.

By incorporating cultural stories, mythologies, or symbols, a designer can make a piece far more evocative—and make the world smaller, but most importantly, richer, for glimpsing or understanding other cultures.

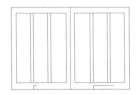

PROJECT
Threaded magazine

CLIENT
Threaded Studio, publisher

DESIGN
Threaded Studio

DESIGNERS, TEAM MEMBERS
Kyra Clarke,
Fiona Grieve,
Reghan Anderson,
Phil Kelly,
Desna Whaanga-Schollum,
Karyn Gibbons,
Te Raa Nehua

IMAGE CREDITS
Threaded Media Limited, 2016/17

New Beginnings, Edition 20 of an international magazine developed, designed, and published by an Auckland-based New Zealand design agency, is dedicated exclusively to the *kaupapa* (topic) of Maori art and designer practitioners.

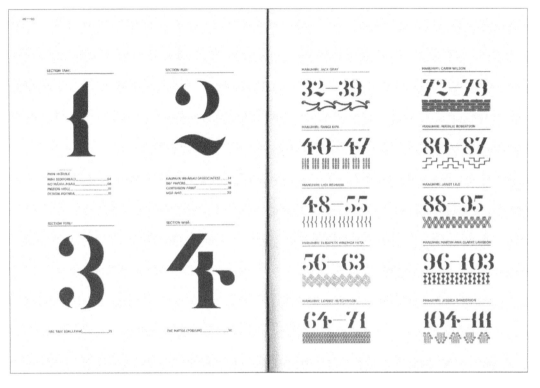

Sans serif typography and lyrical numbers work with symbols derived from Maori culture. The publication's editors created each pattern specifically to reflect the *korero* (talk) of each *manuhiri* (guest) featured in the magazine, making the artwork a unique cultural signifier for each indigenous practitioner.

OPPOSITE PAGE: A simple grid and generous space frame breathtaking Maori art. Ornaments honor the culture, avoiding the banal or stereotypical. Subheads and basic text are spare sans serif typefaces, contrasting with the spectacular images.

REGARDING SCALE:

I work in so many different genres and scales. There are fundamental principles to design but there are so many different ways to exploit them, they have weaknesses and strengths. And they can change as soon as you change scale or your relationship – for example physical proximity or moving from 2D to 3D. There are so many ways in which you can change the nature of the game and it forces you to engage differently with those elements or principles. As I get older in my craft and sense of self (if you're fortunate enough to be given the freedom in your practice to pursue your own sense of design truth) you find that as you journey along eventually as you refine based upon your own sensibilities, as you refine your craft you find the sweet spots. You find what works and what doesn't. What works for me in moko, using line at that proximity – you're working within one foot of your hand guiding the gun as its laying ink in the skin – works differently when you're standing away doing a large mural or a 6 metre bronze sculpture. So you can't use and engage the same principles in the same way, you're forced to renegotiate your own axis or your own sense of gravity to your work.

ON LINE:

I'm acutely aware of how much the power of a line can influence how people read visual material. For me, when I'm working in a sculptural sense I'm assigning everything by the nature of those lines, if they're low reported into low relief or 3D we're talking about edges. Edges are everything. You create a deep or powerful sense of space, direction and form with something that's relatively shallow. The edge of the line enables you to use light to give the impression of depth. I'm aware of it and I just try to exploit it I suppose. There's a beauty in line that's difficult to explain, but I get seduced by the ability to reduce down to linear forms and play with it, there's so much you can do it's really just up to your imagination and over a period of time you get to a point where you can master it. And then people, they follow it, they get it. They're not necessarily able to interpret it or explain it but they get it.

The energy contained in the line is no different than the principle of physics. It's the same as how you use your arm to develop a centrifugal force to throw something. The line can do that as well. You can use that energy to influence and to give the impression (of that force) in the same way whether in 2D and 3D.

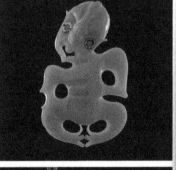

CONNECTIONS AND PATHWAYS:

My artistic practice is strongly influenced by my political belief that we need to be relevant and that we have a role to bridge the past and the future. I'm lucky enough to grow up in my tribal area. I've had strong cultural connections to my community so I have a sense of allegiance to my culture and community that manifests itself in the work. But I can't change the past. I'm trying to visualize a pathway in the future and trying to use my art as a tool to help lay down some of that pathway. I'm trained as a social scientist as well so if you connect that to my cultural background it's part of my imperative to drive my art to always be forward focused. I believe we have a role to visualize the future and make it happen. If you look over my practice over the past 20-30 years, moko was like that, taonga

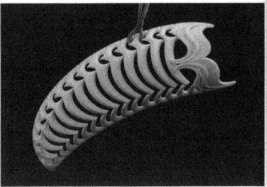

puoro – Māori musical instruments – was like that, my role in waka in Taranaki was like that. So by kicking those things off and by continuing to push them – the same with taonga whakairakau (adornment arts) – restoring those art forms but restoring them in a way that continues to have relevance not only for now and being present in your work but also into the future. I'm trying to push my work so far ahead that it actually looks futuristic, that people can go 'wow – I really like that'. They can see the footprint of our old world in it but it's also out there tugging on them so the materiality, the aesthetics and the cultural imperative that's subtly locked in there pulls at them.

NEW MATERIALS:

The interesting thing was about seeing how the Māori community would respond to media that wasn't seen as valuable, that didn't have a valuable (cultural) attribution, so creating beautiful stuff out of it, it enables itself to be relevant. The beautiful thing about Corian is you can get a great sense of colour – and if you're really good at finishing the work – it's as seductive as what whale tooth, whale bone or pounamu can be. That was the beauty of that exercise, seeing that material being adopted as a taonga. These approaches to materials are interesting journeys, they're not necessarily answers to questions but they're part of the journey.

> **" ...you're working within one foot of your hand guiding the gun as its laying ink in the skin... "**

78. Devise a Versatile System

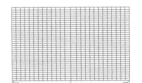

A versatile system allows different sizes, shapes, and information to work in numerous configurations.

PIONEERS
Ellen Lupton notes that the Swiss grid pioneers Josef Müller-Brockmann and Karl Gerstner defined a design "programme" as a set of rules for constructing a range of visual solutions. Lupton nails the crucial aspects of Swiss design. "The Swiss designers used the confines of a repeated structure to generate variation and surprise. A system allows for both dense and spacious pages within the same project.

This systematic grid allows the page to be broken into halves, thirds, and quarters; it can also be subdivided horizontally.

The strong grid controls image sizes and supports variations.

PROJECT
étapes: magazine

CLIENT
Pyramyd/*étapes:* magazine

DESIGN
Anna Tunick

This magazine article employs a flexible system in its visual review the work of the great gridmeister Josef Müller-Brockmann.

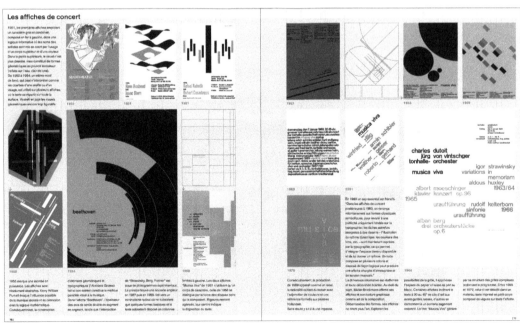

Strict grids do not preclude excitement. Arresting images and rhythmic placement create variation and surprise.

This spread shows how the grid can easily accommodate a sidebar and illustrates how the grid can also support a page with ample white space.

Überholen…?
Im Zweifel nie!

Automobile-Club de Suisse

protegez l'enfant !

❝ En une fraction de seconde, l'affiche doit agir sur la pensée des passants, les contraignant à recevoir le message, à se laisser fasciner avant que la raison n'intervienne et ne réagisse. Somme toute, une agression discrète, mais soigneusement préparée. ❞

est capable de remises en cause profondes. Malgré le succès de son style illustratif, il sait que les progrès dans cette voie sont déterminés par des talents artistiques dont il ne s'est départis. Le dessin, le plaisir de créer, le goût de la nouvelle surprise et la joie de la communication spontanée, satisfactions personnelles du graphiste, ne sont un langage formel le plus apte à répondre aux aspirations de l'époque, à qui les lois du design et d'un graphisme objectif seraient plus adaptées. La raison essentielle du renoncement à l'illustration réside dans le fait qu'aucune illustration ne résout totalement les problèmes que présente un travail. La conception illustrée à elle toute se veut pas l'indispensable caractère documentaire de la publicité et confère au dessin une note personnelle qui ne s'harmonise pas avec le style publicitaire moderne.

En 1950, la commande de la salle de concert (Tonhalle-Gesellschaft) de Zurich contribue à ce virage déterminant. Samuel Hirschi, secrétaire du lieu, a programme des compositeurs modernes et cherche à actualiser le lieu. Les deux hommes nouerout une amitié solide et durant près de vingt-cinq ans, saison après saison, le graphiste vo y expérimenter les possibilités de l'abstraction et de l'art de la construction typographique.

La relation du graphiste à la musique, qu'il estime fort le plus abstrait, y a certainement sa part de responsabilité. Mélomane, figure d'une visionnaire, il pousse ses élèves à s'y intéresser et invite dans ses cours des compositeurs comme John Cage. Autre domaine d'élection, l'art concret, dont l'influence est sensible dans les affiches pour le festival Juni Festwochen ou la programmation Musica Viva, organisée chaque année au Tonhalle et dans les lieux de la ville. Les plus grandes œuvres d'art nous impressionnent par leur équilibre, leur harmonie et leurs proportions, tout ce qui peut être mesuré. En 1960, il cesse de citer les formes de l'art moderne et met en place sa propre écriture: la composition d'affiches exclusivement typographiques. Expressions artistiques, ces travaux sont pourtant vus comme un cas à part par leur auteur, soucieux de moderniser la communication visuelle, le design graphique et la publicité, pour accroître leur efficacité et inscrire leurs formes fortes dans le temps présent. Dans cette perspective, ils sont aussi un territoire d'exploration formelle et d'expérimentation sur la fonction informative de l'affiche et les possibilités de la grille. Autant de découvertes, qui transformées en principes, constitueront la matière de ses livres et de son discours.

nationalité, objectivité et efficacité

Les progrès sont et restront déterminés par des créateurs susceptibles de presentir, au travers des tensions latentes, les possibilités nouvelles et de les transformer en certitudes visuelles.

La parution des écrits de Müller-Brockmann coïncide avec les tournants de son parcours professionnel. En 1956, il entreprend un voyage en Amérique, donne des conférences aux États-

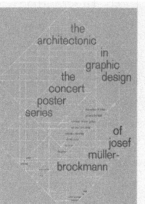

Philosophie de la grille et du design

L'usage de la grille comme système d'organisation est l'expression d'une certaine attitude en ce sens qu'il démontre que le graphiste conçoit son travail dans des termes constructifs et orientée vers l'avenir.

C'est là l'expression d'une éthique professionnelle, le travail du designer doit avoir l'évidente, objective et esthétique qualité du raisonnement mathématique.

Son travail doit être la contribution à la culture générale dont il constitue lui-même une partie.

Le design constructiviste qui est capable d'analyse et de reproduction peut influencer et rehausser le goût d'une société et la façon dont elle conçoit les formes et les couleurs.

Un design qui est objectif, engagé pour le bien-être collectif, bien composé et raffiné constitue la base d'un comportement démocratique. Un design constructif signifie la conversion des lois du design en solutions pratiques. Un travail accompli de façon systématique, en accord avec de stricts principes

formels, permet ces exigences de droiture et d'intelligibilité et l'intégration de tous les facteurs aussi vitaux pour la vie sociopolitique.

Travailler avec un système de grille implique la soumission à des lois valides universellement.

L'usage du système de grille implique la volonté de systématiser, de clarifier; la volonté de pénétrer à l'essentiel; de concentrer; la volonté de cultiver l'objectivité au lieu de la subjectivité; la volonté de rationaliser les modes de production créatifs et techniques; la volonté d'intégrer des éléments de couleur, de forme et de matière; la volonté d'accomplir la domination de l'architecture sur l'espace et la surface; la volonté d'adopter une attitude positive et visionnaire; la reconnaissance de l'importance de l'éducation et les effets du travail conçu dans un esprit constructif et créatif.

Tout travail de création visuelle est une manifestation de la personnalité du designer. Il est marqué de son savoir, de son habileté et de sa mentalité. ~ Josef Müller-Brockmann

the architectonic
in
graphic
the design
concert
poster
series
of
josef
müller-
brockmann

↔ Stellwerk **Bern Wylerfeld**

↔ **CFF Cargo**

SBB CFF FFS

Gleis **1**

→

Unis, visite le Mexique et prend des contacts à New York, où il songeait à s'établir, devant la difficulté pour la Suisse à reconnaître et à laisser s'épanouir ses talents, du fait de son esprit de villageois et de paysans. Il retourne finalement à Zurich, où il prend la suite de son professeur à l'école des arts et métiers, Ernst Keller, et met en place la revue qu'il songeait à monter depuis 1965. D'abord approchées, des personnalités comme Armin Hofmann ou Emil Ruder sont écartées, leurs productions étant jugées trop diversifiées par le quarteron de puristes. Une idéologie formelle et fonctionnelle se met en place. Les trois mots-clefs en sont rationalité, objectivité et efficacité: *J'en suis venu à apprécier l'Akzidenz Grotesk davantage que ses successeurs Helvetica et Univers. Il est plus expressif et ses

bases formelles sont plus universelles. La fin du "e", par exemple, est une diagonale qui produit des angles droits. Dans le cas de l'Helvetica et de l'Univers, les terminaisons sont droites, produisant des angles aigus ou obtus, des angles subjectifs.* Après la Seconde Guerre mondiale et le désordre nazi, le graphisme espère un retour à l'harmonie et ambitionne un rôle constructeur. La subjectivité du dessin est écartée au profit de l'objectivité de la photo et de la construction. Les règles de la nouvelle typographie constituent avec le fer à gauche une dynamique vers le progrès technique et social: *La symétrie et l'axe central sont ce qui caractérise l'architecture fasciste. Le modernisme et la démocratie rejettent l'axe.* Le savoir-faire du designer se précise et quitte la théorie pour passer à le réel au service des entreprises: *Un design constructif signifie la conversion des lois du design en solutions pratiques.* C'est dans ce sens que s'oriente son premier livre Problèmes d'un artiste graphique, dont la publication en 1961 correspond à son départ de l'école des arts et métiers de Zurich, où il n'est pas parvenu à installer son enseignement. Dix ans plus tard, il publie une Histoire de la communi-

cation visuelle et (avec sa seconde épouse) une Histoire de l'affiche, qu'il organise de nouveau avec l'affiche constructiviste en ligne de mire et l'efficacité en lieu et place de l'expressivité: *En une fraction de seconde, l'affiche doit agir sur la pensée des passants, les contraignant à recevoir le message, à se laisser fasciner avant que la raison n'intervienne et ne réagisse. Somme toute, une agression discrète mais soigneusement préparée.* Quatre ans plus tôt, Müller-Brockmann a fondé avec trois associés l'agence Müller-Brockmann & Co, qui intègre la publicité dans son activité régulière, aux côtés de l'identité visuelle, la signalétique et la communication culturelle. Au terme de dix années supplémentaires, en 1981, il publie son ouvrage de référence: Raster systeme für die

programme d'identité, de signalétique et d'informations visuelles des chemins de fer suisses (sbb). assortis de recommandations typographiques (un helvetica modifié), le gabarit permet de garantir l'uniformité du système dans le temps et d'en tirer bénéfice sur une multiplicité de supports, projet réalisé par müller-brockmann (; on va en rester spalingas, primé en 1993 par le swiss design prize.

visuelle Gestaltung. Ses expérimentations dans les affiches du Tonhalle ainsi que son récent travail pour les chemins de fer suisses lui ont permis de forger une théorie mais aussi une éthique de la grille. Derrière son apparence de manuel technique, l'ouvrage est un manifeste. Le livre est introduit par un texte sur la philosophie de la grille et du design (voir encadré) qui conclut par un envoi à l'individualité du créateur: *Tout travail de création visuelle est une manifestation de la personnalité du designer. Il est marqué de son savoir, de son habileté et de sa mentalité.* Les progrès qu'il contient et propose ne seront pas perçus comme les choix déterminés d'un graphiste ou comme des règles parfois comprises proposées à la profession, mais plus souvent

79. Show Weights and Measures

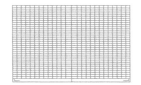

Agridded piece with Swiss design foundations can make a lot of text a delight to read. This system visually broadcasts information so that it reads loud and clear. Multicolumn grids can contain copious amounts of information and accommodate images and color boxes for sectional information. The system also allows for variation; what is left out enhances the material that is put in.

7 GREAT SERIES. 7 GREAT EXPERIENCES!

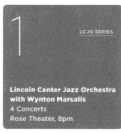

Lincoln Center Jazz Orchestra with Wynton Marsalis
4 Concerts
Rose Theater, 8pm

JJ SERIES

Jazz Jam
4 Concerts
Rose Theater, 8pm

MM SERIES

Music of the Masters
4 Concerts
Rose Theater, 8pm

COLTRANE

Blue tranes run deeper. Ecstatic and somber, secular and sacred, John Coltrane's musical sermons transform Rose Theater into a place of healing and celebration with orchestrations of his small group masterpieces "My Favorite Things," "Giant Steps," "Naima," and more. Join us as the **LCJO** with **Wynton Marsalis** marks the 80th year since the birth of one of

WYNTON AND THE HOT FIVES

Hearts beat faster. It's that moment of pure joy when a single, powerful voice rises up from sweet polyphony. Louis Armstrong's Hot Five masterpieces—"West End Blues," "Cornet Chop Suey," and others—quicken the pulse with irresistibly modern sounds. **Wynton Marsalis, Victor Goines, Don Vappie, Wycliffe Gordon,** and others re-imagine the recordings that defined jazz, and then bring that pure joy to the debut of equally timeless new music inspired by the original.

RED HOT HOLIDAY STOMP

Tradition gets fresher. When Santa and the Mrs. get to dancin' the "New Orleans Bump," you know you're walking in a *Wynton Wonderland*—a place where joyous music meets comic storytelling. **Wynton Marsalis, Herlin Riley, Dan Nimmer, Wycliffe Gordon, Don Vappie,** and others rattle the rafters with holiday classics swung with Crescent City style. *Bells, baby. Bells.*

THE LEGENDS OF BLUE NOTE

Bop gets harder. The music is some of the best ever made—Lee Morgan's *Cornbread,* Horace Silver's *Song for My Father,* Herbie Hancock's *Maiden Voyage*—all wrapped up in album cover art as bold and legendary as the music inside. The **LCJO** with **Wynton Marsalis** debuts exciting and long-overdue big band arrangements of the best of Blue Note, complete with trademark cracklin' trumpets, insistent drums, and all manner of blues.

IN THIS HOUSE, ON THIS MORNING

Tambourines testify. It's that sweet embrace of life—sometimes celebratory, sometimes solemn—rising from so many houses on so many Sundays. We mark the 15th anniversary of Wynton's first in-house commission, a sacred convergence of gospel and jazz that

FUSION REVOLUTION: JOE ZAWINUL

Grooves ask for mercy, mercy, mercy. Schooled in the subtleties of swing by Dinah Washington, keyboardist **Joe Zawinul** brought the fundamentals of funk to Cannonball Adderley, the essentials of the electric to Miles Davis, and carried soul jazz into the electric age with his band Weather Report. Now the **Zawinul Syndicate** takes us on a hybrid adventure of sophisticated harmonies, world music rhythms, and deeply funky grooves. *Mercy.*

BEBOP LIVES!

Feet tangle and neurons dance. Fakers recoil, goatees sprout, and virtuosos take up their horns. Charlie Parker and Dizzy Gillespie set the bebop revolution in motion, their twisting, syncopated lines igniting the rhythms of jazz. Latter day fakers beware as the legendary **James Moody** and **Charles McPherson,** the alto sax voice of Charlie Parker in Clint Eastwood's *Bird,* raise battle axes and *swing.*

CECIL TAYLOR & JOHN ZORN

Souls get freer. Embark on a sonic voyage as the peerless **Cecil Taylor** navigates us through dense forests of sound—percussive and poetic. He is, as Nat Hentoff proclaimed, "a genuine creator." The voyage banks toward the avant-garde as **John Zorn's Masada** with **Dave Douglas** explores sacred and secular Jewish music and the "anguish and ecstasy of klezmer." Musical wanderlust *will* be satisfied.

THE MANY MOODS OF MILES DAVIS

Change gets urgent. "I have to change," Miles said, "It's like a curse." And so his trumpet voice—tender, yet with that *edge*—was bound up in five major movements in jazz. The LCJO's **Ryan Kisor** opens with bebop and the birth of the cool. GRAMMY®-winner **Terence Blanchard** interprets hard bop and

PROJECT
Subscription brochure

CLIENT
Jazz at Lincoln Center

DESIGN
Bobby C. Martin Jr.

Typography readably wrangles a rich offering of programs.

DETAIL (ABOVE) AND OPPOSITE PAGE: This brochure shows a controlled variation of weights, leading, labels, heads, and deks. Hierarchy is clean and clear. Color modules signal the seven different series. The typography within each color module is clear and well balanced, with sizes and weights that clearly denote the series information. The color modules are successful subset layouts within the overall layout of the brochure. Within the modules, an elegant choice of typefaces and alignments act as minibanners.

From Satchmo's first exuberant solo shouts to Coltrane's transcendent ascent, we celebrate the emotional sweep of the music we love by tracing the course of its major innovations. Expression unfolds in a parade of joyous New Orleans syncopators, buoyant big band swingers, seriously fun beboppers, cool cats romantic and lyrical, blues-mongering hard boppers, and free and fusion adventurers. From all the bird flights, milestones, and shapes of jazz that came, year three in the House of Swing is a journey as varied as the human song itself, and the perfect season to find your jazz voice.

4
Afro-Latin Jazz Orchestra with Arturo O'Farrill
3 Concerts
Rose Theater, 8pm

BEBO VALDES

Mambo migrates. Bebo Valdes is a true legend...

5
Singers Over Manhattan
4 Concerts
The Allen Room
7:30pm & 9:30pm

STEPHANIE JORDAN & THE WESS ANDERSON QUARTET

Standards get fresher. Every so often a new voice stands up and proclaims itself...

WILLIE NELSON SINGS THE BLUES

Blues get democratic. It's not the right to sing the blues. As folk legend **Willie Nelson** told the great B.B. King...

CUBANA BE CUBANA BOP

Cultures collide and rhythm explodes....

TODO TANGO

Being gets sultry. Dancers step closer when jazz travels to South American shores...

DIANNE REEVES

Latin shimmers divinely. At once shimmer and sultry, four-time GRAMMY-winner...

DARIN ATWATER GOSPEL

Spirits run deeper. The rhythms of the sanctified church...

6
Singin' & Swingin'
3 Concerts
The Allen Room
7:30pm & 9:30pm

COLTRANE/HARTMAN

Life gets lusher. Softness...

PAQUITO D'RIVERA

Streams converge. The jazz-meets-classical clarinet tradition of Benny Goodman...

THE BIRTH OF COOL

Whispers shout louder. Cool...

7
Jazz for Young People
5 Concerts
Rose Theater, 11pm & 2pm

WHAT IS AN ARRANGER?

Brass and reeds reconcile....

WHAT IS LATIN JAZZ?

Rhythm becomes everything....

HOW DO WE CREATE JAZZ MOODS?

Moods mingle. Jazz is more than a mere indigo...

---

7 GREAT SERIES. 7 GREAT EXPERIENCES!

2
Jazz Jam
4 Concerts
Rose Theater, 8pm

WYNTON AND THE HOT FIVES

Hearts beat faster. It's that sweet moment of pure joy when a single, powerful voice rises up from sweet inspiration. Louis Armstrong's Hot Five masterpieces—"West End Blues," "Cornet Chop Suey," and others—quicken the pulse with impossibly modern sounds. **Wynton Marsalis, Victor Goines, Don Vappie, Wycliffe Gordon,** and others re-imagine the recordings that defined jazz, and then bring that pure joy to the debut of equally timeless new music inspired by the original.

RED HOT HOLIDAY STOMP

Tradition gets fresher. When Santa and the Mrs. opt to dance the "New Orleans Bump," you know you're making it a Wynton Marsalis-style jolly holiday...

THE LEGENDS OF BLUE NOTE

Bop gets harder. The music is some of the best ever made—Lee Morgan's *Cornbread*, Horace Silver's *Song for My Father*, Herbie Hancock's *Maiden Voyage*...

IN THIS HOUSE, ON THIS MORNING

Tambourines testify. It's that special embrace of life—sometimes celebratory, sometimes solemn—living high as many hands on so many Sundays. We mark the 15th anniversary of Wynton's first in-house commission...

3
Music of the Masters
4 Concerts
Rose Theater, 8pm

FUSION REVOLUTION: JOE ZAWINUL

Grooves ask for mercy, mercy, mercy....

BEBOP LIVES!

Feel temple and neurons dance....

CECIL TAYLOR & JOHN ZORN

Souls set free. Embark on a sonic voyage...

THE MANY MOODS OF MILES DAVIS

Change gets urgent. "I have to change," Miles said. "It's like a curse."...

1
Lincoln Center Jazz Orchestra with Wynton Marsalis
4 Concerts
Rose Theater, 8pm

COLTRANE

Blue tunes run deeper. Ecstatic and sorrowful, secular and sacred, John Coltrane's musical animals transform Rose Theater into a place of healing and catharsis in John orchestrations of his sonic group masterpieces "My Favorite Things," "Giant Steps," "Naima," and more. Join us as the **LCJO** with **Wynton Marsalis** marks the 80th year since the birth of one of the most somber, influential, and adventurous artists in the history of jazz.

GERSHWIN

Rhapsodies get bluer. "Composers have been walking around jazz like a cat around a plate of soup," said legendary conductor Walter Damrosch...

JAZZ AND ART

Sound bleeds color. The bebop's hints of a bebop texture and midnight blues of a slow down drips syncopate our musical canvas. Inspired by the Museum of Modern Art's collection, the LCJO with **Wynton Marsalis** performs the music that moved Matisse...

THE SONGS WE LOVE

Perfection endures. They are arranged his perfection—"April in Paris" arranged by Jodd Bill Evans, "Summertime" by Gil Evans...

80. Use Helvetica

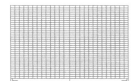

In 2007, Helvetica's fiftieth anniversary helped make this classic and clean sans serif typeface a star. Why is Helvetica so clearly associated with the Swiss grid? Aside from its name, tweaked from *Helvetia*, the Latin name for Switzerland, the functional lines of the face originally christened as Neue Haas Grotesk, worked in tandem with the orderly grids that defined modernism in the 1950s.

A thin, elegant weight of Helvetica can look quiet yet sophisticated.

Various showings of Helvetica

CLIENT
• Designcards.nu by Veenman Drukkers
• Kunstvlaai/Katja van Stiphout

PHOTO
Beth Tondreau

Helvetica can be used in a range of weights and sizes. The medium and bold weights often signal a no-nonsense approach to quotidian information. Thinner weights can conjure simplicity, luxury, and a Zen-like calm.

Vuurrood zoekt stagiaires die niet willen werken

K_nst VI__. | A.P.I.

Art Pie International

Een boek navertellen
op video in precies
één minuut of kom
naar de Kunstvlaai A.P.I.
bij de stand van The One Minutes en
maak hier jouw boek in één minuut.
Van 10–18 mei 2008

Win 1000 euro

Westergasfabriek
Haarlemmerweg 6-8
Amsterdam
www.kunstvlaai.nl

Helvetica's readable features render it as typographically elemental as air and water.

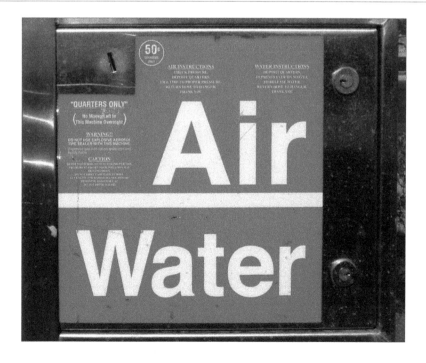

81. Vary Rule Weights

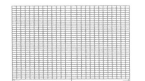

R ules are versatile. They can function as

- navigation bars
- containers for headlines
- grounding baselines for images
- separation devices
- mastheads

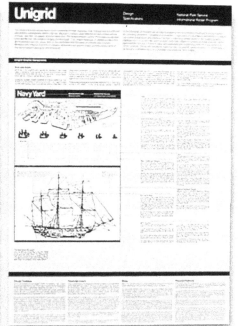

PROJECT
www.vignelli.com

CLIENT
Vignelli Associates

DESIGN
Dani Piderman

DESIGN DIRECTOR
Massimo Vignelli

A master of grids and rules, the late Massimo Vignelli showed his trademark Unigrid on his website. This spread in the updated edition of *Layout Essentials* is a tribute to Vignelli and his associates.

| Home | Recent | News | Clients | Awards | Contact |

**Acerbis
Serenissimo Table
1985**

This table stresses the contrast
between the heaviness of the legs
and the thinness of the top. The legs
are in steel covered with "Venetian
stucco", an interesting revival of
a traditional technique. The top, in
glass, creates the look of thin and
thick not dissimilar from that of a

Bodoni typeface. Another example
that "Design is One".

Furniture Design   1 of 2 ►

| Home | Recent | News | Clients | Awards | Contact |

**Malma Pasta
Packaging**

Made with the best wheat in the
world and processed in their own
mills, this is one of the very best
quality of pasta, made in Poland
with Italian equipment.

We designed a new logo and all
the packages, which are red for the
large market, and clear for the
gourmet line, with the identification
on a hanging booklet describing
the product.

Packaging Design   ► more

Rules of varying weights
both separate and contain
information.

| Home | Recent | News | Clients | Awards | Contact |

Transportation Graphics

To design architectural or transportation graphics means
mostly to convey the information at the point of decision.
Never before, never after.
How the information is conveyed is a matter of
interpretation, but even then there are quite precise
rules for legibility, distance, and size of type.

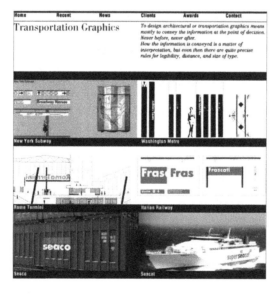

New York Subway   Washington Metro

Rome Termini   Italian Railway

Seaco   Seacat

| Home | Recent | News | Clients | Awards | Contact |

Furniture Design

We design furniture either because
we can not find in the market what
we need for a specific use, or
because we are asked by a furniture
manufacturer to design something
for them. In the first case, we select
the materials; in the second, we
articulate the manufacturer's

resources. The manufacturer
establishes certain parameters
related to his market position and
we work within or beyond them,
to solve the problem at hand.

Casigliani   Acerbis   Bernini

Knoll   Poltrona Frau   Poltroneva

Poltrona frau Teatro   Poltrona Frau CEO   Casigliani

OPPOSITE PAGE BOTTOM:
Headings set in Franklin Gothic
Bold contrast with and
complement Bodoni and Bodoni
Italic, providing Swiss design with
an Italian accent.

82. Employ Vertical and Horizontal Hierarchies

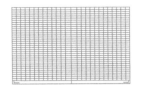

Dividing a page into clearly delineated areas can make stationery, forms, and receipts beautiful as well as utilitarian. Horizontal and vertical grids can coexist successfully, ordering units of information in a way that differs from a more expected approach but contains all of the necessary elements.

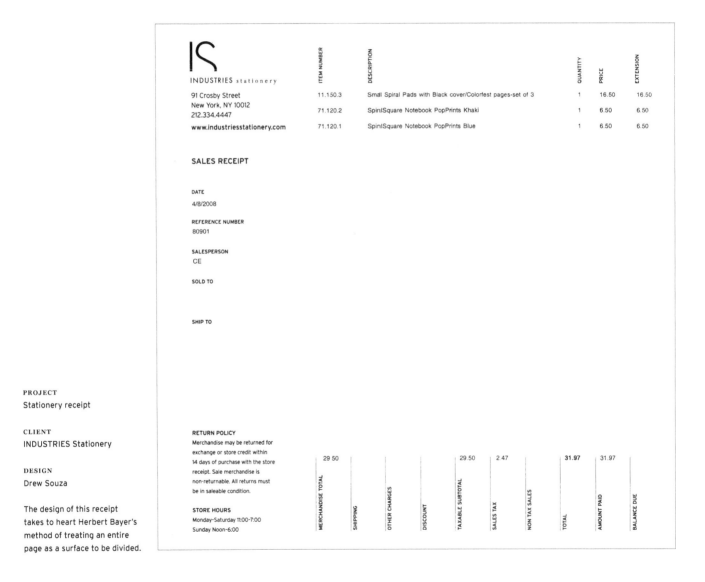

PROJECT
Stationery receipt

CLIENT
INDUSTRIES Stationery

DESIGN
Drew Souza

The design of this receipt takes to heart Herbert Bayer's method of treating an entire page as a surface to be divided.

IS

INDUSTRIES stationery

91 Crosby Street
New York, NY 10012
212.334.4447

www.industriesstationery.com

ITEM NUMBER	DESCRIPTION	QUANTITY	PRICE	EXTENSION
11.150.3	Small Spiral Pads with Black cover/Colorfest pages-set of 3	1	16.50	16.50
71.120.2	SpinlSquare Notebook PopPrints Khaki	1	6.50	6.50
71.120.1	SpinlSquare Notebook PopPrints Blue	1	6.50	6.50

SALES RECEIPT

DATE
4/8/2008

REFERENCE NUMBER
80901

SALESPERSON
CE

SOLD TO

SHIP TO

RETURN POLICY
Merchandise may be returned for exchange or store credit within 14 days of purchase with the store receipt. Sale merchandise is non-returnable. All returns must be in saleable condition.

STORE HOURS
Monday–Saturday 11:00–7:00
Sunday Noon–6:00

MERCHANDISE TOTAL	SHIPPING	OTHER CHARGES	DISCOUNT	TAXABLE SUBTOTAL	SALES TAX	NON TAX SALES	TOTAL	AMOUNT PAID	BALANCE DUE
29.50				29.50	2.47		31.97	31.97	

Employing horizontal and vertical hierarchies in one piece, the stationery system and receipt creates a clearly divided container for many chunks of data. Without the sales information, the receipt is a beautiful abstract composition. With the nuts-and-bolts info, the receipt is a functional system.

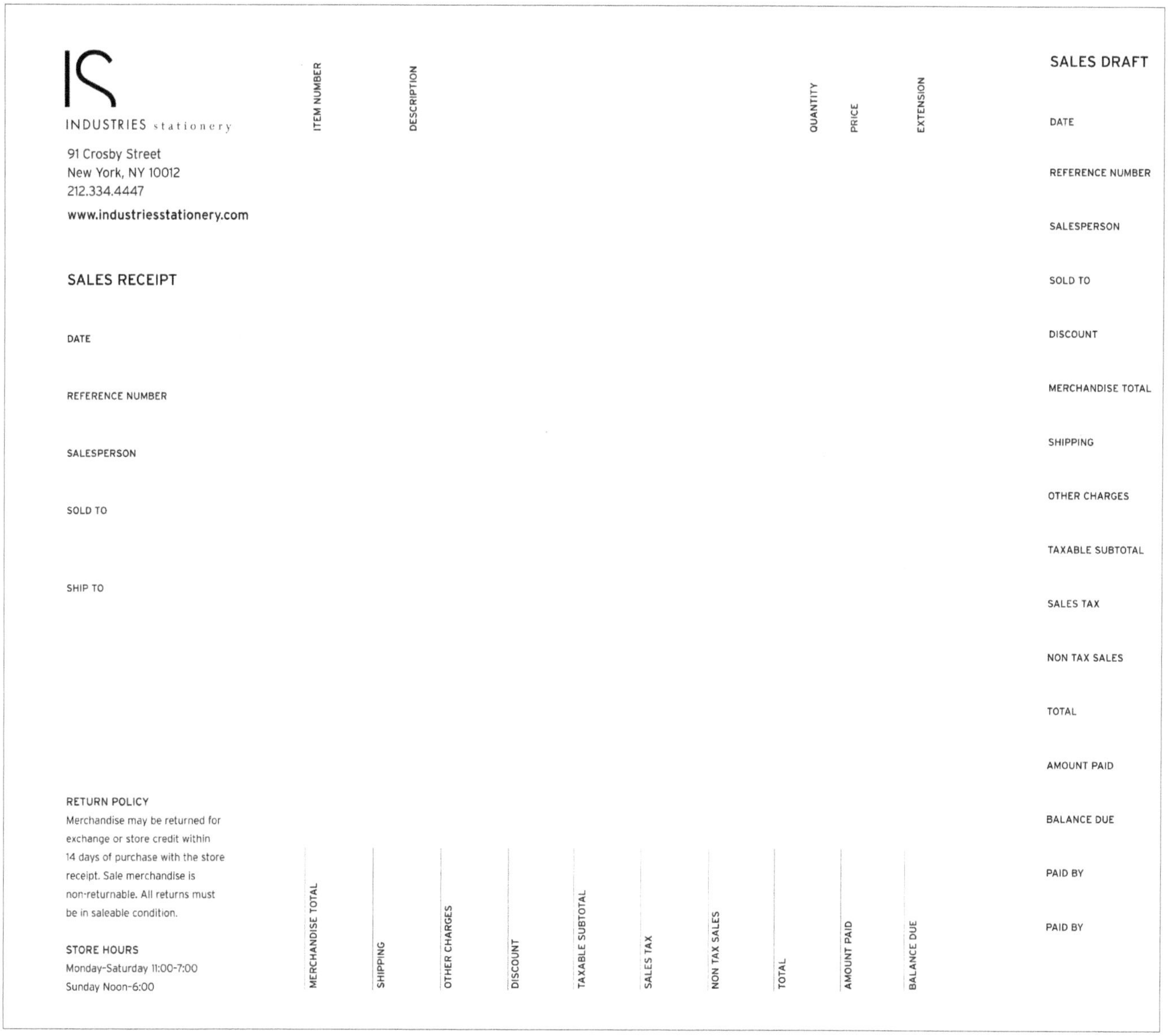

IS

INDUSTRIES stationery

91 Crosby Street
New York, NY 10012
212.334.4447

www.industriesstationery.com

ITEM NUMBER

DESCRIPTION

QUANTITY

PRICE

EXTENSION

SALES DRAFT

DATE

REFERENCE NUMBER

SALESPERSON

SOLD TO

DISCOUNT

MERCHANDISE TOTAL

SHIPPING

OTHER CHARGES

TAXABLE SUBTOTAL

SALES TAX

NON TAX SALES

TOTAL

AMOUNT PAID

BALANCE DUE

PAID BY

PAID BY

SALES RECEIPT

DATE

REFERENCE NUMBER

SALESPERSON

SOLD TO

SHIP TO

RETURN POLICY
Merchandise may be returned for
exchange or store credit within
14 days of purchase with the store
receipt. Sale merchandise is
non-returnable. All returns must
be in saleable condition.

STORE HOURS
Monday–Saturday 11:00–7:00
Sunday Noon–6:00

MERCHANDISE TOTAL

SHIPPING

OTHER CHARGES

DISCOUNT

TAXABLE SUBTOTAL

SALES TAX

NON TAX SALES

TOTAL

AMOUNT PAID

BALANCE DUE

83. Build in a Surprise

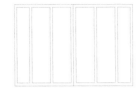

The rigorous underpinnings of a magazine's grid system give it an overall plan, but too much structure can render any publication uninvitingly dull. An unexpected insert, interrupted grid, or use of space keeps readers nimble.

PROJECT
No Man's Land

CLIENT
The Wing

DESIGN
Pentagram

CREATIVE DIRECTION
Emily Oberman

PARTNER
Emily Oberman

SENIOR DESIGNER
Christina Hogan

DESIGNER
Elizabeth Goodspeed

DESIGNER
Joey Petrillo

PROJECT MANAGER
Anna Meixler

The designers mapped out a strong overarching grid but willfully interrupt the system by inserting posters, stickers, and designnng typographic visual puns.

No Man's Land

Feature

Three stacked ramps spring forth from small hills, scattering cars in all four directions. This is the junction between normal L.A. and the parts of L.A. that we always see in movies—the beaches and hills and the very big houses. No doubt my fondness for its ramps has something to do with how they often lead to fun.

This past spring, driving on the 10, preparing to change to the 405, I noticed a light green highway sign with the junction's formal municipal name: the Marilyn Jorgenson Reece Memorial Interchange. Sitting in traffic, I typed the honorific into Google, hoping to learn what a woman must do in order to win a junction for herself. The search results were few—an obituary, some blog posts—and all seemed to draw from the same pool of facts: the first licensed female engineer in California, designed the Santa Monica-San Diego interchange, died at 77 in 2004. Reece was a readymade Woman of the Month, a frequent subject of those bland but nice blurbs that often say more about corporate obligation than the actual women they seek to reward.

Her image results were far more compelling, or at least lent some inadvertent texture to her life. Reece, it seems, was a snappy dresser—a fan of polka-dot blouses and smocks before the era of easy office separates. In one photo of the interchange under construction, she wears a linen skirt suit with a Peter Pan collar. Cranes and pylons rise from the dirt, casting her ballet flats as comically flimsy. It's hard to overstate the strangeness of the photo. The scene looks cribbed from a B-movie—a woman swept up from the pew of her church and set down unharmed at the helm of a job site. Archives are full of such photos of men, surveying big holes in their hard hats and surls. Reece looks more focused than photo-op ready. A gentle breeze ruffles her jacket but scarcely moves her hair-sprayed hair.

Back at my house, I tried to learn more. As the daughter of a working mother and the Spice Girls, I still feel a surge of neoliberal pep at the thought of a female-designed highway junction (or, if you prefer, a she-way interchange). Reece, like most private citizens of her time, barely makes a blip in the searchable

The worst-designed freeways make you wrestle for this thrill; the best, like Reece's, induce it without effort.

news, despite the relative high profile of her work. The day-to-day details of her life and career are less readily available than the same information for any given ex-boyfriend's new girlfriend. I tracked down a colleague from her time at CalTrans who never responded to my interview request. I tweeted at the former Secretary of State who sponsored the light green freeway sign. Deep in the text of a press release, I learned of a $1,000 prize in her name, awarded to a Pomona middle school student for her "Empirical Analysis of Wooden Structures."

It's nice how women cross paths across time but not especially interesting. (I suppose this was the inadvertent message of *The Hours*.) Getting more serious, I filed a public records request. Dredging up some nouns that might pertain to engineering, I wrote: "Any correspondence, designs, photos, or proposals would be useful." The CalTrans librarian emailed me back, asking me to clarify the nature of my interest. The records form acknowledged litigation research but didn't have a box for vague curiosity relating to the life of a former employee. The librarian said she'd see what she could do, but she sounded overworked and confused by my request. I didn't expect to hear from her again.

T
welve miles from downtown and five miles from the sea, I-10 arrives to cross the I-405 at the most beautiful freeway interchange in L.A.—the Santa Monica-San Diego interchange. On a satellite map, these intertwined roads look something like a game of cat's cradle between fingers. The scale, from head-on, is vast and monumental, as striking as the Gateway Arch in repose. In a more pastoral setting, it might have been called land art. In a city defined by its lack of a center, it seems to both enable and pay homage to the sprawl.

72

73

Striving to connect with readers/users/browsers in a dauntingly digital market, publications increasingly vary tactics. Building a community through a print magazine—in this case for a community of women with a shared philosophy—is risky in the digital age. Enter tactile treats such as stickers or a sly fold-out. The poster, which features an accomplished politician, upends clichés of the centerfold by changing the "Miss" of the month from calendar to power girl.

OPPOSITE PAGE AND ABOVE:
A feature story headed with "California's First Female Overpass Designer Created Poetry with Pavement" plays with a little concrete poetry itself by breaking the grid and echoing the shape of overpasses in its typography. (Off the grid comment: the article is as fascinating as it is fun.)

84. Vary Sizes

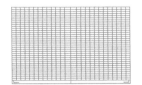

Once an overall grid is determined, there is room to play with scale, space, size, and typography. Springing from the intent and importance of the text, the sizes of images and text can be dynamic or dull, depending on the amount of space the material needs.

PROJECT
What Is Green?

CLIENT
Design within Reach

DESIGN
Design within Reach Design

CREATIVE DIRECTOR
Jennifer Morla

ART DIRECTOR
Michael Sainato

DESIGNERS
Jennifer Morla, Tim Yuan

COPYWRITER
Gwendolyn Horton

"Green-ness" and sustainability are hot (globally warmed) topics, addressed by many companies, including DWR, which has been ecologically conscious for years. The first thirteen pages of this project provide a sense of flow for a story with one related issue and a variety of layouts.

As if it wasn't challenging enough to choose between one color and another, now there's green, which comes loaded with its friends: sustainable, eco-friendly, cradle-to-cradle, recycled, recyclable, small footprint, low-VOC, Greenguard, LEED and FSC-certified. Being a design company, we're encouraged by the increasing number of smart solutions to improve the planet. But we know that not all items fit into every category of ecological perfection. At DWR, we believe in honestly presenting our assortment so you can choose what's best for you. We also believe in selling products that last. We're all doing our part, and we welcome your response when we ask, "What is green?"

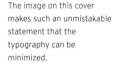

The image on this cover makes such an unmistakable statement that the typography can be minimized.

On the first page, the typography makes a statement—and a lengthy proclamation—filling the entire area of the grid.

In a dramatic shift of scale, the contents page employs a horizontal setup for easy flow. Leaders—rules, for example—direct the eye to the contents. Thumbnails act as quick signals for the content.

These layouts show the shifts in text sizes. Note that one spread has a very wide text measure, which is generally undesirable in text setting. In this case, however, style and message trump normal design precepts. If you want to read about the recycled aluminum chairs, you will. The payoff is that the description of the chairs is very pithy.

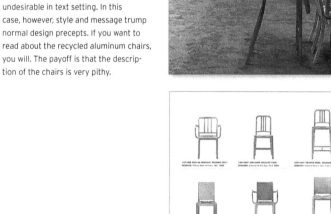

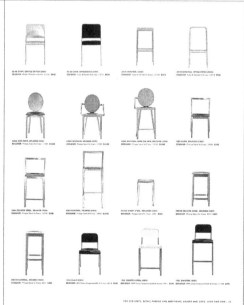

85. Ask What You Can Leave Out

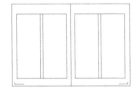

When you have a fabulous photo, don't wreck it. Sometimes the best solution is to make a photo as large as possible, crop very little or avoid cropping altogether, and leave the image free of surprinted type or graphic gimmicks. In other words, relate it to your grid, but, otherwise, let it have its day.

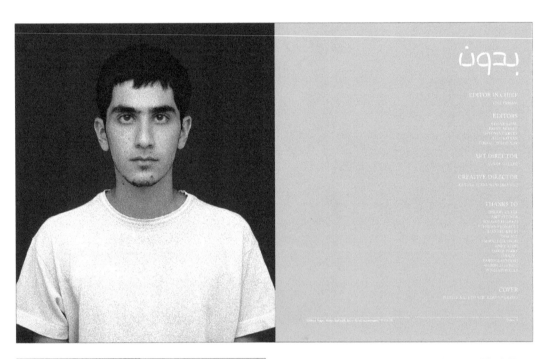

PROJECT
Magazine

CLIENT
Bidoun

CREATIVE DIRECTOR
Ketuta-Alexi Meskhishvili

DESIGNER
Cindy Heller

PHOTOGRAPHERS
Gilbert Hage (portraits) and
Celia Peterson (laborers)

THIS PAGE AND OPPOSITE PAGE: There is no need to do anything to these photos, which speak volumes on their own without graphic devices.

Cautious Radicals

Art and the
invisible majority

By Antonia Carver

At the 2005 Sharjah Biennial, artist Peter Stoffel attempted to get himself framed. Taking inspiration from the notices placed by employers in local newspapers, featuring the names, nationalities, passport numbers and mug shots of ex-employees, Stoffel requested that the biennial's organizing body fire him and announce his occupational demise in the same way. Other potential employers—presumably those organizing another biennial in the UAE—would be hiring him "at their own risk and responsibility." At the same time, the biennial would give Stoffel a recommendation letter "acknowledging his reliable services as an artist," which would be freely available to visitors to the biennial.

The artist's consent turned out to be more potent than the proposed work itself. In keeping with the generally taboo nature of discussion surrounding the rights of the Gulf's underclass of foreign maids and laborers, the biennial organizers declined to go along with Stoffel's ruse. During the exhibition, he showed two panels of text – one a narrative explaining his concern and the outcome, the other a page from a local newspaper with advertisements placed by "sponsors" of Sri Lankans and Pakistanis who had "absconded from duty" and were therefore now outside the employer's responsibility.

For Gulf-based biennial visitors, Stoffel's project was audacious in its attempt to query the region's strict racial and financial hierarchy of workers' rights. (Since the biennial, new legislation has begun to address both the rights of the employee in the transferral of sponsorship and the prerogative of sponsors to impose the customary six-month ban – from the country, and/or from working for a competitor company – on some employees.)

As he describes it, Stoffel attempted to establish a connection between the smallest minority in the UAE, that of the immigrant artist, and the largest, the immigrant laborer. (About two-thirds of the UAE's work force comes from abroad, and about a quarter of all expats work as unskilled laborers for construction companies.) Stoffel concluded that the "two parallel lines of the biennial artist and the Pakistani worker never cross, and that is the paradox of the paradox: that even at an imaginary point, within an artwork, it's impossible to establish a connection."

Despite being the largest segment within the UAE population, the foreign working class remains by and large a faceless majority, known only to the wealthy minority through increasingly balmy local media stories. Every week, the usually self-censoring UAE newspapers detail gory tales of: trafficking, suicide, and rape; of false promises made by dubious foreign employment agencies and mounting debts; of dehydration while working in extreme summertime heat and humidity; of industrial accidents and loan sharks; of depressed, desolate labor camps. The Indian Embassy's official list of its functions includes such grisly tasks as "processing applications received for providing free air tickets by Air India Indian Airlines for transportation of dead bodies of destitute/stranded/absconded Indian nationals."

In many ways, the situation faced by the Gulf's legions of indentured laborers is mirrored worldwide, from Chinese cocklepickers in the UK to Mexican meatpackers in US abattoirs. But the particular state of affairs in Dubai, with its rapid growth and surface profligacy, takes a microscope to what's vaguely termed globalization.

Photos of laborers in Dubai by Celia Peterson, 2005, courtesy of Celia Peterson and unhindsEye

86. Say It with Sidebars

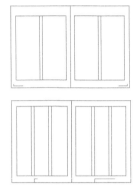

A sidebar, a box that contains a subset story expanding on the main feature, is a common way to set off information that relates to, but needs to be separate from, the main text. Boxes can work within the grid; they function as adjunct information as opposed to interruptions.

A well-organized grid can generally accommodate sidebars, or boxes, in varying sizes: all columns, two columns, or one column.

PROJECT
Nikkei Architecture

CLIENT
Nikkei Architecture magazine

DESIGN
ar

Boxes and charts control technical information in an architectural trade magazine.

労務費動向

[鉄筋・型枠・左官工事]
職人不足で鉄筋、型枠工事は市況上伸

建築工事の施工数は、昨年に比べてマンション、オフィスビルともに微増傾向にあり堅調に推移している。鉄筋工、型枠工の専門工事業者は底堅い工事需要、材料費の値上がり、職人不足などを背景に、安値受注を回避し契約価格の改善に努めており、市況は上伸基調に転じている。今後も首都圏を中心に大型物件を控え、繁忙期の業務ひっ迫が懸念されるため市場には先高感が強い。

一方、左官工事は外壁パネルなどユニットによる仕上げが中心となったことから需要は減少している。業者の廃業が続き、一部に職人が不足する状況が見られるものの、工事費が上昇するまでには至っていない。

建設物価調査会
建築調査部
建築調査一課
総括主任
木谷 彰利

● 工事単価の推移（東京地区）
（資料：建設物価調査会）

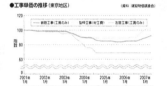

（注）指数は2001年1月を100とし、鉄筋100での単価は、鉄筋工4万円・t、型枠工3060円／m²。左官工事は420円・m²、調査は四半期ごとに実施

● 建物種類別にみた受注動向指数*の推移

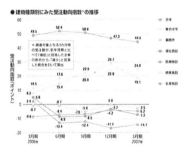

から労務単価も上昇している。アンケート調査では、資材単価ほどではないが、労務単価が値上がりしたとの回答が多かった。

目立つのは「鉄筋工」と「型枠工」。「非常に値上がり」と「やや値上がり」と回答した建設会社の割合を足すと、「鉄筋工」が59.4％、「型枠工」が74.2％を占める。

「専門工事会社も職人の数が足りないので、信用力の低い施工会社の工事は単価を上げても引き受けたがらない」（大手建設会社の担当者）という状況だ。型枠工事では、減少した土木工事から需要が旺盛な建築工事に職人が移っている。

ところが、工事需要が増えても、左官工事は状況が異なる。外壁パネルなどのユニットによる仕上げが多くなってきたことから、需要自体が減少してきた。そのため、鉄筋工や型枠工と同様に職人は減っているものの、工事単価は横ばいが続く。

建設物価調査会の調査によると、鉄鋼・金属類や木材は、世界的な市況の影響を受けて、資材単価の上昇は続く気配。労務単価も、鉄筋や型枠工事では今後の工事需要を見越して、値上げ基調にある。今後も建設コストは上昇しそうだが、建築需要の増減を示す「受注動向指数」は1ポイントだった。　（森下 慎一）

図表の見方
（調査概要は103ページを参照）

▶図表における各期のデータは、特記なき限り、直近1年間（4四半期）の集計値を使用している。例えば、「2007年3月期」は2006年4月~2007年3月、「2006年12月期」は2006年1月~2006年12月を表す。
▶施工物価は設備や外構などの工事費も含む総工費（消費税込み）を比近望実へ速遠移で除した値で、建設会社の受注設計への価格。

● 建物種類別にみた施工単価の構成比の推移

集合住宅

平均値 54.5　55.4　56.8　58.2　59.7（万円／坪）

事務所

平均値 57.7　58.2　59.9　61.6　64.3（万円／坪）

福祉施設

平均値 61.1　61.6　61.9　61.1　61.4（万円／坪）

医療施設

平均値 68.9　71.3　71.7　72.4　74.6（万円／坪）

商業施設

平均値 51.5　50.5　52.4　50.6　53.0（万円／坪）

生産施設

平均値 37.9　39.2　41.4　43.5　44.8（万円／坪）

Often, the boxes or sidebars function as discrete designs, but they always relate graphically to the main story by using common colors, typefaces, or rules.

87. Observe Masters

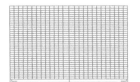

Making a close study of the work of graphic pathfinders can result in layouts that are similar to the work of the masters and yet offer fresh interpretations of grid systems.

Layouts designed as an homage, with echoes of original Swiss masters, can have a fresh feeling thanks to a deep and basic understanding of the overall precepts rather than a slavish copying of specific elements.

PROJECT
étapes: magazine

CLIENT
Pyramyd/*étapes:* magazine

DESIGN
Anna Tunick

A spread from a magazine article about the designer Josef Müller-Brockmann is a trove of grid basics, from the chronology of his life to book jackets and seminal images.

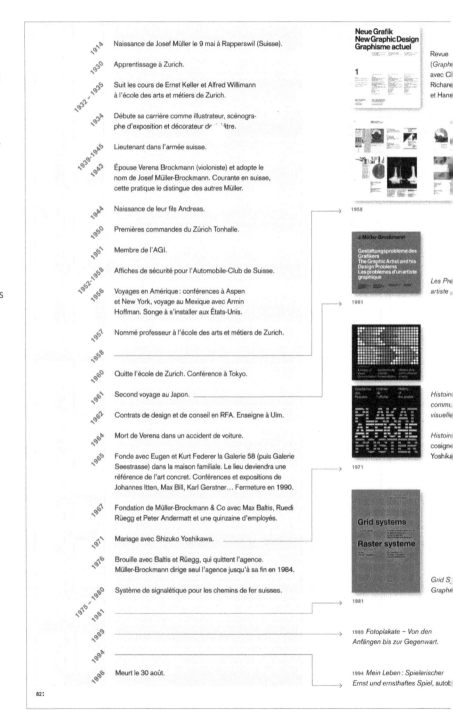

> *Plus la composition
> des éléments visuels est
> stricte et rigoureuse, sur la
> surface dont on dispose,
> plus l'idée du thème peut
> se manifester avec effi-
> cacité. Plus les éléments
> visuels sont anonymes et
> objectifs, mieux ils affirment
> leur authenticité et ont dès
> lors pour fonction de servir
> uniquement la réalisation
> graphique. Cette tendance
> est conforme à la méthode
> géométrique. Texte, photo,
> désignation des objets,
> sigles, emblèmes et
> couleurs en sont les
> instruments accessoires
> qui se subordonnent d'eux-
> mêmes au système des
> éléments, remplissent, dans
> la surface, elle-même créa-
> trice d'espace, d'image et
> d'efficacité, leur mission
> informative. On entend
> souvent dire, mais c'est là
> une opinion erronée, que
> cette méthode empêche
> l'individualité et la perso-
> nnalité du créateur de
> s'exprimer.*

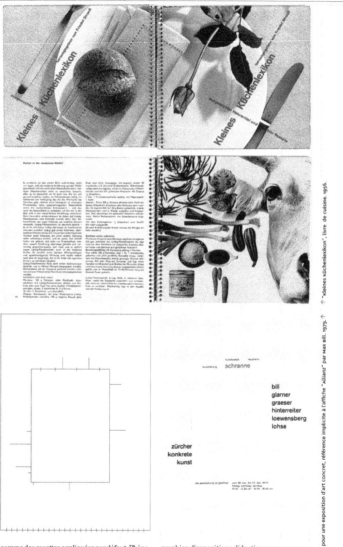

comme des recettes appliquées par défaut. Phéno-
mène encore appuyé par la structure des logiciels
de PAO, qui recourent au gabarit comme point
de départ à l'édition de tout document. L'efficacité radicale de l'abstraction sera quant à elle
escamotée au profit d'effets plus spectaculaires
et moins préoccupés.

ceci dit, au boulot

Depuis ses débuts de scénographe, Müller-
Brockmann a réalisé un grand nombre de travaux,
seul ou à la tête de son agence (1965-1984): scéno-

graphies d'expositions didactiques ou commer-
ciales, identité, communication et édition (brochures, publicités et stands) d'entreprises pour
des fabricants de carton (L + C: lithographie
et cartonnage, 1954 et 1955), de machines-outils
(Elmag, 1954), de machines à écrire (Addo AG,
1960) pour des fournisseurs de savon (CWS,
1958) de produits alimentaires (Nestlé, de 1956 à
1960) ou pour la chaîne de magasins néerlandais
Bijenkorf (1960). En 1962, il décroche d'importants
contrats auprès d'entreprises allemandes: Max
Weishaupt (systèmes de chauffage) et Rosenthal

88. Get Close; Crop

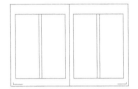

Grids can overwhelm a project and become an overriding force, or they can be subtle underpinnings that, in the words of one author, contribute "a layout that is elegant, logical, and never intrusive."

Also see page
18

The strength of the cover lies in its simplicity and its focus on the artist and his work. Note the overall layout of a book jacket, prior to folding and wrapping around the bound book.

PROJECT
Chuck Close | Work

CLIENT
Prestel Publishing

DESIGN
Mark Melnick

An unobtrusive design elegantly presents big-personality paintings.

Images on the endpapers move from the artist at work to the artist in profile.

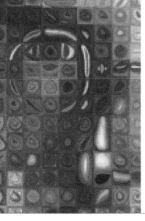

CHUCK CLOSE | WORK

CHRISTOPHER FINCH

Chapter 5.

PRISMATIC GRIDS

THIS PAGE TOP LEFT: For the title page spread, an enlargement of the eye captures the artist, while the title is, again, simple.

THIS PAGE TOP RIGHT: Here, the obvious grid is in the subject matter and its title.

THIS PAGE TWO MIDDLE IMAGES: Again, the grid of the subject matter reigns supreme.

89. Change Boundaries

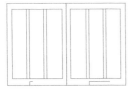

Auxiliary material can be as beautiful as the main text—and can change the boundaries between primary and supporting material. Back matter, that is the material at the end of a book or catalog such as appendixes, timelines, notes, bibliography, and index, can be complex. Details throughout a project define a thorough design, including a clear and handsome design for pages that are sometimes less noticed.

PROJECT
Exhibition Catalog
Show Me Thai

CLIENT
Office of Contemporary
Art and Culture, Ministry
of Culture, Thailand

DESIGN
Practical Studio/Thailand

DESIGN DIRECTOR
Santi Lawrachawee

GRAPHIC DESIGNERS
Ekaluck Peanpanawate
Montchai Suntives

An exhibition catalog contains a number of useful grids, with an especially interesting treatment of the list of participants.

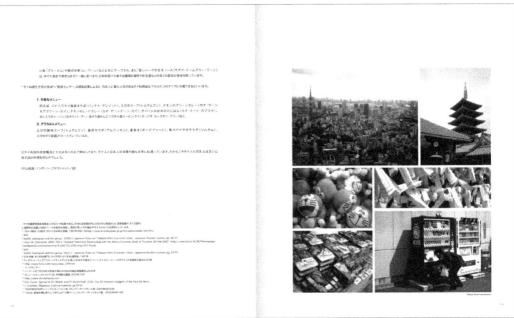

OPPOSITE PAGE TOP: A spare photo contrasts with a highly gridded page.

OPPOSITE PAGE BOTTOM: On the left page, the text measure, or width of the set type, is the same as the width of two images combined. Wide measures are generally not encouraged, but the layout works.

A three-column grid and a chart artfully provide a sense of order.

The tabular material on the spread is clear, handsome, and interesting, with an ornamental motif that lends texture.

90. Trust the Module

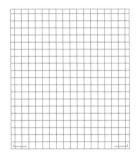

Also see page
29

The near-impossible can be designed if you break down the steps. Color can create shapes and spaces. A receding color is, essentially, a negative space. A dominant color becomes part of the foreground. Plot out how various overlaps can create another dimension for the entire piece. Allow yourself to experiment with layers and shapes. The result may epitomize the golden ratio.

The ultimate grid, a puzzle, gets depth via the skilled hands of Marian Bantjes, who likes "to push those rules that I know and try and make something that is making me uncomfortable, but in a good way."

PROJECT
Cover for the Puzzle
Special of *The Guardian's G2*

CLIENT
The Guardian Media Group

DESIGN
Marian Bantjes

This cover for the puzzle issue of *G2*, uses layers of lines and squares.

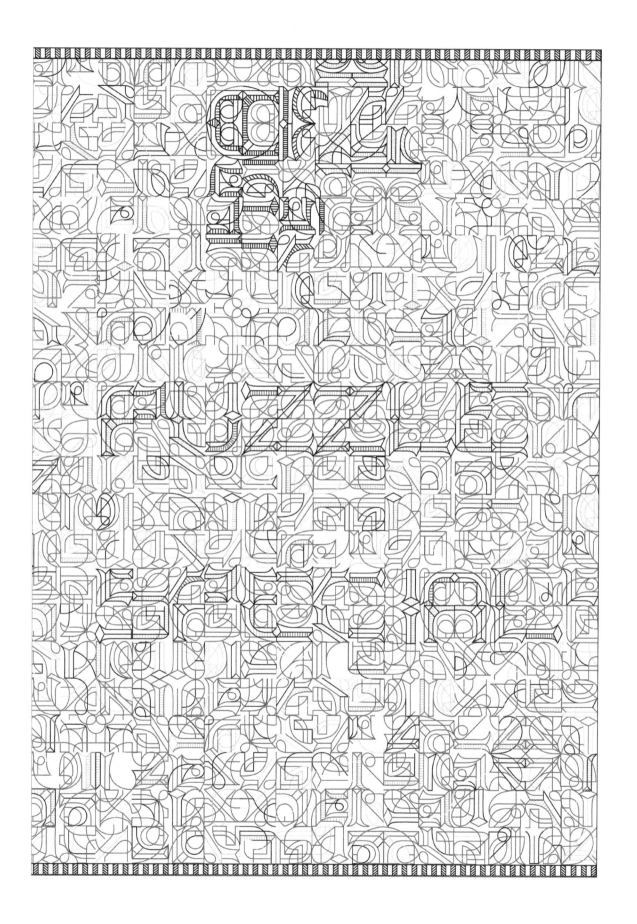

91. Work in Multiple Dimensions

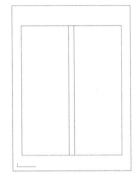

Although most layouts using grids are flat, whether on a printed page or a computer screen, they need to capture the dimensions of the work they illuminate. A brochure can be produced in a format other than a book or booklet or flat page. Conceived three-dimensionally but designed as a flat piece, brochures with accordion or barrel folds can give additional depth to a piece.

PROJECT
Exhibit Catalog for Stuck, an art exhibit featuring collages

CLIENT
Molloy College

GALLERY DIRECTOR
Dr. Yolande Trincere

CURATOR
Suzanne Dell'Orto

DESIGNER
Suzanne Dell'Orto

Cleverly conceived as a fold-out piece, this brochure for an exhibit of collages evokes some of the playful art in the gallery show.

stuck
THE INFLUENCE OF COLLAGE ON 21ST CENTURY ARTISTS

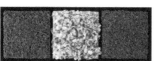

A traditional grid provides a spine for the various quirky collages in an exhibit. The straight-faced (literally) treatment of the type and well-planned space work together to frame the lively art. The top image shows the exterior of the piece; the bottom image is the interior. Printed on two sides, the accordion-folded brochure takes on a three-dimensional air.

OPPOSITE PAGE: One of the four panels on the interior side of the brochure shows a deconstructed art history book, situated tidily in one of the columns. The type combination of the stately Gill Sans and the jocular P. T. Barnum calls to mind the juxtaposition of elements found in collages.

92. Think Globally

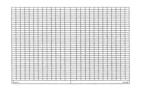

The framework of the grid can support many superimposed elements. Keep in mind that

- informational typography needs to be readable
- open space is crucial to the success of a composition
- it is not necessary to fill every pixel or pica

On the most literal level, layers can intrigue the reader. On a deeper level, they are an invitation to mull over combinations of elements.

Achieving Sustainable
Development in the 21st Century

The Earth Institute
AT COLUMBIA UNIVERSITY

PROJECT
Branding posters

CLIENT
Earth Institute at
Columbia University

CREATIVE DIRECTOR
Mark Inglis

DESIGNER
John Stislow

Illustrator
Mark Inglis

Layered photos, line illustrations, and icons add depth and imply levels of meaning, as well as interest, in this project.

Carbon, Climate
and the Race
for New Energy
Technology

THIS PAGE BOTH IMAGES: Layering adds dimension but keeps the message clear in this cover and inside spread of a brochure.

Elements superimposed over a photo and the use of transparent areas of color enhance the three columns of typography.

Typography is only the top layer on a poster for a talk about complex health issues.

93. Support All Platforms

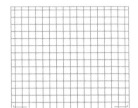

Fields and colors can deliver information in byte-size containers. Occasionally, using the metaphor of a client's name can help determine colors and movement. Categories of information can be located in boxes, or neighborhoods, with navigation bars all around the site. In a densely populated site, results can be like a metropolis: gridded but busy, but sometimes a dizzying ride is just the ticket.

Black headline bars and taxi-yellow boxes form the signature look of Design Taxi.

PROJECT
Website

CLIENT
Design Taxi

DESIGN
Design Taxi

DESIGN DIRECTOR
Alex Goh

The website for Design Taxi, which hails from Singapore, shuttles the user from one grid to the next, in a high-density digitopolis loaded with frames, rules, boxes, guides, colors, shades, links, and searches—but no Starbucks.

With a lot of offerings, the site controls information through framed fields and various shades of gray. The ride can be a bit bumpy, at times. Finding the title that corresponds to the html can be tricky.

Typography is designed for functionality, rather than finesse, for constant and easy updating.

94. Stagger It

Based on a module, shapes can be skewed, repeated, or deleted to keep an overall identity system fresh and forward thinking.

SANTA EULALIA
175 ANIVERSARIO
1843—2018

PROJECT
Santa Eulalia
Identity

CLIENT
Santa Eulalia

DESIGN
Mario Eskenazi Studio

DESIGNER
Mario Eskenazi

For Santa Eulalia, a multibrand luxury fashion retail store from Barcelona, the design agency based the identity on a pattern that suggests an X. (The X is the symbol for Santa Eulalia in Catalunya, who was crucified by the Romans on a cross of the same shape.)

Over the years since the original 2006 identity design, Mario Eskenazi Studio has been adding different elements (numbers and pictograms) based on the original pattern.

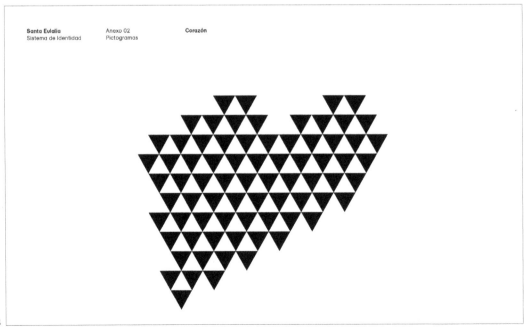

Santa Eulalia
Sistema de Identidad   Anexo 02
                             Pictogramas   Corazón

The stylized X pattern of the
Santa Eulalia identity is offset by a
straightforward serif and clean grid
for the brand name and dates and
cover of the identity system

Expansion of the identity's basic
patterns become ever more complex
grids, while still implying an X.

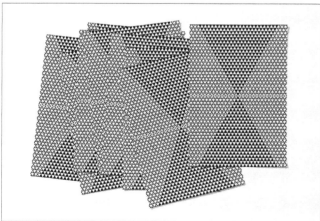

95. Super Size It

Supergraphics are large-scale examples of typographic rules to live by.

- Play sizes, weights, and color values against each other to create dynamic layouts.

- Consider the dimensions of the letterforms.
- Take into account the dynamics; compared to type on a page, type that moves requires extra letterspacing to remain legible

PROJECT
Bloomberg Dynamic
Digital Displays

CLIENT
Bloomberg LLP

DESIGN
Pentagram, New York

**ART DIRECTOR/DESIGNER,
ENVIRONMENTAL GRAPHICS**
Paula Scher

**ART DIRECTOR/DESIGNER,
DYNAMIC DISPLAYS**
Lisa Strausfeld

DESIGNERS
Jiae Kim, Andrew Freeman
Rion Byrd

PROJECT ARCHITECTS
STUDIOS Architecture

PROJECT PHOTOGRAPHY
Peter Mauss/Esto

Big, bold supergraphics on electronic displays, with moving messages, couple information with brand.

BOTH PAGES: The supergraphics combine substance, statistics and style.

The dynamic signs on the four horizontal panels change colors; the sizes of type and colors of the letters vary with the message, creating a point of view as well as data points.

96. Move the Modules

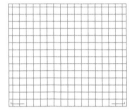

On the web, as in print, equal modules provide a versatile way to compartmentalize content, including areas for videos that help animate the site.

FLUIDITY

In the brave new world of interactive design, a topic worth mentioning is fluid grids and layouts. What do you do when paper size is no longer relevant? Do you stick to arbitrary dimensions and center the layout on the screen? Or do you create layouts that are fluid—that reconfigure themselves for different screen sizes? Web experts may prefer the latter, but keep in mind that the technical aspects of setting up such layouts are more complex.

PROJECT
Website

CLIENT
Earth Institute at
Columbia University

CREATIVE DIRECTOR
Mark Inglis

DESIGN
Sunghee Kim, John Stislow

Modular sections allow the presentation of rich and varied information.

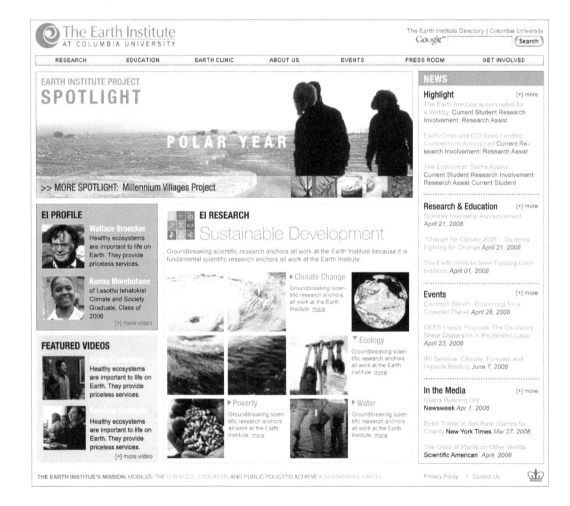

THIS PAGE AND OPPOSITE PAGE:
Designed to appear below the
main navigation bar, modules on
a home page can be combined
into versatile configurations.

- All modules across the width
  can be used as a masthead,
  links included.
- A single module can present
  one subject.
- Two modules together can
  form a sidebar.
- Modules on the side of the
  page can form a long vertical
  column to serve as a bulletin
  board for news and events.
- Modules can contain videos.

Navigating away from the home
page can provide a reader with
a deeper reading experience.

Subpages use a modular
organization and diverge
slightly into a horizontal
hierarchy, depending on the
needs of the information.

97. Play to Your Strengths

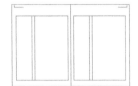

Many fine designers claim to work without using grids. Yet their designs are spacious, textured, and heroic. Without consciously doing so, most designers adhere to the basic tenets of good design to enhance the material and make it clear.

Also see page
29

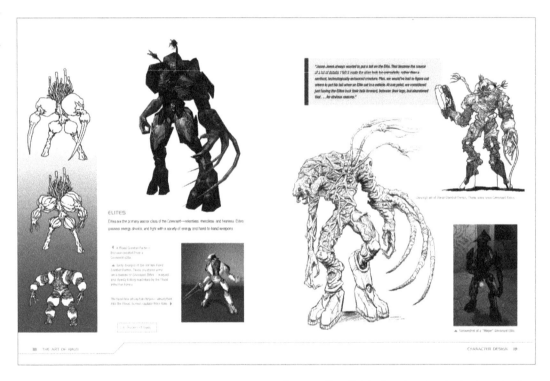

Numerous silhouetted drawings show character development and hint at the animation in the game. Horizontal rules ground the figures, with a downward jog giving movement to the spread.

PROJECT
The Art of Halo

CLIENT
Random House

DESIGN
Liney Li

Heroes become doubly immortal in this book featuring the art of Halo, the game.

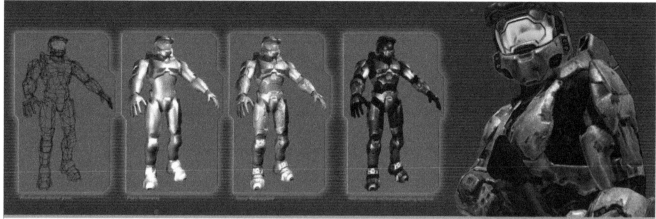

▲ The evolution of Master Chief from wire frame, rendering, and finally clad in his battle armor.

The collaborative process at Bungie wasn't confined to the *Halo* team. There were several Bungie artists and programmers working on other titles during the various stages of *Halo*'s development. "I didn't do a lot on *Halo*—I was assigned to a team working on a different project," said character artist Juan Ramirez. "But most of us would weigh in on what we saw. I like monsters and animals and creatures—plus I'm a sculptor, so I did some sculpture designs of the early Elite.

"When I came on, I wasn't really a 'computer guy'—I was more into comics, film, that kind of thing. I try and apply that to my work here—to look at our games as more than just games. Better games equals better entertainment. A lot of that is sold through character design."

▲ One of the public's first looks at Halo came in the November, 1999 issue of Computer Gaming World; the evolution of Master Chief from wire frame, rendering, and finally clad in his battle armor.

THE MASTER CHIEF

Seven feet tall, and clad in fearsome MJOLNIR Mark V battle armor, the warrior known as the Master Chief is a product of the SPARTAN Project. Trained in the art of war since childhood, he may well hold the fate of the human race in his hands.

MARCUS LEHTO, ART DIRECTOR: *"At first, Rob [artist Robt. McLees] and I were the only artists working on Halo. After that we hired Shek [artist Shi Kai Wang], who's just great from the conceptual standpoint. I'd do a preliminary version of something, then Shek would work from that, and really enhance the concept.*

"The Master Chief design sketch that really took hold came after heavy collaboration with Shi Kai. One of his sketches—this kind of manga-influenced piece, with ammo bandoliers across his chest, and a big bladed weapon on his back—really caught our imagination.

"Unfortunately, when we got that version into model form, he looked a little too slender, almost effeminate. So, I took the design and tried to make it look more like a modern tank. That's how we got to the Master Chief that appears in the game."

The Spartan was huge, easily seven feet tall. Encased in pearlescent green battle armor, the man looked like a figure from mythology—otherworldly and terrifying. Master Chief SPARTAN-117 stepped from the tube and surveyed the cryo bag. The mirrored visor on his helmet made him all the more fearsome, a faceless, impassive soldier built for destruction and death.

The technician felt a pang of fear—and sorrow for the Covenant troops that would have to face this Spartan in combat.

—Excerpt from *Halo: The Flood* by William C. Dietz, the novelization of the game.

An integral part of creating a good story is the creation of believable and interesting characters. Bungie's 3-D modelers craft designs of the various characters that appear in-game, which must then be "textured"—telling the game engine how light and shadow react with the model. From there, the models must be rigged so they can be animated. Overlap is vital, particularly among modelers and animators," says animator William O'Brien. "We depend on each other for the final product to work—and none of us can settle. We always have to up it a notch."

"Our job is to bring the characters to life in the game," said Nathan Walpole, animation lead for Halo 2. "It's what we're best at. We don't use motion capture—most of us are traditional 2-D animators, so we prefer to hand-key animation. Motion capture just looks so bad when it's done poorly. We have more control over hand-keyed animation, and can produce results faster than by editing mocap."

Crafting the animations that bring life to the game characters is a painstaking process. "Usually, we start with a thumbnail sketch to build a look or feel," explained Walpole. "Then you apply it to the 3-D model and work out the timing."

Sometimes the timings are off, it's hilarious," adds animator Mike Budd. "Everyone comes over and has a good laugh. Working together like we do keeps us fresh. There's such a variety of characters—human and alien. And you work on them in a matter of weeks. You're always working on something new and interesting."

▲ A pair of Grunts prepare to engage the viewer. Screen capture from Halo.

To design the characters' motions, the animators study virtually any source of movement for inspiration—though this can create some challenges for animator William O'Brien. "Just being surrounded by people with good senses of humor makes it easier to do your job. The drawback is, I've always had my own office. To animate a character, I often act out motions and movements; this gives you a sense of what muscle and bone actually do. But now, I have an audience. 'Key, look at the crazy stuff Bill's doing now!' So now I tend to do that kind of work on video, in private."

◄ Opposite page: Captions reverted for illustrations 1, 2, 3, and 4.

The book combines classic with stylized futuristic typography. Captions are differentiated from the text through the use of a different color, blue. Rules and directionals (arrows and words such as "left" and "right") appear in an orange accent color.

Screened areas along the side of the page create sidebars and set one character off from another.

98. Be Flexible

S ometimes, the formal aspects of design, such as ample margins, readable type, and correct italics, need to be tossed aside. In certain contexts, a "wrong" design can be right. If a communication is meant to be provocative or visionary, a solution that breaks the rules can be perfect.

Design and the Elastic Mind

RIGHT: Elastic.
Layered. Intriguing.

PROJECT
Design and the Elastic Mind

CLIENT
Museum of Modern Art

DESIGN
Irma Boom, the Netherlands

COVER TYPE
Daniël Maarleveld

In this catalog for the exhibit "Design and the Elastic Mind," the designer eschews the traditional formal aspects of design. The result is as provocative— and, sometimes, as irritating— as the show.

Foreword

With Design and the Elastic Mind, The Museum of Modern Art once again ventures into the field of experimental design, where innovation, functionality, aesthetics, and a deep knowledge of the human condition combine to create outstanding artifacts. MoMA has always been an advocate of design as the foremost example of modern art's ability to permeate everyday life, and several exhibitions in the history of the Museum have attempted to define major shifts in culture and behavior as represented by the objects that facilitate and signify them. Shows like Italy: The New Domestic Landscape (1972), Designs for Independent Living (1988), Mutant Materials in Contemporary Design (1995), and Workspheres (2001), to name just a few, highlighted one of design's most fundamental roles: the translation of scientific and technological revolutions into approachable objects that change people's lives and, as a consequence, the world. Design is a bridge between the abstraction of research and the tangible requirements of real life.

The state of design is strong. In this era of fast-paced innovation, designers are becoming more and more integral to the evolution of society, and design has become a paragon for a constructive and effective synthesis of thought and action. Indeed, in the past few decades, people have coped with dramatic changes in several long-standing relationships—for instance, with time, space, information, and individuality. We must contend with abrupt changes in scale, distance, and pace, and our minds and bodies need to adapt to acquire the elasticity necessary to synthesize such abundance. Designers have contributed thoughtful concepts that can provide guidance and ease as science and technology proceed in their evolution. Design not only greatly benefits business, by adding value to its products, but it also influences policy and research without ever reneging its poietic, nonideological nature—and without renouncing beauty, efficiency, vision, and sensibility, the traits that MoMA curators have privileged in selecting examples for exhibition and for the Museum's collection.

Design and the Elastic Mind celebrates creators from all over the globe—their visions, dreams, and admonitions. It comprises more than two hundred design objects and concepts that marry the most advanced scientific research with the most attentive consideration of human limitations, habits, and aspirations. The objects range from

Tiny margins, mutant type, disappearing page numbers, and running feet (or footers) are all part of a plan to intrigue, provoke, and mirror the subject matter.

sometimes for hours, other times for minutes, using means of communication ranging from the most encrypted and syncopated to the most discursive and old-fashioned, such as talking face-to-face—or better, since even this could happen virtually, let's say nose-to-nose, at least until smells are translated into digital code and transferred to remote stations. We isolate ourselves in the middle of crowds within individual bubbles of technology, or sit alone at our computers to tune into communities of like-minded souls or to access information about esoteric topics.

Over the past twenty-five years, under the influence of such milestones as the introduction of the personal computer, the Internet, and wireless technology, we have experienced dramatic changes in several mainstays of our existence, especially our rapport with time, space, the physical nature of objects, and our own essence as individuals. In order to embrace these new degrees of freedom, whole categories of products and services have been born, from the first clocks with mechanical time-zone crowns to the most recent devices that use the Global Positioning System (GPS) to automatically update the time the moment you enter a new zone. Our options when it comes to the purchase of such products and services have multiplied, often with an emphasis on speed and automation (so much so that good old-fashioned cash and personalized transactions—the option of talking to a real person—now carry the cachet of luxury). Our mobility has increased along with our ability to communicate, and so has our capacity to influence the market with direct feedback, making us all into arbiters and opinion makers. Our idea of privacy and private property has evolved in unexpected ways, opening the door

top: James Powderly, Evan Roth, Theo Watson, and HELL. Graffiti Research Lab. L.A.S.E.R. Tag. Prototype. 2007. 60 mW green laser, digital projector, camera, and custom GNU software (L.A.S.E.R. Tag V1.0, using OpenFrameworks)

New forms of communication transcend scale and express a yearning to share opinions and information. This project simulates writing on a building. A camera tracks the beam pointer of a laser pointer and software transmits the action to a very powerful projector.

17 bottom: James Powderly, Evan Roth, Theo Watson, DASK, FOXY LADY, and BENNETT4SENATE. Graffiti Research Lab. L.A.S.E.R. Tag graffiti projection system. Prototype. 2007. 60 mW green laser, digital projector, camera, custom GNU software (L.A.S.E.R. Tag V1.0, using OpenFrameworks), and mobile broadcast unit

for debates ranging from the value of copyright to the fear of ubiquitous surveillance.[2] Software glitches aside, we are free to journey through virtual-world platforms on the Internet. In fact, for the youngest users there is almost no difference between the world contained in the computer screen and real life, to the point that some digital metaphors, like video games, can travel backward into the physical world: At least one company, called area/code, stages "video" games on a large scale, in which real people in the roles of, say, Pac Man play out the games on city streets using mobile phones and other devices.

Design and the Elastic Mind considers these changes in behavior and need. It highlights current examples of successful design translations of disruptive scientific and technological innovations, and reflects on how the figure of the designer is changing from form giver to fundamental interpreter of an extraordinarily dynamic reality. Leading up to this volume and exhibition, in the fall of 2006 The Museum of Modern Art and the science publication Seed launched a monthly salon to bring together scientists, designers, and architects to present their work and ideas to each other. Among them were Benjamin Aranda and Chris Lasch, whose presentation immediately following such a giant of the history of science as Benoit Mandelbrot was nothing short of heroic, science photographer Felice Frankel, physicist Keith Schwab, and computational design innovator Ben Fry, to name just a few.[3] Indeed, many of the designers featured in this book are engaged in exchanges with scientists, including Michael Burton and Christopher Woebken, whose work is influenced by nanophysicist Richard A. L. Jones; Elio Caccavale, whose interlocutor is Armand Marie Leroi, a biologist from the Imperial

Images are lost in the binding, which is normally verboten in a less-elastic project.

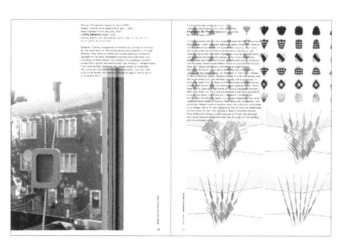

Art superimposed over type is laid out with a purpose in this book.

Ghosted bars containing text surprint images.

99. Follow Your Heart

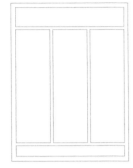

Determing the grid for a project is like working a puzzle. Sometimes, the concept itself is a puzzle, both in its subject matter and its charge to convey an important idea. Such a meaningful cause can inspire strong work that communicates a valuable message and feeds heart and soul—a big factor in devising work that reflects love for and interpretation of the communication necessary to engage an audience.

PROJECT
Conundrum

DESIGNER
Dayna Iphill,
New York City College
of Technology, 2018

PROFESSOR
Douglas Davis

Conundrum is an organization that helps raise autism awareness. Because the developmental disorder can be confusing to those who are unaware of what autism is, the design presents the idea as a typographical puzzle. The Conundrum Identity system includes the logo, posters, brochures, website, and social media platforms.

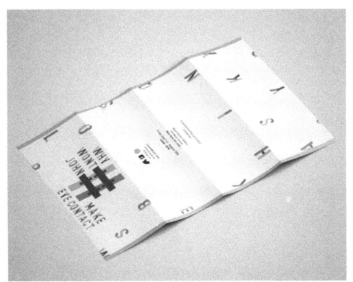

THIS PAGE: Balancing Conundrum's puzzle logo/lockup, the brochure employs a clear two-column grid that guides readers. Blue vertical rules recur throughout components.

OPPOSITE PAGE: Echoing the brochure, blue rules head the website. Screens are simplied for social media. Subway and bus posters incorporate text into the logo's puzzle.

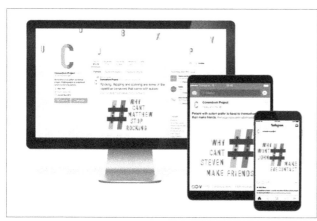

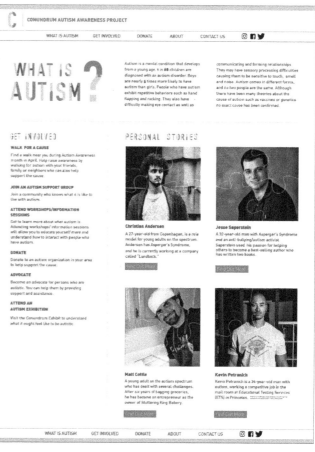

100. Ignore the Rules

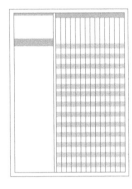

Covering layout essentials such as typography, space, and color, this book shows a range of communications that use grid systems. As noted earlier, the primary rule is to make certain your grid system relates the design to the material. Make the hierarchy of information clear, paying attention to typography, whether it's classical and clear or a lively mix of different faces and weights. In layout, craft counts. Work in balance and with consistency.

Learn from the nuggets in this book, but think for yourself. As crucial as it is to know formal principles, it's also necessary to break the rules occasionally. No book or site can teach everything. Observe. Ask questions. Collaborate. Learn from others. Request help if necessary. Keep a sense of humor. Be flexible and persistent. Practice. Keep practicing. The success of a design depends on reiteration while enjoying in the process. Feel free to ask me questions.

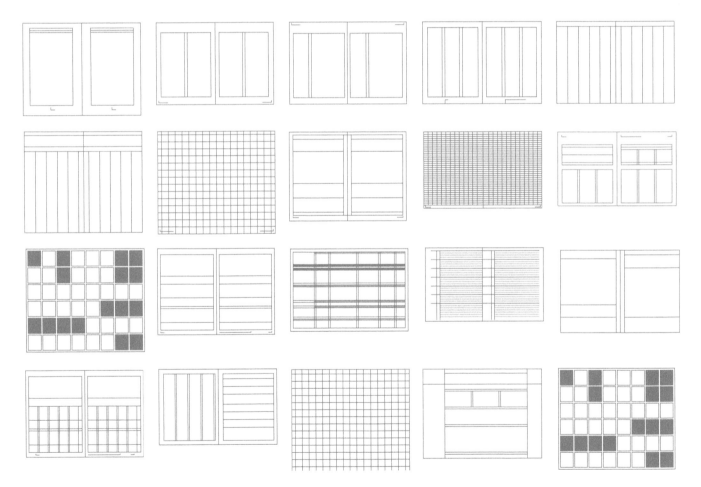

"Don't be governed by the grid, govern the grid. A grid is like a lion cage—if the trainer stays too long it gets eaten up. You have to know when to leave the cage—you have to know when to leave the grid. —MASSIMO VIGNELLI

"The grid system is an aid, not a guarantee. It permits a number of possible uses and each designer can look for a solution appropriate to his personal style. But one must learn how to use the grid; it is an art that requires practice."

—JOSEF MULLER-BROCKMANN

"A grid is like underwear, you wear it but it's not to be exposed."

—MASSIMO VIGNELLI

Glossary

A SELECTION OF TERMS USED THROUGHOUT THE PRINCIPLES

Back Matter—Supportive material that is not part of the text and can includes items such as the appendix, notes, bibliography, glossary, and index.

CMYK—Cyan, magenta, yellow, and black (K), the four colors used in full-color process printing.

Column—A vertical container that holds type or images. Text in a column is measured horizontally.

Deck—Similar to a tagline

Flush Left—Text that is aligned (straight) on the left margin, with a right margin of varied—but not too greatly varied—widths. Uneven margins are also called "ragged."

Flush Right—Text that is aligned (straight) on the right margin, with a left margin of varied widths.

Font—Digitally, a font is a single style of one typeface and is used in typesetting. Font is often used interchangeably (and incorrectly) with typeface. Think of font as production and typeface as design in hot metal, a complete assortment of type characters of one face and size.

Front Matter—In a book, copy preceding the main text, such as title page, copyright, and contents.

JPEG—Acronym for Joint Photographic Experts Group. A compression format used for images used on the Internet and not suitable for traditional printing.

Justify—To align text on both left and right margins of a column.

Layout—The arrangement of elements such as type and visuals on a page or screen.

Masthead—A list of people involved with a publication, along with their job titles. A masthead also contains information about the publication.

Negative Space—The space between shapes and masses, used mostly in referring to fine art, sculpture, or music.

Orphan—The first or last line of a paragraph that has become separated from the rest of its paragraph and is positioned at the bottom or top of a page or column, alone.

Perfect Binding—An adhesive binding technique. Edges of printing signatures are glued, then covered. The covered book is then trimmed cleanly on the remaining three sides.

Pica—A unit of measurement used for type. A pica is equal to 12 points. In Postscript printers, a pica is $\frac{1}{6}$th of an inch.

Pixel—A square dot that represents the smallest unit displayed on a computer screen. (Stands for picture elements).

Point—A unit of measurement in typography. There are 12 points in a pica and approximately 72 points to the inch

RGB—Red, green, blue, the colors on computer monitors. Photoshop provides images in RGB when scanning. For most web offset printing, images must be printed as CMYK tiffs.

Running Head—Headings at the tops of pages that indicate the section and locations of materials. A running head can contain a page number, or folio. A running foot is the same element positioned at the page foot.

Running Text—Solid copy, normally not interrupted by headings, tables, illustrations, etc.

Saddle Stitched—Binding with wires, similar to staples.

Saturated—A color that contains little gray; an intense color. As saturation increases, the amount of gray decreases.

Silhouette—An image where the background has been eliminated, leaving only a figure or object.

Sink—Also called sinkage. The distance down from the topmost element on a page.

Spec—Formally called specification. Instructions for typesetting, now most often determined using the style sheets function of page layout programs.

Surprint—To lay down one ink on top of another.

Tagline—A slogan or a few lines extracted from text.

TIFF—Acronym for Tagged Image File Format. A format for electronically storing and transmitting bitmapped, grayscale, and color images. TIFF is the format desired for traditional printing.

Typeface—A type design with specific characteristics. Typefaces can have characteristics in common. One typeface can include designs for italic, bold, small caps, and different weights. The typeface is the design. *See* Font.

Typography—The style, arrangement, or appearance of typeset matter. The art of selecting and designing with type.

Web—The Internet.

Web Offset—Printing on a press designed to use paper supplied in rolls (printers use "web" to refer to the roll of paper). The image is offset from a blanket onto the paper.

White Space—Blank areas on a page or screen that do not contain text or illustrations.

Widow—A short line, word, or part of a word left bereft at the end of a paragraph. People often use widows and orphans interchangeably. The definition in this glossary is from *The Chicago Manual of Style*.

Recommended Reading and Listening

BOOKS

Antonelli, Paola. *Design and the Elastic Mind.* Museum of Modern Art, 2008.

Bierut, Michael. *How to use graphic design to sell things, explain things, make things look better, make people laugh, make people cry, and (every once in a while) change the world.* Harper Design, 2015.

Birdsall, Derek. *Notes on Book Design.* Yale University Press, 2004.

Bringhurst, Robert. *The Elements of Typographic Style.* Hartley & Marks Publishers, 1992, 1996, 2002.

Heller, Steven, and Fili, Louise. *Stylepedia. A Guide to Graphic Design Mannerisms, Quirks, and Conceits.* Chronicle Books, 2007.

Heller, Steven. Any of his 150+ (and counting) books.

Kidd, Chip, *Work: 1986–2006; Book One.* Rizzoli International Publications, Inc., 2005.

Kidd, Chip, *Work: 2007–2017; Book Two.* Rizzoli International Publications, Inc., 2017.

Lawson, Alexander. *Anatomy of a Typeface.* David R. Godine Publisher, Inc., 1990.

Leborg, Christian. *Visual Grammar.* Princeton Architectural Press, 2004.

Lee, Marshall. *Bookmaking: Editing, Design, Production.* Third Edition. W. W. Norton & Co., 2004.

Lidwell, William; Holden, Kristina; Butler, Jill. *Universal Principles of Design.* Rockport Publishers, 2003.

Lupton, Ellen. *Thinking with Type.* Second, Revised and Expanded Edition. Princeton Architectural Press, 2010.

Müller-Brockmann, *Grid Systems in Graphic Design.* Niggli. Bilingual Edition, 1996.

Rand, Paul. *Design Form and Chaos.* Yale University Press, 1993.

Samara, Timothy. *Making and Breaking the Grid.* Second Edition. Rockport Publishers, 2017.

Spiekermann, Erik, and E. M. Ginger. *Stop Stealing Sheep & Find Out How Type Works.* Peachpit Press, 2003.

Stevenson, George A., Revised by William A. Pakan. *Graphic Arts Encyclopedia.* Design Press, 1992.

Updike, Daniel Berkeley. *Printing Types; Their History Forms, and Use.* Volumes I and II. Harvard University Press, 1966.

WEB ARTICLES OR SITES

Haley, Allan. "They're not fonts!" www.aiga.org/content.cfm/theyre-not-fonts

Vinh, Khoi. "Grids are Good (Right)?" Blog Entry on subtraction.com

PODCASTS

The Observatory. Design Observer

Design Matters with Debbie Millman

Contributors

PRINCIPLE NUMBERS ARE IN BOLD

Quick Start Guide

1

ASSESS THE MATERIAL

❏ What is the subject matter?

❏ Is there a lot of running text?

❏ Are there a lot of elements? Section headings? Subheads?
   Run in heads? Charts? Tables? Images?

❏ Has an editorial staff determined and marked the hierarchy of
   information, or do you need to figure it out yourself?

❏ Does art need to be created or photographed?

❏ Will the piece be printed traditionally or posted online?

2

PLAN AHEAD.

KNOW PRODUCTION

SPECIFICATIONS

❏ How will the material be printed?

❏ Is it one color, two color, or four color?

● ● ● If the material will be printed traditionally, you must work
         with or assemble 300 dpi tiffs at reproduction size.

● ● ● 72 dpi jpegs are not suitable for printing; they're suitable
         for the Web only

❏ Are there a lot of elements? Section headings? Subheads? Run
   in heads? Charts? Tables? Images?

❏ Will the piece be printed traditionally or posted online?

❏ What is the trim size of your piece and your page?

❏ Does the project need to be a specific number of pages? Is
   there any leeway?

❏ Does your client or printer have minimum margins?

3

CHOOSE FORMAT, MARGINS,

AND TYPEFACE(S)

❏ Work with the number of pages/screen you have and
   determine best format.

● ● ● If the material is technical or on a larger size page, it may
         warrant two, or multiple, columns

❏ Determine your margins. This is the trickiest part for beginners.
   Allow yourself some time for trial and error. Keep in mind that
   space helps any design, even when there's a lot of material to fit
   onto the page.

❏ Given the subject matter, which you assessed in step 1,
   determine your typeface. Does the material warrant just one
   face with different weights or a number of typefaces?

● ● ● Most computers have a lot of resident fonts, but familiarize
         yourself with fonts and families. Dare to be square some-
         times. You don't always need to use funky faces.

❏ Think about the type sizes and the space between lines.
   After visualizing and maybe sketching, go ahead and flow (pull)
   the text into your document to see how it fits.

4
KNOW THE RULES OF TYPOGRAPHY AND TYPESETTING

❏ In typesetting, there's only one space after a period.

● ● ● Working in layout programs differs from word processing; you're setting correct typography now. The double spaces originally set up to mimic typewriters are history.

❏ Within a paragraph, use only soft returns if you need to break text to eliminate too many hyphenations or odd breaks

❏ Use the quotation marks in the typeface, not the hatch marks (those straight marks used to denote inches and feet)

❏ Use the spell checker

❏ Make certain your italic and bold setting is the italic of the typeface. If your layout program enables you to bold or italicize the words, don't be tempted. It's wrong.

❏ Watch out for bad line breaks, like splitting names, or more than two hyphens in a row, or a hyphen followed by an em dash at the end of a line

● ● ● And yes, if you catch bad breaks in this book, I'll be happy to hear from you and rectify any gaffes in the next printing

❏ **Dashes make a difference.**

    Em Dash. Use for grammatical or narrative pauses. The width of the letter m in the chosen face
        (Shift-Option-hyphen)

    En Dash. Use for the passage of time or to connect numbers. Half an em; the width of the letter n in the chosen face
        (Option-Hyphen)

    Hyphen. Connect words and phrases; break words at ends of lines
        (Hyphen key)

GET SMART; AVOID "DUMB QUOTES"

"Dumb Quotes"
"Smart Quotes"

"Dumb Quotes"
"Smart Quotes"

5
KNOW THE RULES OF GOOD PAGING

PAGING

❏ When paging, avoid widows and orphans (*See* Glossary)

❏ See, but don't copy, the examples in the previous pages

❏ Be aware that when you send a project to a printer, you'll need to collect (if you're working in QuarkXPress) or package (if you're working in InDesign) the fonts along with your document and images

---

SPECIAL CHARACTERS AND ACCENT MARKS

SPECIAL CHARACTERS

-	Option - hyphen	en dash
–	Option - Shift - hyphen	em dash
…	Option - ;	ellipsis (this character can't be separated at the end of a line as three periods can)
•	Option - 8	bullet (easy to remember as it's the asterisk key)
■	n (*ZapfDingbats*)	black ballot box
□	n (*ZapfDingbats, outlined*)	empty ballot box
©	Option - g	
™	Option - 2	
®	Option - r	
°	Option - Shift - 8	degree symbol (e.g. 102°F)
¢	Option - $	
"	Shift - Control - quotes	inch marks (same as dumb qoutes)

ACCENT MARKS

´	Option - e	(e.g. Résumé)
`	Option - ~	
¨	Option - u	
~	Option - n	
^	Option - i	

Acknowledgments

Curating a book like this is an adventure in humility. I thank Steven Heller for suggesting me for the task. I also wish to thank Judith Cressy for her patience and David Martinell for his diplomacy.

The many professionals featured in the book took time to assemble materials, answer questions, and graciously grant the use of their projects. I thank and admire all of them and have learned from their talent and work.

I am grateful to Donna David for the opportunity to teach years ago. It was an intense experience which taught me a lot. Donna also provided glossary terminology used in this book.

Throughout, I've noted that graphic design is a collaboration. Janice Carapellucci provided support, as she did in the first edtion. George Garrastegui Jr., reviewed the first edition and offered insightful comments and suggestions that helped make this edition more useful for students and practitioners alike. I'm also grateful to Punyapol "Noom" Kittayarak, Suzanne Dell'Orto—and especially Patricia Chang, who is eagle-eyed, talented, reliable, responsible, and a paragon of an associate.

My favorite life collaborator, Pat O'Neill, was, again, characteristically as kind as he is funny, which are essentials in my book.

Printed in the USA
CPSIA information can be obtained
at www.ICGtesting.com
LVHW072331120424
776530LV00022B/16